W9-AQB-147

The Logical Way of Doing Things

The Logical Way of Doing Things

edited by Karel Lambert

New Haven and London, Yale University Press, 1969

Published with assistance from the Louis Stern Memorial Fund.

Copyright © 1969 by Yale University

Library of Congress catalog card number 69-15450
Designed by Marvin Howard Simmons,

set in Times Roman type,
and printed in the United States of America by
The Carl Purington Rollins Printing-Office of the
Yale University Press, New Haven, Connecticut.

Distributed in Great Britain, Europe, Asia, and
Africa by Yale University Press Ltd., London; in
Canada by McGill University Press, Montreal; and
in Latin America by Centro Interamericano de Libros
Académicos, Mexico City.

This volume is dedicated to
the memory of Henry S. Leonard

Preface

Henry S. Leonard was a philosopher logician whose concerns were largely nonmathematical. He thought of himself as primarily a metaphysician who believed formal procedures indispensable in philosophical inquiry. But the relation between logic and philosophy was not a one-way street for him. Convinced as he was of the enormous power and utility of formal languages to deal with the entire range of philosophical problems, he felt nevertheless that metaphysical considerations showed the insufficiency of the traditional syntactical and semantical treatment of formal logic proceeding from *Principia Mathematica*. Accordingly his published papers consisted not only of purely logical investigations, as in his prophetic paper of 1942 "Two-valued Truth Tables for Modal Functions," and of applications of mathematical logic to philosophical problems, as in his classic paper of 1940 with Goodman, "The Calculus of Individuals and its Uses," but also of arguments and suggestions for altering what he called "the modern mathematical logic." His most ambitious attempt in the latter direction was the construction of "the wide language W" in his presidential address to the Western Division of the American Philosophical Association in 1964, entitled "Essences, Attributes and Predicates." Further, more than anyone else in America, he is responsible for reawakening interest in the logic of existence and in the subsequent construction of a nonstandard formal language called "free logic," a species of formal logic which is devoid of existence assumptions with respect to its terms, singular or general.

The essays in this volume fall into these two categories of Leonard's interests, and not surprisingly are the areas of interest where Leonard's influence has been most dominant. Thus, some essays consist of purely logical investigations or are applications of logic to matters of philosophical importance; others fall in that broad area called the philosophical foundations of logic. Of course, these areas of interest often are not sharply separated, and conceivably some of the essays could be justifiably placed in either category.

In this volume I have also tried to capture the chronological breadth of Leonard's influence. Most of these essays have been contributed by former students of Leonard, by former students of his students, or by scholars who have acknowledged the influence of Leonard's thought on their own. The remainder of the list of contributors consists of distinguished contemporaries of Henry Leonard who, though perhaps in disagreement with his particular philosophical views, shared his general attitude about the strengths and weaknesses of the prevailing logic as a tool in philosophy.

August 1968   K.L.
Laguna Beach, California

Memorial Note

Nelson Goodman

Henry Leonard was my closest associate during our years as students at Harvard. Our introduction to philosophy included the historic running debate over idealism versus realism between W. E. Hocking and Ralph Barton Perry, and over monism and pluralism in logic between C. I. Lewis and Harry Sheffer. We were absorbed by Lewis' courses in the theory of knowledge, based on the just published *Mind and the World Order*; and we were at first exasperated and then enthralled by the nearly incoherent but inspired and profound lectures of James Houghton Woods on Plato. We sharpened our philosophical teeth in almost daily discussions of such matters as Berkeley's idealism, Plato's theory of ideas, Whitehead's extensive abstraction, and problems in logic.

Leonard went on to study with Whitehead and to become a perceptive expositor of *Process and Reality*. But the main activating factor in Leonard's own work was the new logic. Nowadays it is hard to realize how novel symbolic logic was then. Few American universities had any courses at all in the subject; and of the two main undergraduate courses in logic, one was concerned entirely with traditional Aristotelian logic, while the other, taught by Lewis in Sheffer's absence, covered parts of the *Survey of Symbolic Logic* and of the first volume of *Principia Mathematica*. Those who went further were largely self-taught; and in my own efforts, I depended heavily on Leonard. He also first proposed trying direct application of symbolic logic to some philosophical problems we had been working on. This resulted in our joint article "The Calculus of Individuals," and in other material incorporated in his doctoral thesis, "Singular Terms," and in my own later work. Definitions, axioms, proofs were invented, tried, and convicted weekly in nearly all-night conferences in various holes-in-the-walls that served as residences for graduate students and instructors in those days.

Active collaboration between us ended when Leonard left Cambridge for the University of Rochester; and circumstances never again gave me the opportunity of working with this dedicated philosopher, notable for perspicacity and patience of mind, for absolute intellectual integrity, and for unfailing gentleness of spirit.

Contents

Contributors

Nuel D. Belnap, Jr.

William J. Callaghan

Roderick M. Chisholm

Milton Fisk

Frederic B. Fitch

Nelson Goodman

David Harrah

Herbert E. Hendry

Jaakko Hintikka

Karel Lambert

R. M. Martin

Gerald J. Massey

Wilfrid Sellars

Richmond H. Thomason

Bas C. van Fraassen

John Vickers

Part I

Interests, Questions, and Beliefs

1. Erotetic Logistics

David Harrah

Our subject in this paper is the information-gathering process. Our concern is with the person who is in a certain kind of situation and is rational in certain respects. We are concerned with how he specifies his interests, how he communicates these interests to others, and how he uses messages from others to satisfy his interests. We want to know what counts as a rational procedure for doing these things, and what apparatus our man must have if he is to be well equipped.

The situation may be outlined as follows: The man we are concerned with, whom we shall hereafter call C, is a member of a community of persons. Some members of the community are peers of C, some are subordinate to him in various ways, some are superordinate; some try to help, and some do not. The members of the community share one or more languages. Because of their scientific, economic, legal, or other activities, they need at least one language that is clear and precise in the relevant respects; so they adopt a formalized language L. To fix our ideas at the outset, we shall assume that the logical apparatus of L includes the first-order predicate calculus. In many of the examples below, however, we shall be tacitly assuming that L includes more than just the predicate calculus, and the English idioms used in these examples are intended to suggest what sort of further apparatus L might have. In any case we shall assume that the syntax of L is of the usual sort, with a finite alphabet and expressions of finite length, with formula, derivation, and proof effective (recursive), and with theorem constructive (recursively enumerable).

In addition to the apparatus such as languages which he shares with other members of the community, C has an apparatus which might be peculiar to him. He has a set B of beliefs and a set Int of interests. He has many kinds of interest, but Int consists of his cognitive interests—his interests in knowing whether, or knowing how, or knowing about, and the like. He makes these interests definite for his own thinking by expressing them in L, or at least by describing them in the metalanguage of L. Then to obtain help toward satisfying these interests, C expresses some of them in L and communicates them to other persons. He might have several ways of doing this, but for definiteness we shall assume that C's equipment includes a system for expressing interests through questions. Some questions, comprising a set QE, he communicates to other persons; other questions, comprising a set QI, he keeps to himself. On this basis he can construct an interpretation procedure, which we may think of in terms of an interpretation set IS. When C receives a message m, he examines m for consistency, usability, and the like; specifically, he determines whether the combination of m and B is consistent, and whether he can use it to satisfy his cognitive interests. In particular he determines whether he can use it to deduce answers to questions in QI. Any answers thus deduced, together with any further consequences of m and B that are "interesting" for other reasons, are placed in a set IA of interest acquisitions. Speaking metaphorically, C builds IA by passing m through a series of amplifiers and filters; B amplifies m, and Int filters the result.

Throughout his career, C is an almost perfect logician. He does not know all the theorems of L, but he has a theorem-proving machine that he runs occasionally, in order to generate new theorems which he then stores in his memory. His memory too is almost perfect; at any one time there are only finitely many things in it, but its capacity is indefinitely great, no item is ever lost, and being in the memory of C at time t is effective for C at t and later.

On the other hand, all members of the community suffer certain economic limitations. It costs money (or time, or energy, or whatever) to run a theorem-proving machine, to search a memory, to send messages, and to process replies; and each person has only a limited budget of money, time, and energy. Moreover, taking economics in a broad sense, we may view certain logical relations as imposing economic limitations. For example, if L is such that F implies G or presupposes G in some sense, then the users of L might say that a person who asserts F is thereby committed to G, and accordingly that commitment to G is part of the price one pays for asserting F. For many kinds of activity, therefore, C and his fellow citizens must consider costs and commitments; and for some activities they might be willing to bear the costs and commitments only if these are compensated for in some way or other.

Now given that C is in a situation of this sort, the main problem of our study is how C is to construct a rational system for satisfying his cognitive interests. Let us first note that C might be able to satisfy his interests in a way which appears to be unsystematic. He might want certain pieces of information, and he might acquire these by chance, regardless of whether he has communicated to others what it is that he wants: he might, for example, intercept a message intended for someone else, or someone might give him the information gratuitously. Also, it might be that C's interest, instead of being obviously systematic and calling for some specifiable piece of information, appears rather unsystematic and satisfiable by messages whose satisfactory quality could not have been predicted in advance. And further C might satisfy his interests in an obviously systematic but apparently non-rational way. He could choose sentences F at random and ask "Is it the case that F?" Or he can say things to the respondent R which are calculated to elicit some response from R because they make R garrulous or angry or the like. There are situations in which even a rational man wants to appear unsystematic or nonrational in these respects; examples arise in situations of conflict or competition, where a person wants to prevent others from discovering his current interests or predicting his future behavior. Because of this C would like to have an interest system which is general enough to accommodate these apparently nonsystematic and nonrational interests and expressions of interest, and correspondingly we must try to achieve this degree of generality as we develop our theory of interests.

Next we should note some considerations which lead C to want a community-wide system for specifying and expressing interests. These considerations are of fundamental importance because they affect not only the choice of system but also the concept of cognitive interest itself. Let us begin by looking at some simple information-supply systems which involve minimal theory and minimal linguistic apparatus. Suppose that C finds a respondent R and makes an agreement with him; R will supply C with information of a certain kind, and C will pay R for it at certain times and at a certain rate. The kind of information which is to be supplied is specified at the beginning, before the communication process commences; after the agreement is made, no further specifications or qualifications are added. The agreement is made in the metalanguage of L; the information-supply itself is to be effected via a stream of sentences of L sent by R to C, and these latter sentences do not have to use metalinguistic terms like 'information' and 'interest'. The question we must ask at this point is, exactly

how does C specify what it is that he wants R to give him?
Of the many possible specifications, let us note five:

(1) Give me all the true sentences of L.
(2) Give me at each time t all the true sentences which
     I do not already know at t.
(3) Give me at each t all the true sentences which are
     about X, Y, or Z, and which I don't already know at t.
(4) Give me at each t all the true sentences which are
     about X, Y, or Z, which I don't already know at t,
     and which will be interesting or useful to me at t or
     later.
(5) Give me at each t all the true sentences which you
     believe I ought to be interested in at t.

These different specifications have different advantages for
C and R. Specification (1) does not require that R know
anything about C's knowledge or interests, and C will eventually have the information he wants (perhaps!), but he might
have to wait a long time, and he might have to pay for information which does not interest him. Specification (2) secures
that any transmitted item will be news, but not that it will be
interesting. Specifications (3), (4), and (5) require concepts of
aboutness, interest, and usefulness; the easiest for R to follow
is (5), but the most accurately "expressive" one is (4). Unless C
has extraordinarily broad interests and can afford to make
specification (1) or (2), he will need to use something like
(3), (4), or (5); if so, he and R must reach an agreement on
what they mean by 'about,' 'interesting,' and the like.
    Further, suppose that C wants to be able to change, curtail,
or qualify his interests; suppose that he decides he will not
try to specify his interests wholesale, in advance, but will
specify them one at a time, as he needs to. Perhaps he wants to
be able to define some interests in terms of what happens after
he makes his initial information agreement in terms, for

example, of what happens during the course of his communication with R. Finally—and most important—C might want to be able to turn to other sources of information besides R.

Considerations of this sort lead C to favor a community-wide system for indicating interests. He wants a standard theory for describing interests; this theory might be expressible only in the metalanguage of L, but it must be understood and agreed on by all users of L. In addition, C wants a standard system for expressing interests. Given an interest as described in the metalanguage, C wants an expression of L which in some systematic way expresses that interest. By this means any user of L can communicate with any other user concerning the content and satisfaction of interests. To the problem of developing such a theory and such a system we now turn.

In ordinary English, if a person is asked what he is interested in, or what his cognitive interests are, he might say something like: "I am interested in what my salary will be next year, I am interested in prime numbers, I am interested in how I should plan my research, and I am interested in whether my son will do well in mathematics." This suggests that we should represent a set of cognitive interests as a set of phrases, like "prime number" and "My son will do well in mathematics," or alternatively as a set of things, like prime numbers. If we do represent interests in either of these ways, however, we shall have difficulty in analyzing the satisfaction of interests. What satisfies the interest "prime number"? One might say that anyone who announces "prime number" as an interest is in effect calling for all sentences which are about prime numbers, but then we have the problem of analyzing aboutness. This suggests that we should look at interests in the opposite way— that we should first look for the things which satisfy an interest and then look for a way of expressing the interest. Let us adopt and formalize this suggestion in the following definitions. Roughly, we represent an interest as a set consisting of three items, namely, the area of interest, the things that satisfy the interest, and the things that partially satisfy the interest. Our formal definitions are:

D1 An *area of interest* is a nonempty set of sentences of L.
D2 An *interest* is an ordered triple $\langle A, Sat, Prt \rangle$ such that:
1. A is an area of interest.
2. Sat (and likewise Prt) is a set each of whose members is a sequence of sentences of L.
3. If S is a member of Sat, then the members of S constitute a subset of A.
4. If S' is a nonempty member of Prt, then there is a nonempty member S of Sat, such that every member of S' is derivable in L from the set of members of S.

Given an interest I, the first member of I may be called the *area of* I. For D2 we understand that among the possible sequences which can be in Sat or Prt, there is in particular the empty sequence, which may be identified with the empty set.

Particular examples of interests are usually best characterized in terms of how the interest is expressed, so we shall consider expression now and look at examples later. We shall use the phrase "interest-expression system" in an informal way to refer to all of the apparatus and procedures which are used in connection with expressing interests and communicating about them. The central item in an interest-expression system is the set of one or more interest-expression functions. Each of these functions is a function from interests to sequences of expressions; that is, given an interest I, the function assigns to I some sequence Z of expressions of L, and we say that Z *expresses* I (with respect to that function). If the function assigns only one-membered sequences, we call the function *finitary*. In most of the examples below we shall be tacitly assuming that the expression-function is finitary, and we shall speak of the function as assigning to I a single expression E. Later we shall note the importance of nonfinitary functions.

In one type of system interests are coded, or denoted by names; this is the system adopted when a library and its users agree on a scheme for classifying books. Under such a system one can use names of interests to form sentences of any kind, as "I am interested in Interest Number 29." In another kind of system interests are indicated via sentences of some standardized form; the interest itself, qua set-theoretical entity, might or might not be named or described by a term occurring in the sentence, but from the sentence as a whole one can determine by some procedure *that* an interest is being expressed and *what* the interest is. This kind of system is exemplified by standard interrogative systems. The interrogative, "Which mountain did Evans climb in 1956?" would naturally be interpreted as containing terms which refer to Evans and 1956, but as containing no term which refers to any interest, while according to the rules of the system the interrogative as a whole indicates or expresses the interest (see example 10, below).

Interests might be expressed via declarative, interrogative, or imperative sentences. An expression system might have one expression function which expresses some interests via declaratives and another which expresses other interests via interrogatives; or a system might have several functions which parallel each other, so that the same interest is expressed by all of "Someone discovered boron," "I am interested in the discoverer of boron," "Who discovered boron?" and "Describe the discoverer of boron." If one decides that he will allow nondeclarative sentences to express interests, he must then decide how these nondeclaratives can be joined syntactically with declaratives. Also, if F is to express an interest I, and F is to have semantic properties such as truth-conditions, one must decide whether the semantic properties of F are to be connected with the content of I in a systematic way. Thus, if F is a declarative, does it describe the area of I? the Sat component? the Prt component? just these, or these and other things as well? The decisions made concerning these matters affect certain other properties of the system, and it is these other properties which are the crucially important ones. We should note three types.

In the first place there are *completeness properties*: Given a set Int of interests, an expression system may be said to be *complete for* Int if, for every I in Int, there is in the system an expression-function which assigns some Z to I. The system would be *absolutely complete* just in case it were complete for every Int.

In the second place there are *consistency properties*. Let us say that W is a *satisfaction set for* Int if W has in it exactly one member of Sat for each interest in Int whose Sat is non-empty. Intuitively, a satisfaction set for Int is a way of satisfying all the members of Int which can be satisfied in a nonvacuous way. We can then say that Int is *consistent* if it has a consistent satisfaction set (i.e. if no contradiction is derivable from the set of all members of members of W). Next we need a concept of consistency appropriate for sets of the expressions (such as interrogatives or imperatives) which express interests. If such a concept is available, we may say that an interest-expression function is *consistent* if it never happens that both Int is consistent and Exp is inconsistent, where Exp is the set of expressions which express the members of Int.

In the third place there are *effectiveness properties*. Let I be an interest $\langle A, Sat, Prt \rangle$, and suppose that Z expresses I. Then: If there is an effective method whereby, given Z and any sentence F, one can determine whether F is in A, then we say that Z is *area-effective for* I. If there is an effective method whereby, given Z and any sequence S of sentences, one can determine whether S is in Sat, then we say that Z is *Sat-*

effective for I (and likewise for *Prt-effective*). If there is an effective method whereby, given Z, one can construct A (i.e. generate the members of A one by one), then we say that Z is *area-constructive for* I (and likewise for *Sat-constructive* and *Prt-constructive*). Using the notions of *effective, constructive, nonconstructive, partially effective, partially constructive, constructive for initial segments,* and the like, we may specify a variety of further properties which expression systems might have.

Now let us look at examples. Under the above definitions of interest and expression, it is possible that:

(1) *Both Sat and Prt are empty.* An interest of this sort would be the extreme case of interest; the interest is there (i.e. the area is nonempty), but nothing can satisfy it to any degree.

(2) *The empty sequence is in Sat or Prt or both*: intuitively, "I'll be satisfied with silence." If silence would in fact be ambiguous, it might be best to express the empty sequence by a special symbol interpreted as "the null assertion."

(3) *Sat is empty but Prt is not.* In this case Prt can have only one member, and that member is itself empty.

(4) *Prt is empty but Sat is not*: "I want a complete report, and I won't accept an incomplete one."

(5) *Sat has A as one of its members*—Sat has some sequence whose members are the members of A: "I want to know about X," meaning thereby that one will be satisfied to have the whole truth about X, though perhaps he will also be satisfied to have some incomplete description of X.

(6) *Sat has A as its only member*: "I want the whole truth about X."

(7) *Sat has members which do not exhaust A*: "I want some truths about X." This is the standard case.

(8) *Some finite S and some infinite S' are both in Sat.*

(9) *Every member of Sat is infinite*: "I am interested in mathematics, but I'll be satisfied if I know all the truths of any one branch of mathematics."

(10) *Each member of Sat has exactly one member.* This case is of special interest for the logic of questions. We may regard many of the logics of questions which have thus far been developed as logics of interests, and in particular as expression systems which use interrogatives to express interests where Sat consists of one-membered sequences. The interrogative is said to express a question; the question has a set of direct answers, and the interrogative calls for the respondent to assert one direct answer. In terms of our theory of interests, the interrogative expresses an interest which can be satisfied by any one sentence out of the indicated set of sentences. Further, our definition allows the particular case where Sat consists of one-membered sequences, but the members of these sequences do not exhaust the area of interest. It might be in terms of this case, among others, that we can obtain a logical explication of the proposition that a question is more than its answers.

(11) *The area consists of a single sentence, and Sat consists of a single sentence.* This case suggests that our definition of *interest* might be general enough to accommodate noncognitive interests of a certain sort. Suppose that C wants the world to be such that F is true. We could say that he has an interest whose area consists of just F and whose Sat likewise consists of just F; in other words, he hopes that F is true, he does not want to be told that F is false, and he will be satisfied only by being told that F is true. Or suppose that C knows that F is true, and he wants other people to know or believe that F is true. His area of interest then consists of sentences of the form "——— knows that F," and Sat consists of sentences of the form "——— knows that F" or "——— believes that F" or simply "F."

(12) *Sat is effective while Prt is not.* This is perhaps the usual situation for interrogative systems. There is an effective method whereby, given the interrogative and any other sentence, one can determine whether that sentence is a direct answer

to the question expressed by the interrogative. On the other hand, logical consequences of a direct answer count as partial answers to the question, and the set of logical consequences is constructive but not effective.

(13) *Both Sat and Prt are merely constructive.* This situation is tolerable if the interest does not have to be satisfied quickly, or if there is no need for a method of showing that a given S does *not* satisfy the interest.

(14) *Sat is nonconstructive.* Many interest systems in ordinary language are of this sort. In the statement "I want all the books in section n of the library," Sat is effective, but in "I want all the books which are relevant to the study of X," and "I am interested only in true assertions about X," Sat is neither effective nor constructive. The predicate "interesting to C at time *t*" might be effective or constructive for C at time *t* and thereafter, but nonconstructive for C at times prior to *t* and perhaps nonconstructive at all times for persons other than C. In the directive, "Start talking about X, and I'll tell you when to stop," Sat might be nonconstructive for both C and R; C gives the directive, hoping that something will turn up in the response from R which will then be seen to satisfy C's interest.

(15) *The area, or Sat, or Prt, is defined via conditionals*: "If Arnold was always a traitor, then I am interested in his positive contributions; and if he was not, then I am interested in why he turned traitor"; or, "My interest in Arnold will be satisfied by an account of his army service if he was always a traitor, and by an account of his turning traitor if he was not." It is important to distinguish between a conditional interest and the conditional expression of an unconditional interest. In practice, C might have an unconditional interest but also have some reason for asking for help conditionally; he might say "If you already know the answer, what sort of family life did Arnold have?" Probably C and R have agreed that C will

pay R for an answer to a conditional question only when the antecedent of the question is true, and possibly that the question *has* answers only when the antecedent is true. Suppose this is so, and that R volunteers a reply which would be an answer if the antecedent were true, but C and R do not know whether the antecedent is true; C cannot yet accept this reply as answering the conditional question, but he could accept it as answering the unconditional question (in the consequent of the conditional) and satisfying his unconditional interest.

(16) *The area, or Sat, or Prt, is defined via disjunctions*: "I'm not sure what will satisfy my interest in Arnold; it might be an account of his treason, or it might be an account of his positive contributions." Compare also "There is something about his story that puzzles me, though right now I can't say exactly what it is."

(17) *The interest I is expressed by an infinite sequence Z.* We allow this case for the sake of generality in our theory, and completeness in certain of our interest-expression systems. In practice, if C begins sending to R an infinite Z, it might be possible for R to examine initial segments of Z and thereby make correct guesses about the content of Sat and Prt.

Clearly the seventeen examples listed above do not exhaust the cases of interest and expression that are possible in our theory. They have been listed only to indicate the variety of possibilities, relative to interest and its expression per se. With these examples, furthermore, we have been considering only relatively simple examples of interest system. To develop a general theory of interest systems we must consider more than just interests and interest-expression functions; we must take into account additional factors which introduce new dimensions of possibility. This can be seen as follows.

To express an interest is not thereby to request that the interest be satisfied, or to motivate the respondent to satisfy it. Of course one could specify in advance that an expression of interest is to be interpreted as calling for satisfaction of the interest; but the important point here is that it would require the separate specification, and, furthermore, that there are advantages to keeping expression separate from request. One use that C has for a "bare" or "abstract" expression system is to provide for filters in his interpretation set IS. He must include in IS some specification of his interests, so that IS can filter out from an incoming message the parts of the message which help to satisfy his interests. The neatest way to do this is to express the interests in L as questions of L, so that answering a question is equivalent to satisfying an interest. The point again is that these interests are expressed by C to himself, and the expressions thus need not include a request to anyone that the interest be satisfied. It might be possible to develop a reasonably simple semantics for questions such that the questions in QE (public questions) could be interpreted as both having answers and calling for them, while the questions in QI (private questions) have answers but don't call for them; but here we shall not assume that this is possible, and we shall assume that in any case we want a more general theory. We assume, then, that if C wants R to help him satisfy his interests, either he must make some general provision in advance, covering all interest expressions or at least certain types of interest expression, or he must be able to add an expression of request to an expression of interest, as in "I am interested in Arnold's family life; give me an account of it."

Further, whatever formal system of expression is used, C will want to be sure that R is motivated to respond promptly and fully. In some situations R will be subordinate to C, and C can then command R to help him. If R is free, however, not subordinate to C, and if R must consider the costs of answer-finding, message-sending, and so on, then C must be prepared to compensate R for what it costs R to respond to C's request. In most cases it will be advantageous for C to help R to some extent, depending on his own cost parameters; e.g. instead of saying merely, "Exactly where is Yungay located?" he says, "Exactly where in Peru is Yungay located?" This sort of consideration becomes most important in cases where R does not know that the interest is satisfiable. In these cases the crucial piece of help which C can give R is to assure R that there does exist a finite, discoverable, and communicable way of satisfying C's interest. In the case of questions, C must assure R that the question has a true direct answer. He might say "What are all the things which are so-and-so? I know there are only seven of them, and I know that each has a name in L." Or he might offer a wholesale assurance in advance: "I promise that, for every question I ask, *direct answer* will be effective, and one direct answer will be true." Or, in a more interesting example, "I promise that, for every question I ask, *direct answer* will be constructive, and either there will be one true direct answer or there will be infinitely many true partial answers."

Now C and R can strengthen, objectify, and standardize the system of promises and assurances by converting it into a system of commitments. More generally, they will supplement the promise-and-assurance system by adding a commitment system. They agree on a system whereby certain commitments are attached to certain types of interest expression. These commitments are attached in advance; they are specified in the metalanguage as part of the interpretation of the interest expressions. These commitments might or might not be expressible via declarative sentences in the language L, and they might or might not be effectively determinable from the interest expression itself, but the important thing is that they are concessions made by C to compensate and thus motivate

R. Among the commitments which users of the system agree on, there might be some which are felt to be logically necessary, as when we say that to assert a statement is to be committed to all of the logical consequences of that statement. Other commitments, ranging from assurances of communicability to promises of monetary reward, might be regarded as "purely pragmatic" and more or less dependent on user and context. In these terms we might explicate 'presupposition'; the presuppositions of an expression are its logical commitments. Alternatively we might say that all the commitments, being made in advance, are presuppositions. Nothing in our theory of interests, however, depends on how we relate presuppositions and commitments, and it will probably be most useful to work only with the general notion of commitment.

The assurances, promises, and commitments mentioned thus far all serve as positive inducements for R. Let us now generalize one step further to allow for cases of negative inducement. These include the cases where C threatens to penalize R if R does not respond satisfactorily. Perhaps C and R agree in advance on a system of standardized rewards and penalties, or C attaches ad hoc threats to particular interest expressions. In all cases of inducement, whether the inducement is positive or negative, C and R in effect have an interest contract.

D3   An *interest contract* is an ordered triple $\langle I, K, P \rangle$ such that I is an interest, K is a set, and P is a function whose arguments are sequences of sentences of L.

The set K is the set of commitments, including presuppositions; it might consist of sentences of L. The function P is the payoff function, which assigns positive or negative rewards to possible replies. If P is completely defined, so that every sequence of sentences of L has some value assigned to it by P, then we may call the contract *complete*. In the case where C wants only to reward R for replies which satisfy or partially satisfy I, he will confine his P-function to the sequences which are members of the Sat or Prt components of I; we could call this a *positive* interest contract. Intuitively we think of a contract as *fair* if the payoffs and inducements are equitable and satisfactory to both C and R. A problem for research is to develop a precise explication of *fairness*. We should expect, for example, that a necessary condition for a question contract to be fair is that K include all the presuppositions of the question; another is that every member of Sat and Prt is assigned a value by P.

As with interests, so with interest contracts: it is one thing to specify them in the metalanguage of L, and a different thing to express them in L itself. Suppose that C wants to be able to express all of his interests and all of his interest contracts in L; what sort of apparatus must L contain? The answer of course depends partly on what C's interests are, or what sorts of interests he is willing to confine himself to; so we can approach a complete answer only by making more and more detailed assumptions about C's interests and about the initial content of L. At this point it will be useful to make one observation and one suggestion.

The observation is that finitary expression-functions are severely limited in their ability to express interests, and a fortiori in their ability to express interest contracts. Suppose that C uses only finitary expression-functions, so that each interest, if expressed at all, is expressed by one expression of L. Suppose also that C expresses interests in such a way that no two interests are expressed by the same expression—each expression of L expresses at most one interest. We have been assuming from the start that L has certain finitary properties, so that L has only denumerably many expressions. This means that C can use the expressions of L to express at most denumerably many interests. But, if we allow interests to have areas which are infinite, there are more than denumerably many interests, and a fortiori more than denumerably many interest contracts. It is true that in practice, in request situations, the important component of an interest is not the area but Sat, and that an expression-function concentrates on differentiating the different Sats rather than the different areas; unfortunately, however, Sat contains sequences constructed from the area, so the number of possible Sats is not smaller than the number of possible areas.

The suggestion we may offer as advice to C is this: first specify the domain D of things you want to talk about. Then construct a language OL for talking about the things in D. Then construct the language L by extending OL in such a way that L is a syntactic and semantic metalanguage for OL. In addition, let L have some set-theoretical apparatus. Thus L can talk about the things in D, just as OL can, but in addition L can talk about the expressions of OL, sets and sequences of these expressions, their truth-values, and so on. Moreover, let L also contain such further operators as are wanted for the particular interests and expression modalities you need: you might add interrogative operators, imperative operators, and perhaps some epistemic operators such as knows, believes, or asserts. After you have specified the syntax and semantics of L and assured yourself that L is consistent, then construct your interest-expression system, allowing yourself the use of nonfinitary interest-expression functions. Don't be afraid of interests whose expression requires an infinite Z; in many cases you will find, after you have transmitted a reasonably short initial segment of Z, that R has discovered and sent you something which satisfies the interest. You do run the risk of growing old in the futile transmission of some infinite Z, but that is the price you must pay for being able to have infinite interests, and infinitely many of them.

This advice is sketchy and vague, and easier to give than to receive. Watching how C makes it precise, fills in the details, and follows it in the development of his interest system, is the next phase of our inquiry.[1]

1. For further discussion of the logistics of erotetic systems, discussion of interrogative systems in particular, and bibliographic references, see my *Communication: A Logical Model* (Cambridge, Mass., M.I.T. Press, 1963), and "On Completeness in the Logic of Questions" (forthcoming).

Research for this project was supported by an Intramural Research Grant from the University of California.

2. Questions: Their Presuppositions, and How They Can Fail to Arise

Nuel D. Belnap, Jr.

Leonard was one of the first of the modern erotetic logicians, his *Principles of Reasoning* being unique among texts of its era in having a separate section on questions. Presupposition is one of the topics he discusses there, so that it is especially appropriate to take up this topic in this place. Presupposition has also had more than a run for its money in declarative logic, particularly in connection with theories developed by Strawson. According to the technical Strawsonian use of the word "presupposition," the use of a sentence A presupposes B if the truth of B is a necessary condition for A's being successfully used to make a statement capable of being either true or false. Since we are interested only in standard uses of sentences, and since we are also interested in the comparison of presupposition with other logical relations, it is simpler to say that the sentence A itself has the presupposition B, and is itself—derivatively, if you like—either true or false when its presupposition is true. Then the doctrine is to be contrasted with Tarskian logical implication: *A logically implies B if B* is a necessary condition of A's being true, while *A presupposes B if B* is a necessary condition of A's having a truth-value. It is obvious that the notion of presupposition is only useful for a codification of language in which not all sentences have truth-values—a codification allowing "truth-gaps," as Quine somewhere says. A standard example is "The present King of France is bald," which Strawson parses in a gappy way as having a truth-value only if its presupposition, that there is now a unique French king, is satisfied, and which Russell parses in a gapless way as invariably having a truth-value, but as logically implying the existence of a unique French king.

What I first want to point out is that there is an extremely important root notion of question-presupposition that is wanted even on a gapless view, and which is more analogous to logical implication than to Strawsonian presupposition. From this it will emerge that the Strawsonian account draws no prima facie aid and comfort from erotetic considerations. I shall use 'presupposition' for sentences in the modified Strawsonian sense explained above, but for questions I reserve this word for what I take to be the more important notion, using 'S-presupposition' for a notion of question-presupposition analogous to the Strawson notion for sentences. In the second part of the paper I indicate some of the different ways in which questions can fail to arise.

Before proceeding let us agree on some terminology. By an *interrogative* I mean an interrogative sentence, whether of English or of some formal language. By a *question* I mean "what is asked" by the use of an interrogative, hence something more abstract, so that a single question can be put by the use of any one of several interrogatives. Question then stands to interrogative as proposition or statement stands to sentence. There is also the *concrete questioning*, from which we may abstract the concept or family of concepts, *the asking of question q in circumstances* (of kind) *C, the use of interrogative I in circumstances C,* etc.

Let us begin with some examples: The question "Has John stopped beating his wife?" presupposes that John used to beat his wife; the question "Is the present King of France bald?" presupposes that there is now a king of France; the question "What is the width of the desk?" presupposes that a width is the sort of thing a desk has, and to use a second example of Leonard's,[1] "How fast did Jones drive down Main Street last night?" presupposes that Jones drove down Main Street last night. Also, asking the question "How many bones in a lion?" ordinarily implies that the questioner doesn't know the (true) answer and thinks it likely that the respondent either knows or can find out the number of bones in a lion.

The last-mentioned relation is radically different from the others, since it describes the questioner, the respondent, and the empirical context in which the question is asked rather than the topic of the question. We may call such implications "pragmatic," since they are so closely related to the speaker involved in erotetic situations. Pragmatic implications attach not to questions bare, but to asking-questions-in-circumstances, so that it is illuminating (if inaccurate) to say that the asking of a question q in circumstance C has A as a pragmatic implicate if A is ordinarily true when q is asked in circumstance C. Since when one asks "How many bones in a lion?" in the usual information-seeking circumstances, it is ordinarily true that one doesn't know the answer, we may say that the questioner's not knowing how many bones there are in a lion is in standard circumstances a pragmatic implicate of the asking of that question.

1. Henry S. Leonard, *Principles of Reasoning* (New York, Dover, 1967), p. 34. Hereafter parenthetical page numbers refer to this volume. This research has been supported in part by the System Development Corporation, Santa Monica, for whom I prepared *An Analysis of Questions: Preliminary Report* (1963), which contains a detailed discussion of the question–answer relationship. I am grateful to Richard Gale for many helpful conversations, and to Dorothy Grover for a variety of useful suggestions.

Other sorts of pragmatic implications attach more properly to uses-of-interrogatives-in-circumstances than to questions, since they depend on linguistic details of interrogatives, independent of questions put. We should think that the interrogative "Is snow puce?" puts the same question as "Isn't snow puce?," or "Snow *is* puce, isn't it?"—namely the question as to whether or not snow is puce—but in usual circumstances the use of the second or third seems to imply that the questioner tends to believe, but isn't sure, that the answer should be "yes."

We are not going to concern ourselves further with pragmatic implications of either the asking of a question or of the use of an interrogative, but only with those presuppositions, such as those resident in the other examples, which attach indiscriminately to question or interrogative, and which are not about the context of interrogation.

Consider the examples again: "Has John stopped beating his wife?" presupposes, we say, that John used to beat his wife; "Is the present King of France bald?" presupposes that there is now a king of France; "What is the width of the desk?" presupposes that a width is the sort of thing a desk can have; and "How fast did Jones drive down Main Street last night?" presupposes that Jones drove down Main Street last night. Note that these presuppositions, unlike those in the "lion" example, do not describe in any specific way the questioner, respondent, or circumstances of interrogation. That this is so can be seen by noticing that each one of these questions has exactly the same presuppositions even when asked for non-standard purposes, for example as a test-question to see if the respondent is on his toes, or as a rhetorical device when both questioner and respondent know the true answer, as often happens in the court room. Unlike pragmatic implications they do not need to be relativized to circumstances.

Leonard[2] suggests that presuppositions can be divided into primary and the secondary ones, so that "How fast was Jones driving down Main Street last night?" has a primary presupposition that Jones was driving down Main Street last night and has as a secondary presupposition that there is such a place as Main Street. The idea is that the secondary presuppositions are implied by the primary, while "any presupposition which is not a secondary presupposition is called a **primary** presupposition." It may sometimes or even often be useful to look at the matter in this way, in attempting to assay the worth of asking or trying to answer a particular question, but still what is really needed is a unified theory of presuppositions.

It is not only possible but easy to formulate such a theory once one has articulated the notion of a *direct answer* to a question. Briefly, a direct answer to a question is a sentence which is directly and precisely responsive. Such a sentence may, indeed, be either true or false, but in either case it is the sort of thing which if true would tell anyone asking the question exactly what he wants to know, neither more nor less. There are many indirect ways in which to respond to questions, as with "I don't know," "Ask your old man," or with illuminating comments about the topic at hand which do not precisely match the question; but central to the erotetic enterprise is the possibility of responding in exact accord with the question. By putting one question rather than another, a questioner defines the kind of response he would like to have.

It is to be noticed that we take sentences as direct answers to questions, though the analogy with declaratives might suggest that statements would be equally appropriate. In order to allow a way of talking about answer-statements, let us say that such statements are *real* (as opposed to *nominal*) answers. We should recognize the possibility that to some direct

2. Leonard, p. 39.

answers (answer-sentences) there may correspond no real answer because of a failure of a Strawsonian presupposition, and that because of some poverty in the particular language at hand there may be real answers not corresponding to any direct answers.

The direct answers to "Has John stopped beating his wife?" are two: "John has stopped beating his wife," coded by "yes" and "John has not stopped beating his wife," coded by "no." Any other response is indirect. The direct answers to "What is the width of the desk?" are infinite: any substitution-instance of the matrix, "The width of the desk is _____," where the blank is to be filled by a numeral followed by an indication of scale, e.g. "$32\frac{1}{2}$ inches." A long and complicated chapter of the logic of questions concerns the details of the question–answer and interrogative–answer relationships, and the analysis and classification of questions and interrogatives derivative therefrom, but all of that can be suppressed for now except for the observation—useful in avoiding misunderstanding of parts of what follows—that some questions have more than one true direct answer. An example of such a question would be the one put by "What is an example of a question having more than one true direct answer?"

One further item before getting back to presuppositions: so that it will be clear that the notion of erotetic presupposition defined below has nothing to do with truth-gaps, we shall suppose we have a codified language in which every declarative sentence has a unique truth-value.

Beginning with Leonard, we note that he defines a presupposition of a question as "any proposition whose truth is necessary to the validity of the question."[3] But what does it mean to say that a question is "valid"? Once we begin to think that a fruitful way of ascribing properties to questions is via the answers thereto, we are almost driven to Leonard's own

3. Ibid., p. 35.

account of "validity": a valid question is one "that has a correct answer."[4] When we put these two together there emerges what seems to be the most useful concept of presupposition:

> A question, *q*, *presupposes* a sentence, *A*, if and only if the truth of *A* is a logically necessary condition for there being some true answer to *q*.

The definition makes sentences presuppositions, but of course one can have statements play this role as well (or instead). Evidently it is a consequence of this definition that *A* is a presupposition of *q* if and only if every direct answer to *q* logically implies *A*. Questions have in general many presuppositions, but in spite of this we sometimes speak of *the* (unique) presupposition of a question. What we ought to have in mind in these cases is a condition which is not only necessary but also sufficient for there being some true answer, so that *the* presupposition of a question should always be that at least one of its answers is true. Less exactly though more pointedly, a question presupposes that it can be answered truly. Usually, however, we do not pick out the metalinguistic sentence "At least one of *q*'s answers is true" in this connection, but use instead some topical sentence in the same vocabulary as *q*, which is true just exactly when *q* has a true answer. The choice of the sentence we call "the presupposition" of *q* is then a mixture of logic and grammatical convention. In order to isolate the logical part, we may define "*A* expresses the presupposition of *q*"[5] by "*A* is true exactly when *q* has at least

4. Ibid., p. 616.

5. The defined expression "*A* expresses the presupposition of *q*" is to be taken as the result of applying a two-place predicate to *A* and *q*, so that its grammatical analysis is into the three parts "*A*," "expresses-the-presupposition-of," and "*q*." In particular, one should not construe it as composed of "*A*," "expresses," and "the-presupposition-of-*q*."

one true answer," which is to say, the truth of A is both sufficient and necessary for the true answerability of q. And we can go on to observe that in most languages, one among the many A's which express the presupposition of q is uniquely picked out by grammar as deserving of the title, "*the* (unique) presupposition of q."

Consider "Has John stopped beating his wife?" with direct answers "John has stopped beating his wife" and "John has not stopped beating his wife," which we wish to interpret in a non-truth-gappy way as equivalent respectively to "John used to beat his wife and has now stopped" and "John used to beat his wife and hasn't stopped." Clearly at least one of these sentences is true just in case "John used to beat his wife" is true, which is exactly why that sentence expresses the presupposition of this question and is legitimately chosen by grammar as the unique presupposition of q. Among sentences which are presupposed by this question without expressing the presupposition of it are "John is married" and "John used to beat someone." Again, let the answers to "Is the present King of France bald?" be given Russell's gapless interpretation. Then the question presupposes precisely "There is a present King of France," since that is what it takes to render at least one of its direct answers true. Some questions, of course, such as "Are there any unicorns?" have only logically true presuppositions, e.g. "Either there are some unicorns or there are no unicorns." These are "safe" questions, while questions with substantive presuppositions are "risky." Many, perhaps even most, of the questions we ask are risky, and of course there need be nothing "wrong" with asking such questions, unless perhaps their presuppositions are false. From the logical point of view the wife-beating question is on a par with "How fast was Jones driving down Main Street last night?" which requires, for there to be a true answer, that for some number, n, Jones was driving down Main Street last night at

n miles per hour. The difference is that the style of the wife-beating interrogative wrongly suggests that it is used to put a proper yes–no question which is free of substantive presuppositions, while there is nothing similarly misleading about the "how fast" interrogative, which wears its presuppositions on its sleeve.

It is my view that to ask a question with a substantive presupposition is, in ordinary circumstances, to hold oneself responsible for the truth of the question's presupposition and thus implicitly to make a statement. To ask a question is to convey information—and I do not mean "meta-information." One can learn something "about the world" by being asked for the proportions of sodium to chlorine in common table salt, or for the name of the man who was seen with one's wife. Lawyers are for this reason not supposed to ask questions which presuppose debatable claims not yet established, for in this way they could communicate information to the jury in illegitimate ways.

To ask a question with a false presupposition is very much like making a false statement. One can do it knowingly and maliciously, and be exactly on a par with a liar; or one can do it innocently, and be subject to exactly the same kind of benevolent correction as a maker of false statements. For this reason it seems to me convenient to call a question "true" or "false" according as its presupposition is true or false, i.e. according as it does or does not have some true answer.

This account of the presuppositions of questions has nothing to do with Strawsonian presuppositions, since it makes sense for the gapless codification of language, while the latter has to do with truth-gaps. Erotetic presupposition as described above is instead an analogue to standard logical implication. Suppose now we consider a truth-gappy codification of language, with A being a Strawsonian presupposition of B if the truth of A is required for B's having a truth-value. Then we could define Strawsonian presupposition for questions by the formula,

> *q S-presupposes A* if and only if the truth of *A* is required for at least one direct answer to *q* to have a truth-value.

That is, *A* is an S-presupposition of *q* if and only if *A* is a Strawsonian presupposition of each answer to *q*, just as *A* is a presupposition of *q* just in case *A* is a logical consequence of each answer to *q*. It will turn out that questions like "Is the present King of France bald?" have exactly the same *S-presuppositions* when giving their answers a truth-gappy reading as they have *presuppositions* on the gapless interpretation, which I suppose is a good thing.

But it can also be misleading, for if one pays attention only to these special cases one will overlook some crucial differences. To bring these out we need a clear-cut example of a question whose answers are free of Strawsonian presuppositions. This is not so easy since so many sentences have Strawsonian presuppositions. Simple existential sentences, however, are in their standard uses said to be presupposition free, so we can take as our example something like "Which of the following exist: unicorns or chimeras?" with answers "Unicorns exist" and "Chimeras exist." Here there are no Strawsonian presuppositions, but still the question quite obviously presupposes "Either unicorns or chimeras exist," i.e. that at least one of the answers is true. This example shows that it would be wrong to take over too directly into erotetic logic the Strawsonian notion of presupposition for declarative logic, saying something like "the use of an interrogative presupposes *A* if the truth of *A* is required for the interrogative to be used to ask a question," since clearly the unicorn-chimera interrogative can be used to put an answerable question—even if answers are taken to be statements and not sentences—regardless of whether or not its presupposition is true. Of course, the question put cannot be answered *truly*, but in spite of having a false presupposition it can certainly be answered *truly-or-falsely*.

There is a variation of S-presupposition which some might prefer : let us say that a question, *q*, *S'-presupposes A* just in case the truth of *A* is required for it to be the case that all of *q*'s direct answers have a truth-value. Then "Of the present King of France and the present King of England, which one is bald?" would S'-presuppose the existence of a French king, but it would S-presuppose only the existence of at least one of a French or an English king.

It is interesting to observe that one can give an account of Strawsonian presuppositions of sentences from the gapless point of view. To each sentence there corresponds its 'ordinary denial' :

> The present King of France is bald.
> The present King of France is not bald.
>
> Sugar is soluble.
> Sugar is not soluble.
>
> Lions are tawny.
> Lions are not tawny.
>
> All men are mortal.
> Some men are not mortal.

Let us suppose that each of these is given a gapless interpretation, with the existential claim built in. Then in spite of the fact that in general questions are not most profitably thought of as derived from sentences, it seems plausible to define "the ordinary yes–no question syntactically derived from a sentence" as having as its direct answers the sentence and its ordinary denial. The derived "proper" yes–no question would have the sentence and its contradictory as answers, but of course the ordinary denial is by no means always the same as the contradictory. And just because it is not, the ordinary yes–no question derived from a sentence will often have a substantive presupposition. For example, "Are lions tawny?" will presuppose on this interpretation that there are lions, and that either all or none of them are tawny, while "Are all men mortal?" will presuppose that there are men. (Note the difference between the examples: "Are lions tawny?" is on this account *not* the same question as "Are all lions tawny?") It would then seem that this presupposition, the presupposition of the ordinary yes–no question derived from a sentence, is what Strawson is thinking about: *A* S-presupposes *B* just in case the ordinary yes–no question derived from *A* presupposes *B*. In this way it is possible to give an account of S-presupposition which does not depend on truth-gaps.

By paying attention to the answers to a question, one can throw some light on a favorite locution of some philosophers, namely, "the question does not arise," which we shall find can happen in many ways.

One needs in the first place to contrast "*q* does not arise" with "*q* is not arising" or more usually, "*q* did not arise." The last two are historical remarks about what actually is being or was asked, while the first is a logical or quasi-logical remark about the question in relation to a set of circumstances. Thus we might say "The question of his qualifications did not arise," even when we would be prepared to grant that it sometimes does arise in such circumstances. This example leads one also to see that to deny that a question does not arise is not to affirm that it arises, but rather that it might or could properly arise. As a first approximation, "the question does not arise" means that it ought not arise, or that it would be incorrect to ask the question in such circumstances, while "the question arises" is first cousin to "the question ought to arise."

Of course, the ought-analysis won't do : only certain justifications or explanations of the fact that a question ought not be asked can be described in terms of its not arising. At the table the question of which spoon to use might well arise when it would be incorrect to ask it. There is more to life than asking questions : one wants to isolate those ways in which a question does not arise which are peculiar to the logical side of the erotetic enterprise. There seem to be at least three very different ways.

"When trying to win a knock-down drag-out, life-and-death struggle, the question of fair play does not arise." That is, the answer is irrelevant to the present interests of the questioner.

As Harrah has pointed out, cognitive interests may be reified as questions or sets of questions. (For brevity we omit the greater power and subtlety of his extension of this idea in his paper in this volume.) Thus, the underlying idea is of a question being irrelevant to a set of questions. This in turn can be analyzed by paying attention to answers : a question q is irrelevant to a set of questions Q if no answer to q is relevant to any answer to any question in Q. We thereby reduce the concept of relevance among questions to relevance among sentences, the standard account of which is given in terms of logical implication : A is relevant to B if either A or its contradictory implies either B or its contradictory. For applications we would want to relativize the implication to an appropriate set of sentences, S, representing, say, the beliefs of the questioner, so that putting everything together we would have : q is relevant to Q relative to S just in case, relative to S, either an answer to q or the negation of such implies some answer to some member of Q or the denial of such. Otherwise, q is irrelevant to Q relative to S, and we can say that q does not arise, relative to Q and S, in the Way of Irrelevance. For a man whose interests are codified by Q and whose beliefs are codified by S, there is no point in asking a question irrelevant to **Q** and **S**, since no answer will have any logical relation, relative to his beliefs, to any of the questions in which he is interested.

"As you read these words, the question of the language in which they are spoken does not arise." That is, you already know the answer: relative to your present state of knowledge, the question of language is merely rhetorical or trivial; similarly for "Does 2 + 2 equal 4?" That question does not, for most of us, arise, because we already know the answer. Let us define a question, q, as *rhetorical* relative to a set of sentences, **S**, if **S** logically implies some direct answer to q, and *trivial* relative to **S** if the implication is obvious. (This could be made more rigorous by reifying and at the same time relativizing obviousness in terms of privileged transformations.) Then for a man whose beliefs are codified by **S**, there is no point in asking a question trivial relative to **S**—or even rhetorical relative to **S** if he is a perfect logician—since he already has, at least in immediate potentiality, an answer. In these circumstances we may say that the question does not arise in the Way of Triviality.

"The question as to whether the ink on this page is red or green does not arise." That is, you already know the falsity of presupposition of the question, "Is the ink red or green?" The question is known to have no true answer, and so it would be foolish to ask such a question. Thus the third and perhaps most common way in which a question does not arise is in the Way of Foolishness, where we say a question, q, is foolish relative to a set of sentences, **S**, if **S** logically implies (or perhaps: obviously logically implies) the falsehood of the presupposition of the question. That is, a question is foolish relative to **S** if **S** is such as to guarantee that the question can have no true answer. For that reason, if there is no present King of France, and if we use the Russellian analysis, the question of whether or not the present King of France is bald does not arise, and similarly for the wife-beating question if John never beat his wife, for in each case neither answer is true. Evidently closely related concepts are available from the notions of S-presupposition and S'-presupposition, but these matters seem not to throw much further light on the matter.

In summary and conclusion : The most interesting properties of questions derive from their answers, in terms of which we can illuminate the notion of presuppositions of questions, and some of the different ways in which a question can fail to arise, including the Way of Irrelevance, the Way of Triviality, and the Way of Foolishness.

3. Judgment and Belief[1]

John Vickers

The predecessors who had the most direct influence on Henry Leonard's philosophical interests were his teachers A. N. Whitehead and C. I. Lewis. From them he inherited his conviction that logic included the laws of thought and his abiding and fruitful interest in the metaphysics of modalities. In these and other directions Leonard liked to blur the distinction between traditional and modern logic, and he viewed himself as working on traditional problems which were at the same time problems in modern logic. Among these problems were those concerning the validity of inferences involving intensional contexts. The present paper is concerned in large part with this topic and perhaps for that reason may be counted as relevant to Leonard's interests.

In this paper I wish to consider the nature of judgment and in what ways it may be distinguished from belief. I shall begin by discussing the view of judgment put forth by Hume in the first book of the *Treatise*[2] and go on to argue that this view

1. Gordon Brittan and Daniel Dennett were kind enough to discuss an earlier draft with me. I have talked about this paper with Donald Davidson for some time and the extent to which the paper reflects his criticism—not without distortion, I'm sure—is broad and deep enough to defy documentation. Work on the paper was supported in part by NSF Grant 1180.

2. Citations to the *Treatise* are parenthetical and in the pagination of the Selby-Bigge edition.

requires modification in important respects. With these modifications the view seems to me to be a good representative of a large and interesting class of accounts of judgment. Hume does not distinguish belief from judgment in the *Treatise*, but he does leave room for such a distinction in the ramification of his theory, and I shall try to exploit this opportunity.

HUME'S THEORY OF BELIEF

One makes a judgment, on Hume's view, when he has an idea with the feeling of belief or assent. He insists that this feeling is not distinguishable from the occurrence of the idea (623 f.), and thus his account amounts to identifying belief or judgment and lively conception.

Hume sometimes also uses *belief* to mean the association of a lively idea with a present impression (96, 105), but it is no major modification of his view to call such associations *inferences* made in accordance with the inferential or causal habit of associating ideas of that sort with such impressions. This view of causal inference according to which one may infer causally from an impression of A that B, thus believe B, and yet not believe that A causes B—that is to say, a view of inference according to which the deduction theorem does not in general hold for causal inference—is of great interest, but it is not a feature of Hume's theory of judgment with which the present paper is concerned. In what follows I shall ignore as far as possible the topic of inferential belief and restrict consideration to the simple notion of belief as lively conception.

Hume's identification of belief with lively conception is not implausible. If we insist upon finding conscious occurrences which we identify as judgments then it is hard to fault Hume's introspection; the trace of judgment in consciousness is merely conception. "Whether we consider a single object or several; whether we dwell on these objects or run from them to others; and in whatever form or order we survey them, the act of the mind exceeds not a simple conception . . ." (97 n.).

Peter Geach[3] has taught us to ask an interesting question of theories of belief and judgment: What account is or can be given on the basis of the theory of logical ideas? In particular we should ask what account can be given of the idea of negation. It is for several reasons interesting to face Hume's theory with the question of the negation of *judgments of existence*. Hume claims that we have no distinct idea of existence and holds that to judge that something exists is just to form a lively idea of it (66, 94). Thus to judge that Pegasus exists is simply to form a lively idea of Pegasus. There are the following (neither exclusive nor exhaustive) alternatives for this theory as an account of judging that Pegasus does not exist.

1. The alternative which Hume takes in the *Treatise*, namely that there are no judgments of nonexistence, that "whatever we conceive, we conceive to be existent" (67). I think that Hume is forced into this alternative—and indeed he does not adhere to it consistently—by an inessential feature of his theory, namely the absolute primacy he accords to individual concepts. He insists that every belief must have a particular object (20 ff), and this in company with the lively conception view of judgment and his insistence that existence is not a property, makes the alternative almost inevitable. But if we abandon the primacy of individual concepts and allow in at least some cases their elimination in favor of attributes, following the methods of Quine,[4] then we can continue to view belief as lively conception, deny that existence is a property, and still make sense of judgments of nonexistence. In this case we would take judgment that Pegasus does not exist to be, for example, judgment that there is no unique winged horse.

3. In *Mental Acts* (New York, Humanities Press, 1960).
4. See, for example, *Word and Object* (Cambridge, Mass., M.I.T. Press, 1960), § 37.

2. Another way of avoiding the undesirable conclusion that there are no judgments of nonexistence is to count existence as a property, as does Meinong.[5] Then we can suppose that every judgment has a particular object, and that judgment is lively conception—neither of which is held by Meinong—and still account for judgments of nonexistence.

Both of these modifications of Hume's view make it possible for there to be a component of presentations, which is the presentation of negation; and for the negations of judgments to be, by means of this component, in some way uniformly related to the judgments of which they are negations.

3. Another account of negation in judgment which may not be incompatible with Hume's theory of judgment is to suppose that negation is not conceived or presented in judgment, and that the negation of a judgment is a judgment with the same content, but somehow different in the manner in which the content is conceived or felt. Hume's fundamental analysis of causality is of this sort, and Quine's account of the radical translation of truth-functions in *Word and Object*[6] is a semantic form of this view: One will assent to the negation of *P*, on Quine's view, just in case he will dissent from *P*. If we consider the judgments expressed in assent and dissent, taking dissent to express judging negatively, the view becomes that one judges the negation of *P* just in case he judges *P* negatively. The dificulty with this view of the role of negation in judgment is that of finding the mental characteristic of negation, not to speak of isolating those for other logical operations, and the apparent impossibility—if such characteristics are isolated—of giving an account of the recursive formation of logically complex judgments. Double negations become judgments about mental

5. See "The Theory of Objects," in R. M. Chisholm, ed., *Realism and the Background of Phenomenology* (Glencoe, Ill., The Free Press, 1960), especially § 3.

6. § 13.

attitudes, and there is no compelling reason for the law of double negation. This objection does not apply against Hume's mentalistic account of causality, since causal judgments do not in general permit of reiteration.[7] I shall call this view of negation as a way of judging or conceiving the *mentalistic* view.

4. An obvious fourth alternative is to suppose that there is no uniform component of judgment corresponding to negation. That is—still supposing judgment to be lively conception—that to judge that Pegasus does not exist is to form a conception which is not uniformly related to the conception of Pegasus. Thus we do not suppose that the conception of the negation of Pegasus existing must be formed from the conception of Pegasus existing by negation.

This alternative is inadequate because it gives no account of why one cannot judge *P* and also judge the negation of *P*. The relation of logic to judgment becomes mysterious, and there is no way to identify one judgment as the negation of another.

Of these alternatives the first two, both of which are versions of the uniform-conception view of negation, seem to be the best available accounts of negation open to Hume's theory. His theory can be ramified to give a uniform-conception account either by way of eliminating individual concepts, in accordance with Quine's methods, or by way of a theory such as Meinong's, in which existence is taken to be a property. The first of these is certainly more compatible with Hume's views as a whole, but the second has advantages in suiting some of our intuitions about individual concepts.

One of the interesting features of Hume's theory of belief is the account he gives of partial belief. He allows for two sorts of partial belief, frequentist and subjectivist (132 ff.). Frequentist partial belief involves a habit of less than full strength of making

---

7. Nor does it, for different reasons, apply against Quine's account of the radical translation of truth-functions, which is mentioned here only as an illustration. Quine is not there attempting an account of negation in judgment.

judgments which are of full strength. In this case the judgments made are of invariable causal connection but the habit of making them is not invariable. This frequentist account describes partial belief in terms of the frequencies of judgment.

The second sort of partial belief, subjectivist partial belief, is just the reverse of this; the judgments made are of less than full strength, but the habit of making them is invariable. Thus, for example, I always judge that the chances of a head on a fair flip are $\frac{1}{2}$. In this sort of partial belief chance or probability is found as a constituent of judgment.

The two types of partial belief correspond in their treatment of chance to the mentalistic and uniform-conception accounts of negation. The difficulty with the mentalistic account of negation, that it does not allow for the recursive formation of complex judgments, does not apply against the mentalistic or frequentist account of partial belief for the same reason that the mentalistic account of cause is immune to it: such judgments do not in general permit of reiteration to form other judgments. This is not to say that frequentist judgments can never be reiterated, only that they are to be distinguished from negations in that susceptibility to reiteration is an essential feature of the latter.

Hume puts this distinction of two sorts of partial belief succinctly

> Thus, upon the whole, contrary experiments produce an imperfect belief, either by weakening the habit, or by dividing and afterwards joining in different parts, that *perfect* habit, which makes us conclude in general, that instances, of which we have no experience, must necessarily resemble those of which we have. (135)

Hume sees that he must describe the phenomenology of partial belief if he is to remain true to his goal of giving a natural history of the mind. Further, his account of partial belief is intended to be an account of the place of the laws of probability in belief, and thus he must say how these laws are to apply. In the case of frequentist partial belief, strength of belief can be identified with frequency of judgment. Thus, for example, a frequentist belief of strength $\frac{1}{2}$ that a is F would amount to following a-impressions with F-ideas just half the time.

In the case of subjectivist partial belief this interpretation of probability is not, however, open, since the habit of making the judgment is invariable. In this case, in keeping with his insistence that judgment is no more than conception, Hume identifies strength of belief with strength of conception. As the feeling of belief is not distinguishable from the force and vivacity with which the idea is conceived, so strength of belief is taken to be just the strength of this feeling. Hume sees quite clearly that the comparison of strengths is not precise enough to admit application of the laws of probability to judgment. As Ramsey says in this connection,

> the scale of probabilities between 0 and 1, and the sort of way we use it . . . [are] in no way related to the measurement of an introspected feeling. For the units in terms of which such feelings or sensations are measured are always, I think, differences which are just perceptible: there is no other way of obtaining units. But I see no ground for supposing that the interval between a belief of degree $\frac{1}{2}$ consists of just as many perceptible chances as does that between one of $\frac{2}{3}$ and one of $\frac{5}{6}$, or that a scale based on just perceptible differences would have any simple relation to the theory of probability.[8]

Hume attempts to find units other than just-perceptible differences in terms of which to measure feelings of belief. He

8. F. P. Ramsey, "Truth and Probability," in *Foundations of Mathematics and Other Essays* (London, Routledge, Kegan-Paul, 1931), p. 171.

settles on identifying strength of feeling with frequency in the class of observations which caused the judgment (140 f.). This results in applying the laws of probability to subjectivist partial belief in a quite a priori fashion, and has also the difficulty that it leaves us with no account whatever of partial belief not based upon a sequence of observations.[9] Further, even restricting consideration to cases where there are histories of observations, we must either suppose that the frequency may sometimes fail to give the strength of belief or else admit the reduction of subjectivistic partial belief to frequentist partial belief and hence—since in this case we *define* feeling in terms of frequency—deprive the notion, strength of feeling, of its content.

One has, of course, the choice here of abandoning the concept of subjectivistic partial belief and with it the attempt to account for chance as a constituent of judgment. But for many reasons, not the least of which is the apparent difficulty on the frequentist view of accounting for partial belief in propositions which are clearly not instantiations of propositional functions for which frequencies can be found, I think we should avoid this as far as possible. The place to look for a subjectivistic account of partial belief is in the relation of judgment to action.

BEHAVIORISTIC THEORIES

In Hume's theory the relation between my judgments and my actions is causal. My judgments in conjunction with my passions cause my actions. To see this, according to Hume, I need only reflect upon my own judgments, passions, and actions. If I do this I shall see that there is a constant conjunction between judgment—passion pairs in the form of practical syllogism premises, and actions in the form of the corresponding conclusions.

9. And it is difficult to reconcile with Hume's applications of the principle of indifference. Cf. 128 f.

When we turn to the relation from my point of view between the beliefs of others and their actions, the issue is not so simple. Hume says in arguing that we attribute reason to animals on the same grounds as we do to people;

> We are conscious, that we ourselves, in adapting means to ends, are guided by reason and design, and that 'tis not ignorantly nor casually we perform those actions, which tend to self-preservation, to the obtaining pleasure, and avoiding pain. When therefore we see other creatures, in millions of instances, perform like actions, and direct them to like ends, all our principles of reason and probability carry us with an invincible force to believe the existence of a like cause. 'Tis needless in my opinion to illustrate this argument by the enumeration of particulars. The smallest attention will supply us with more than are requisite. The resemblance betwixt the actions of animals and those of men is so entire in this respect, that the very first action of the first animal we shall please to pitch on, will afford us an incontestable argument for the present doctrine.
>
> This doctrine is as useful as it is obvious, and furnishes us with a kind of touchstone, by which we may try every system in this species of philosophy. 'Tis from the resemblance of the external actions of animals to those we ourselves perform, that we judge their internal likewise to resemble ours; and the same principle of reasoning, carry'd one step farther, will make us conclude that since our internal actions resemble each other, the causes, from which they are deriv'd, must also be resembling. When any hypothesis, therefore, is advanced to explain a mental operation, which is common to men and beasts we must apply the same hypothesis to both; and as every true hypothesis will abide this trial, so I may venture to affirm,

that no false one will ever be able to endure it. The common defect of those systems, which philosophers have employ'd to account for the actions of the mind, is, that they suppose such a subtility and refinement of thought, as not only exceeds the capacity of mere animals, but even of children and the common people in our own species; who are notwithstanding susceptible of the same emotions and affections as persons of the most accomplish'd genius and understanding. Such a subtility is a clear proof of the falsehood, as the contrary simplicity of the truth, of any system. (176–77)

We never encounter directly the passions and judgments of others or animals. These passions and judgments must remain for us constructed or inferred entities, transcendent or theoretical constructs. Thus I cannot in viewing the actions of another make causal *inferences* on the basis of practical syllogism premises which conclude in expectation that the individual will commit an action in the form of the conclusion. In the case of my own actions, an impression (or reflection) of a judgment and a passion leads me to expect that I shall act in the appropriate way, and this is why I say that the judgment and passion cause the action. But since I can never have impressions of the other's judgments and passions, I can never be led by such impressions to anticipate his actions. Thus the analogy between my view of my action and my view of others' actions is not at all complete, and we are left with the problem of explaining how it is on Hume's view, or reconstructions of it, that we do indeed anticipate others' actions.

An exegetical alternative which we should reject here is that of supposing that Hume's use of *cause*, in expressing the relation between others' beliefs and actions, is informal or vulgar and not analyzed in his theory of causality. My reasons for rejecting this alternative are first that Hume explicitly disavows it in "Of Liberty and Necessity" (see esp. 403, 410), and second that he has good grounds for disavowing it, since most of his arguments that judgments and passions cause actions depend upon his account of causality.

The other alternative is more plausible: simply to view others' judgments and passions as constructions from the data of their actions. This has the virtue from an exegetical point of view of leaving intact the arguments in "Of Liberty and Necessity" as well as those in "Of the Reason of Animals." This alternative requires that we reject the second sentence of the above-quoted selection, but this is no great sacrifice since the analogy on which it is based is, from the point of view of Hume's account of cause, insufficient to support the claim.

I have picked Hume's theory about which to make this point because in this respect it is representative of an interesting class of accounts of belief and action: the class of accounts which are based on empirical accounts of causality and which strive to give in outline a scientific account of belief and action.

The decision to view the beliefs of others as constructs from their actions raises the question what the form of this construction should be. We know pretty well in given cases how to perform the construction—supposing that construction is the route from action to beliefs, because we do find out what people believe. But of course an analysis of this capacity is just what we are after.

What we require is a behavioristic account of belief, and the only account of this sort which has been explicitly stated is roughly that an agent's beliefs are such that if they were true then his actions would satisfy his desires.[10] This rough phrasing is inadequate for at least two reasons. First, it implies that everyone believes every false proposition. Secondly, it makes no allowance for beliefs or desires of varying strength. Before

10. By Ramsey, for example, though not quite in this form. See "Truth and Probability," p. 173.

I turn to remedies for these inadequacies let me mention several general features of this account.

1. It does not attempt to correlate belief in a proposition with disposition to act in a certain way.[11] Such attempts are pretty clearly destined to founder in ill-defined collections of *caeteris paribus* clauses and end up as little more than assertions that we do somehow know what others' beliefs are on the basis of their actions.

2. Belief and desire are on this account parameters of action. The agent's access to his beliefs is not in any way privileged.

3. Hume's account of the causal relation between my judgments and my actions makes the practical syllogism a causal principle and thus provides a plausible account of incontinent action on my part, namely when this causal relation breaks down; when, for example, I have the premises—make the judgment and undergo the passion—and do not commit the appropriate action. This is possible because, on Hume's view, causal relations need not be invariable. When belief and desire are taken as parameters of action, however, we can no longer view the practical syllogism as expressing a causal relation. It becomes now a principle of construction and we cannot depict a man failing to act in accordance with his beliefs and desires, because the behavioristic theory translates immediately a change in action into a change in belief or desire. Thus if incontinent action is action not in accord with beliefs and desires, I can never view another as acting incontinently.

Modifications and refinements of this account allow for partial belief and desires of varying strength. These beliefs and desires are related to the agent's action by something like the

11. As do Scheffler and Ryle, for example. See *The Anatomy of Inquiry* (New York, Knopf, 1963), pp. 88–110, and *The Concept of Mind* (London, Hutchinson, 1949), pp. 134 f.

principle of maximization of utility.[12] We define measures s and v of belief and desire and suppose that the agent performs always that action A which maximizes

$$v(A) = \sum_i v(B_i/A)$$

where the B_i are exclusive and exhaustive given A, and $s(Y/X)$ is the strength of the agent's belief that Y will occur given that X occurs.

It is an a priori requirement of these accounts that the measure s be a probability measure.[13] This requirement includes reference to an unanalyzed notion of necessity in the laws.

If Y is necessary, then $s(Y/X) = 1$.
If X and Y are necessarily exclusive, then $S(X \vee Y/Z) = S(X/Z) + S(Y/Z)$.

Now we have in such accounts of partial belief a response to the demand which made us look to action for a measure of strength of belief in the first place, namely that the attempt to identify strength of subjectivistic partial belief with strength of feeling failed. By turning to action we have a notion of partial belief which allows chance to be a constituent of belief and which makes comprehensible partial belief in nonfrequency propositions. From an exegetical point of view this seems to me a further reason for ramifying Hume's account of my view of others' beliefs to make these beliefs constructed or inferred entities from the data of action. Not only do we thereby

12. See Ernest Adams, "Survey of Bernoullian Utility Theory," in M. Solomon, ed., *Mathematical Thinking in the Measure of Behavior* (Glencoe, Ill., The Free Press, 1960), for a thorough introduction to these accounts.

13. I argue for this in some detail in "Remarks on Coherence and Subjective Probability," *Philosophy of Science, 32* (1965), pp. 32–38. See also below. Davidson has been making this point in lectures and discussion for several years.

replace the insufficient analogy between my view of my beliefs and my action and my view of others' beliefs and actions, but we also resolve the difficulties of attempting to define strength of subjectivistic belief in terms of feelings. Further the question lurking behind these difficulties of how to apply the laws of probability to the beliefs of a man who is ignorant of these laws is now answered without having to suppose these laws to be innate knowledge. We can apply them to his beliefs in spite of his ignorance because such application implies nothing about his awareness. Indeed, the agent may also be quite ignorant of the propositional content of his beliefs when these are viewed as parameters of behavior.

I am ignoring here the important and difficult question of the extent to which we describe the agent's awareness when we describe his actions, and thus I ignore what is apparently a conclusive if vague argument that, since utility-maximization theories require description of an agent's actions, they also require description of his awareness. It is safe to ignore this here because it seems doubtful that the awareness described will necessarily include awareness of probability theory.

A further feature of these utility-maximization theories is the difficulty of the rough formulation of the theories, that according to that formulation everyone believes every false proposition has disappeared. We have in its place the essential involvement of an unanalyzed notion of necessity, and I shall return to this involvement later.

Although these theories as I have described them take belief to be a parameter of behavior, I suppose that at least sometimes they are put forward as giving behavioristic indicators of some underlying reality—the structure of the agent's beliefs and desires. In some cases they are perhaps viewed as first approximations to neurological theories. It is not at all clear what form such neurological theories would take, but in any event insofar as utility-maximization theories follow out the program of completing Hume's account of the relation of belief and action, they are not at all theories that indicate some underlying reality in terms of its manifestations, but rather exhaustive characterizations of belief and desire in terms of action.

This completely behavioristic character of utility-maximization theories has interesting implications for the question of the extent to which one's beliefs are determined. Since beliefs are given completely by action, it is just as much up to a man what he believes as it is up to him how he acts.

We have still, of course, the consequence mentioned with respect to the initial formulation of utility-maximization theories—that we can on these theories give no account of failing to act on a belief, and as a consequence that there is no way in them of describing incontinent action.

In sum, when we modify the Humean theory to treat the beliefs of others as constructs we find ourselves with two notions of belief: one—the lively conception account offered by Hume—applies to my own beliefs; and the other—the behavioristic notion of the utility-maximization accounts—applies to the other's beliefs. This ambiguity of the notion of belief leads to the following question: I can with some effort view my beliefs and desires as others would view them, as behavioristic parameters. If I do this, then what is the relation between my beliefs from my point of view and my beliefs from others' points of view?

This question also raises the following issue: if the correct account of subjectivistic partial belief has it that probability is a part of the way in which you view my action, then what possible force is there to the injunction that I ought to make probabilistic computations in deciding how to act?[14] However

14. The issue was discussed by L. J. Savage in a symposium at the Western Division of the American Philosophical Association in May 1967, and in Ian Hacking's paper at the same symposium. Hacking's paper, "Slightly More Realistic Personal Probability," is forthcoming in *Philosophy of Science*.

I act, my beliefs and desires will conform to the laws of probability because you, the observer, will attribute to me only beliefs and desires which do so.

We can, of course, fall back on the frequentist view of partial belief and issue it as a canon of reasonableness that one ought to have beliefs of strength determined by the frequencies of past observation, but this leaves quite untouched the strengths of beliefs in nonfrequentist propositions. The problems that led Hume to distinguish subjectivistic partial belief are unresolved, and such a canon gives no reason why I should obey the laws of probability in basing action on my subjectivistic partial beliefs. There is apparently no point whatever in my deliberating over probabilities, computing likelihoods, and so on, unless I am translating an observed frequency into a course of action. Thus the utility-maximization view of belief has the consequence that the injunctions of the Bayesians are either indistinguishable from frequentist injunctions, and thus not applicable to nonfrequentist propositions, or are pointless because one cannot fail to obey them; my beliefs and desires (viewed as parameters of behavior) will be probabilistic no matter what I do.

The reply to this difficulty in terms of coherence results misses the point.[15] It is that we have a notion of betting function, which is defined in terms of the odds at which one is willing to bet on propositions, that such a function is coherent just in case it is probabilistic, and that it is possible for a man to have an incoherent betting function—simply by being willing to accept sets of bets on which he cannot come out net winner. But as I have argued elsewhere[16] it is not at all a contingent question whether a betting function is a probability measure, and to pretend that it is is to misread coherence

15. The remainder of this section is in response to criticisms by Isaac Levi.

16. See "Remarks on Coherence and Subjective Probability," and "Some Features of Theories of Belief," *Journal of Philosophy, 63* (1966), 197–201.

results. It can be established on the basis of the assumptions needed to define betting functions that all non-negative betting functions are probability measures, and thus that the only way in which a betting function can fail to be coherent (hence probabilistic) is for it to be negative, that is, for the agent to be willing to give away outright what he values. But the way in which value is determined in utility-maximization theories is by what the agent is willing to give away and a fortiori, from this point of view, one cannot give away what one values. Thus it is never possible for a man to have an incoherent betting function so long as we take his actions (that is, his willingness to bet) as defining his belief and desire.

The explanation for this apparently paradoxical situation is that we usually think of a man as being able to tell us what bets he is willing to take; that is to say, we think of his belief as something to which he has access and the strength of which he can express. And if we have an independent account of partial belief this is all well and good, but if we take the utility-maximization theory to define belief and desire then we cannot expect to find sets of beliefs and desires which fail to conform to it, and this is just what incoherent beliefs would fail to do.

The reason behind this is just the reason that behavioristic theories can give no account of incontinence, namely that failure to act on a belief implies on such theories that it is not a belief of the agent. In the same way, incoherence of a set of beliefs implies that one with these beliefs cannot act so as to maximize his expected utility, and hence implies that these beliefs are not the correct parameters for describing the agent's behavior.

If we are to resolve these problems it must be by way of relating my beliefs from my point of view with my beliefs from the point of view of another. Or, in terms of Hume's theory, by relating my lively conceptions with parameters of my action, and it is to this question that I now turn.

STATES OF BEHAVIOR

Working out Hume's theory of belief, to account for the relations between others' beliefs and their actions and to make explicit the sense in which subjectivistic partial belief is probabilistic, results in an ambiguity in the notion of belief. In particular, my belief can be understood by me as a mode of my consciousness or as a state of my behavior. To make this ambiguity clear I shall use 'belief' from now on always in the behavioristic sense, supposing that this sense is explicated in utility-maximization theory, and reserve the term 'judgment' for modes of consciousness, supposing Hume's lively conception account to be an account of judgment. In these terms the problem is now to describe the relation of belief and judgment.

The first step here is to say what in general *states of behavior* are. I shall use Sartre's analysis of *states*[17] in trying to make this clear. Sartre's view is that the state stands to consciousness of it, on the part of the subject, much as an enduring physical object stands to perception of it. Perception provides access to objects, but this access is not infallible—perceptual consciousness may occur, signifying an object as content, while there is no object as signified. Analogously a state such as hatred of someone may be signified or revealed to me in a consciousness or feeling of hatred when in fact I do not hate the person whom at that instant it seems to me that I do hate. As in the case of perception, my consciousness provides an access to the object, hatred, but—also as in the case of perception—this access is not infallible; the question whether I hate a man is still open when I feel hatred of him. This feeling could be described as consciousness of hatred, just as the perception of the chair could be described as consciousness of the chair, so long as in neither

17. As developed in *Transcendence of the Ego*, Eng. trans. F. Williams and R. Kirkpatrick (New York, Farrar, Straus, 1957), pp. 61–68.

case do we take the consciousness to imply the existence of what it is consciousness of.

The relation between hatred and consciousness of it is disanalogous to the relation between a physical object and perception of it in the following respect: hatred is in considerable part a state of my behavior. This is not to say that it must qualify my behavior in fact, but rather that it includes or implies at least certain behavioral dispositions on my part. A part of what it means to say that I hate someone is that I will or would in certain situations act in certain ways. I know of no adequate analysis of the state of hatred, but it is pretty clear that such an analysis would in some way have to describe the behavioral dispositions involved in hatred. The object of my perception, on the other hand, is not in any sense a state of my behavior, and the analysis of such objects need make no reference to my behavior.

Since my hatred is in considerable part a state of my behavior, my feeling or consciousness of hatred must be in considerable part a consciousness of dispositions on my part to behave in certain ways. A part of feeling hatred is to see oneself as acting or prepared to act in certain ways, ways which now, for lack of adequate analysis, we can specify only as "appropriate to hatred." This vision need not of course be precise; I may not be able to specify with any precision in what way I see myself as acting. Indeed, a significant part of the test of adequacy of an analysis of hatred would be the extent to which we saw that it did describe in detail these dispositions which heretofore we have been able to describe only vaguely and by example.

The relation between belief and judgment can be viewed as a case of a state and consciousness of the state. Here the state is, as in hatred, a behavioral state, but in the case of belief we do have an analysis of the state, namely that offered by utility-maximization theories. These theories say quite precisely what the behavioristic meaning of belief is. Roughly put, the behavioristic meaning of believing P is the set of actions for the success of which (in the agent's terms) the truth of P is a necessary and sufficient condition. Here, of course, we encounter inadequacies similar to those from which the first formulation of utility-maximization theories suffered, which inadequacies are avoided in a more detailed account.

When I make a judgment on this view I am conscious of a belief, and thus conscious in some degree of behavioral dispositions. I may be conscious of these dispositions in vague or ill-defined ways or—in some cases such as those involving symmetric gambling devices or where I consider explicitly past frequencies—I may be conscious of the dispositions quite precisely, to the point where I can characterize them numerically. The utility-maximization theory gives this precision in the limit which in some cases, notably those where the proposition believed is of great importance to me, does not exist.[18]

States of behavior are open to dual access; you view my hatred as a construct from my behavior, I view it in consciousness. Similarly, you view my beliefs and desires as constructs from my behavior, and I view them in judgment (and in the evaluative correlate, consciousness of desire). When you view my beliefs in this way you are to some extent making a claim about my judgments, and when I view my beliefs in judgment I am to some extent making a claim about my behavior. This way of viewing belief and judgment makes possible an in-

18. In Ramsey's theory, for example, there is no way to measure extent of belief in a proposition which is extremely important to the subject. Examples of such are some cases of religious beliefs, as when someone believes in the existence of a God, claiming that if there were no God then his life would be pointless. Another instance is provided by the customary refusal of a betrayed wife or cuckolded husband to consider seriously evidence of his partner's infidelity. Festinger's work on cognitive dissonance, in *Conflict, Decision, and Dissonance* (Stanford, Stanford University Press, 1964), is interesting in this connection.

teresting characterization of incontinence, namely when I act so as to make myself believe what I judge to be false, or to make myself fail to believe what I judge to be true. Or, more precisely, when I undertake a course of action which I do not view as the most likely to eventuate in what I want. This view of incontinence accounts for the difficulty we have in attributing incontinence to another, while we see our own incontinence with ease. As Davidson has emphasized,[19] whatever we cite as evidence that a man acted contrary to his beliefs is at least as good evidence that he does not have those beliefs. In the case of my own view, or rather views, of my own beliefs, the belief is revealed or signified in my judgment, and I see myself as incontinent when I see that I do not in a behavioristic sense have that belief.

The question of how a partial belief can be in error—what it means for partial beliefs to be mistaken—is not at all a simple one. I do not at present see how to avoid some reference to frequencies in answering this question and in general, I should try to deal with it along the lines of Ramsey's treatment in "Truth and Probability." I do not intend to try to treat that issue here, beyond some remarks on coherence below. Supposing that some sense can be made of correctness of partial belief, it follows that there are two distinct senses in which a judgment may be incorrect. One of these is incontinence, where the belief signified in the judgment is not in fact believed by the agent; and the other is where the belief signified is incorrect. As far as I can see these two senses of error are independent, and this is in accordance with our intuitions about incontinence: we take a man to be incontinent when the belief which he betrays in his action is false as well as when it is true.

Similarly, there are two senses in which consciousness of

19. Most recently in "How is Weakness of the Will Possible" in J. Feinberg, ed., *Moral Concepts* (Oxford, forthcoming). The account I offer here of incontinence obviously owes much to this paper.

desire can be mistaken: one is when the desire is incorrect, when satisfying it would not satisfy me, and the other is when I do not have the desire which I am conscious of having. This formulation of incorrectness of desire is not directly applicable to partial belief, and hence this notion of correctness is not clearly formulated. The point here, however, is to distinguish the question of the correctness of the desire from the question of the consciousness of it.

JUDGMENT, BELIEF, AND TRANSPARENCY

We can view the transition from judgment to belief as quantitative rather than qualitative, as providing a continuum of notions of belief, ranging from consciousness at one end to pure behavioral state at the other end. This continuum corresponds to the extent to which we can understand or describe another's beliefs; to the extent to which we know what a statement about his belief means, in the sense of knowing what other statements about his beliefs imply and are implied by it. When we look at belief purely behavioristically our grasp of belief is precisely our grasp of behavior. The arguments of the functions in the utility-maximization account are propositions which we express, and—in the limit of purely behavioristic description—the adequacy of our description does not depend upon the extent to which the subject is aware of these propositions.[20] Examples of this abound in the literature of experimental psychology, where the beliefs of subjects are described in terms of stimuli in ways clearly incomprehensible to them, and where, correspondingly, we grant the validity of inferences about these beliefs depending only upon our grasp of the propositions believed. Thus, for example, if a subject is conditioned to respond to heaviness in objects we may infer

20. With the reservation about the extent to which our description of his action has implication about his awareness. See above, pp. 55 f.

also that he is conditioned to respond to the mass of objects, even though he has comprehension neither of heaviness nor mass.

In the other limit, when we think of the judgment end of the continuum, we are much less confident of our ability to comprehend the proposition judged, and we do not in general allow inferences in accordance with our comprehension of the terms of the judgment. In brief, the extent to which we view belief as public and behavioristic corresponds to the extent to which we view belief statements as *transparent*, that is, to the size and nature of the class T of logical transformations such that for t a transformation in T, we take belief in P to imply belief in $t(P)$.[21]

This question of transparency when applied to partial beliefs cannot be put simply: What is the class T such that for t in T $s(P) \leq s(t)P$)? for the following reasons: in making inferences about partial beliefs we require not only that strengths be preserved but also that dependencies be preserved.[22] Thus the question must be generalized to something like the following: What is the class T of transformations such that for $t_1, \ldots, t_k$ in T and $P_1, \ldots, P_k$ objects of belief, the strengths of belief and dependencies among $t_1(P_1), \ldots, t_k(P_k)$ are determined by the strengths and dependencies among $P_1, \ldots, P_k$?

This question can be seen to be equivalent to the following question: What is the class T of transformations such that

1. If A is provable from no premises by T then $s(A) = 1$.
2. If from A as a premise the negation of B is provable by T then $s(A \vee B) = s(A) + s(B)$.

21. See for example Quine's *Word and Object*, §§ 29–33.

22. By 'dependencies' I mean the values of the conditional belief function, $s(x/y)$. Thus the question of transparency includes in the case of partial belief questions about transformations t such that knowledge of $s(x/y)$ permits inference of $s(t(x)/t(y))$.

Thus this question is just the question of what sense is to be given to the notion of necessity in the laws of probability, supposing only that we analyse necessity in terms of transformations. This means that the continuum from judgment to belief can be viewed as a continuum of concepts of probability. At the belief end of the continuum is the class of all valid transformations including those like the relation of heaviness to mass—which depend upon physical laws and other non-logical transformations. At the extreme-judgment end of the continuum is the null class of transformations, where our comprehension of the object believed is not adequate to permit any inferences.

This account also provides an answer to the Bayesian question why I should obey the laws of probability in deliberation about nonfrequentist beliefs.[23] The answer to this question is that in the judgments which signify such beliefs, ways of behaving are signified. Exactly which way of behaving is signified in my judgment is not in general directly evident to me but frequently requires some calculation. My way of behaving depends to a great extent upon what limits nature places upon me, and thus deliberation about these limits is required for me to know what behavior is signified in a judgment. The laws of probability are absolute limits on ways of behaving, in the sense that they are presumed in the description of behavior by utility-maximization theories, and failure to take them into account in judgment means that my judgment may not signify a possible way of behaving, and thus that my action could not be as envisioned in judgment and would of necessity be incontinent.

Thus, for example, a man who judges that the chances of a head are $\frac{1}{2}$, that throws are independent, and that the chances of two heads in a row are $\frac{1}{2}$, cannot in general act in accordance with this judgment. For him to do so would be for him—in

23. See, for example, the papers by Hacking and Savage.

the case of a bet we could offer him which he could not win—to undertake to give us the stake, which would just show that the stake was not what he valued.

The question naturally arises what account can be given of mathematical beliefs. In considering this question we encounter among others the following difficulty: there are some mathematical propositions which apparently are indubitable in the sense that comprehension of the concepts involved implies that the propositions are fully believed. In particular many propositions of elementary arithmetic are of this sort. On the other hand there are many propositions of mathematics which can apparently be clearly understood and still only partially believed; unresolved conjectures of first-order number theory provide an interesting case in point.

This situation is one that must be accounted for in an adequate account of mathematical belief. Without attempting to provide such an account here even in outline, perhaps I can at least mention the direction one might take.

The account I have in mind is based on the notion of a construction, and identifies belief in a mathematical proposition with belief in the existence of a construction. On this view the existence of constructions corresponding to indubitable propositions is a trivial consequence of, for example, the assumption that there are numbers.

On this view, since in at least some cases the question of the existence of a construction of a specified sort is open, in these cases it becomes possible to account for partial beliefs in the propositions which correspond to these constructions. That is to say, the question of the existence of a construction becomes on a par with the question of the existence of other objects for which we may adduce evidence. We could in this way understand Putman's remark that he thought the Fermat conjecture probable because he knew that Fermat had been competent and careful, and he took Fermat's assertion of the existence of a construction to be good reason to suppose there to be a construction.

The program for this account is clearly to provide an adequate analysis of the notion of construction, and an accompanying inventory of the propositions of intuitive mathematics which are to be taken as indubitable.

Part II

Presuppositions, Truth-valuelessness, Modality, and Metaphysics

4. Presuppositions, Supervaluations, and Free Logic*

Bas C. van Fraassen

Professor Leonard brought to the study of contemporary logic concerns from philosophy of logic and traditional logical theory. These concerns led him specifically to develop a new logic of singular terms (the beginning of free logic[1]) and a new logic of general terms.[2] In these two areas, it has been my aim to extend Professor Leonard's work through the application of formal semantic methods.

A few years before the publication of Leonard's work on the "logic of existence," there had appeared a thoroughgoing critique of the logic of singular and general terms by P. F. Strawson.[3] A basic point made by Strawson was that a statement may have presuppositions, and if any of its presuppositions fails to be true, then the statement is neither true

---

*An early draft of this paper was presented at the Symposium on Free Logic at Michigan State University, June 9–10, 1967.

1. Henry S. Leonard, "The Logic of Existence," *Philosophical Studies*, 7 (1956), 49–64.

2. Leonard, "Essences, Attributes, and Predicates," Presidential address, American Philosophical Association (Western Division), Milwaukee, May 1964.

3. P. F. Strawson, *Introduction to Logical Theory* (London, Methuen, 1952); "On Referring," *Mind*, 59 (1950), 320–44.

nor false. Examples of presuppositions given by Strawson are:

(1a) 'All John's children are asleep' presupposes that John has children.

(1b) 'The King of France is wise' presupposes that the King of France exists.

Elsewhere I have presented a general account of the notion of presupposition conceived of as a semantic relation,[4] which will be summarized in the first part of this paper. I then discuss a general characterization of validity and valid consequence in languages in which presuppositions are countenanced, and finally devote a section to the application of this to free logic.

PRESUPPOSITIONS AND PRESUPPOSITIONAL LANGUAGES

The notion of presupposition, as presented by Strawson, is characterized by:

(2) *A presupposes B* if and only if *A* is neither true nor false unless *B* is true.

Thus, "*A* presupposes *B*" is equivalent to the conjunction of

(3a) if *A* is true then *B* is true;
(3b) if *A* is false then *B* is true.

The semantic relation described by (3a) is a familiar one: it is usually symbolized as "*A* $\Vdash B$" and formulated as "*A* semantically entails *B*." Since "entailment" is often used as synonymous with "implication," and semantic entailment is not implication by any account of that complicated subject, I shall sometimes use the term "necessitation" rather than "semantic entailment" for the relation $\Vdash$.

4. B. C. van Fraassen, "Presupposition, Implication, and Self-reference," *Journal of Philosophy*, 136–52 (1968), sections I and II.

If (3a) means just that $A \Vdash B$, can (3b) be put in a similarly familiar form? The answer is *yes*, if the language under discussion has a negation sign ⅂ such that ⅂A is true if and only if A is false. Then (3b) means just that ⅂$A \Vdash B$. In that case we have:

(4) A presupposes B if and only if $A \Vdash B$ and ⅂$A \Vdash B$.

It must be noted that this form of negation is not the only one encountered in the logical literature. Following Mannoury—though narrowing his meaning somewhat—we can draw the following distinction:[5]

   (5a) *choice negation*: (not-A) is true (respectively, false) if and only if A is false (respectively, true);
   (5b) *exclusion negation*: (not-A) is true if and only if A is not true, and false otherwise.

For (4) to be an adequate rendering of (2), ⅂A should be the choice negation of A. Of course if the principle of bivalence holds (that A is always either true or false), then the distinction collapses. In that case, however, presupposition is a trivial semantic relation, being borne exactly by every sentence to every *valid* sentence and to no others.

The idea of rejecting bivalence will suggest that we are now to turn to 'many valued truth-tables' (logical matrices). And this will suggest in turn the appearance of wonderful new 'logical' connectives, and of rules of 'deduction' resembling the prescriptions to be read in *The Key of Solomon*. Since no one expects that standard logic texts shall ever read like witches' grimoires, this inclines one to dismiss the technical study of presuppositions as a mathematical parlor game.

Three remarks are here in order. First, the use of many valued matrices need not lead to a nonstandard logical system.

5. Cf. E. W. Beth, *Mathematical Thought* (Dordrecht, Reidel, 1965), pp. 20–22.

Secondly, their proper use does not involve the identification of any of their elements as 'truth-values other than truth or falsity,' nor any other such philosophically implausible maneuver. Finally, we shall in any case not use the method of matrices to study contexts in which bivalence fails, but rather the method of *supervaluations*.

Since this is only a convenient summary, we shall not repeat the line of thought that leads to the notion of supervaluation, nor the intuitive reasons for holding it to be the proper formal tool in the present context.[6] Rather, we proceed immediately to define a kind of artificial language (*presuppositional language*) in which a nontrivial presupposition relation may connect various sentences. It must be mentioned that we generalize this by allowing that a *set* of sentences may necessitate a given sentence B, although B is not implied by this set.

An artificial language L has a vocabulary and syntax which together define the set of *sentences* $S(L)$ of L. The semantics of L specifies the set of *admissible valuations* for L: a valuation being an assignment of truth-values (T,F) to members of $S(L)$. The basic idea is that such an assignment is an admissible valuation if, intuitively speaking, it correctly identifies the true and false sentences in some possible situation. We admit the possibility that not all sentences have a truth-value in a given situation.[7]

Such a language L will be called a *presuppositional language* if and only if the definition of its class of admissible valuations fits the following pattern. Its semantics specifies a relation **N** of *nonclassical necessitation*, from sets of sentences to sentences, and a class V of *classical valuations*, mapping all the sentences of L into $\{T,F\}$.

6. van Fraassen, "Presupposition, Implication, and Self-reference," sections I and II.

7. The disregard for Strawson's distinction between 'sentence' and 'statement' is not, it seems to me, essential here.

Thus the classical valuations do not admit truth-value gaps; bivalence holds for them. They proceed on the assumption that there is no possibility of a failure of presupposition. On this assumption, a classical valuation gives a faithful picture of which sentences are true and which false in some (possible) situation. The relation **N** completes the picture by exhibiting the presuppositions (and perhaps other cases of necessitation not reflected in the construction of the classical valuations). As an example, suppose that L has only the two atomic sentences

p: The King of France is wise
q: The King of France exists

and as only logical signs $\neg$ and $\vee$. Then the classical valuations are just those mappings of $S(L)$ into $\{T,F\}$ which satisfy:

(6a) $v(A \vee B) = F$ if and only if $v(A) = v(B) = F$
(6b) $v(\neg A) = F$ if and only if $v(A) = T$

and N is the relation borne to q by $\{p\}$ and also by $\{\neg p\}$. Consider now a situation in which q is false. Then the more popular view is that one of the two classical valuations

$v_1(q) = F$; $v_1(p) = F$
$v_2(q) = F$; $v_2(p) = T$

correctly represents the situation, but that *which* of them does so is a matter of convention. Our present view is that neither does so, since in this situation p is neither true nor false.

To define the admissible valuations, we first introduce the relation **C** of *classical necessitation*:

(7) XCA if and only if every classical valuation which assigns T to every member of X, also assigns T to A.[8]

8. Henceforward we use "v satisfies X" for "v assigns T to every member of X," and sometimes "v satisfies A" for "$v(A) = T$."

We maintain that for any possible situation, the set of sentences true in it will be *saturated*, this property being defined by:

(8) A set G of sentences is *saturated* if and only if
    (a) there is a classical valuation which satisfies G,
    (b) if X is a subset of G and $X\mathbf{C}A$, then A is in G,
    (c) if X is a subset of G and $X\mathbf{N}A$, then A is in G

(briefly: G is a classically satisfiable set closed under $\mathbf{C}$ and $\mathbf{N}$). The characterization of "admissible valuation" is now but a step away.

(9) The *supervaluation* induced by a set of sentences X is the function s which
    (a) assigns T to every sentence which is assigned T by every classical valuation satisfying X,
    (b) assigns F to every sentence which is assigned F by every classical valuation satisfying X,
    (c) is not defined for any other sentence.
(10) Every *admissible valuation* for a presuppositional language L is a supervaluation induced by a saturated set of sentences.

Note first that if in (9) X is saturated, then $s(A) = $ T if and only if A is in X (due to closure under $\mathbf{C}$); second that (10) does not define the family of admissible valuations but only limits it. Semantic entailment is of course defined by

(11) $X \Vdash A$ if and only if every admissible valuation which satisfies X also satisfies A.[9]

To return momentarily to our example: our position is that both v_1 and v_2 correctly represent the situation *in so far as they agree*. The admissible valuation which correctly represents

---

9. We shall write "$B \Vdash A$" as shorthand for "$\{B\} \Vdash A$."

the situation is the supervaluation induced by the saturated set

$$\{A : \{\urcorner q\}\mathbf{C}A\}$$

and that is just the common part of v_1 and v_2.

RADICAL AND CONSERVATIVE PRESUPPOSITIONAL LANGUAGES

We will assume that the classical valuations of L satisfy the principle of bivalence. Adjoining $\mathbf{N}$ then permits the definition of (super)valuations which do not satisfy bivalence. Of course, the relation $\mathbf{N}$ can be adjoined even if the classical valuations are not bivalent; in particular, we could form a new language L' with relation $\mathbf{N}'$ and as family of classical valuations the set of admissible valuations of L. I mention the possibility of such generalizations because in all the theorems we intend to prove in this section and the next, we aim to describe the semantic structure of L in terms of the relation $\mathbf{N}$ and the set V of classical valuations for L. The nature of V and $\mathbf{N}$ will be restricted only through assumptions made explicit in the theorems, and these assumptions can often be satisfied in various ways.

In (10) we restricted the admissible valuations for L to supervaluations induced by saturated sets. An obvious way to complete the definition of admissible valuations is to say that every such supervaluation is admissible. We shall call this the *radical* policy; it amounts to the position that any contingent sentence could fail to have a truth-value for reasons not necessarily reflected in $\mathbf{N}$ (say, because of the failure of a presupposition not formulable in L). The *conservative* policy is to admit as few truth-value gaps as possible; to insist that all the reasons for truth-value gaps are reflected in $\mathbf{N}$. There are, of course, intermediate positions (which, continuing our analogical terminology, might be called liberal but not wishy-washy). We shall here study only the radical and the conservative policy.

> (12) A presuppositional language L is *radical* if every saturated set induces an admissible supervaluation.

What happens to the set of sentences which are *valid* (i.e. satisfied by all admissible valuations) under the radical policy? If we define *classically valid* in the obvious way, then in any presuppositional language whatever, classically valid sentences are valid.

> (13) A is *classically valid* in L if and only if every classical valuation satisfies A.

THEOREM 1   If L is a presuppositional language, and A is classically valid in L, then A is valid in L.

Every saturated set is closed under C, hence contains every classically valid sentence. Whether or not there are further valid sentences depends on N. If A is classically valid, and ANB, then B is valid. But B could be made valid as well by restricting the set of classical valuations instead of widening the extension of N. Hence the possibility that N enlarges the set of valid sentences is not an interesting one.

> (14) N is *normal* if and only if, when all members of X are classically valid, and XNA, then A is classically valid.

THEOREM 2   If L is a radical presuppositional language, and N is normal, then a sentence is valid in L only if it is classically valid in L.

For if N is normal, then the set of all classically valid sentences is saturated; since L is radical, this set induces an admissible (super)valuation satisfying only the classically valid sentences.

The second important question is : what happens to semantic entailment under a radical policy? We can again answer the question in part for presuppositional languages in general, and in full for radical languages.

THEOREM 3   Let L be a presuppositional language, and Y the smallest set containing X which is closed under both $\mathbf{C}$ and $\mathbf{N}$. Then if A is in Y, $X \Vdash A$ in L; and if L is radical and $X \Vdash A$ in L, then A is in Y.

For the proof, note that Y is saturated or not satisfiable. This does not rule out the possibility that a proof of A on the basis of X may not be possible in finitely many steps. Let us designate as $\mathbf{Cn}(X)$ the set of all consequences which can be drawn from X by $\mathbf{C}$ or $\mathbf{N}$ in finitely many steps :

(15a) $\mathbf{C}(X) = \{A : XCA\}$
(15b) $\mathbf{N}(X) = \{A : YNA \text{ for some subset } Y \text{ of } X\}$
(15c) $\mathbf{Cn}(X)$ is the union of the sets $X_1, \ldots, X_k, \ldots$ defined by

$$X_1 = X$$
$$X_{k+1} = \mathbf{C}(\mathbf{N}(X_k)).$$

In general, $\mathbf{Cn}(X)$ is the set of all consequences of X only if $\mathbf{C}$ and $\mathbf{N}$ are finitary relations.

(16) A relation R is *finitary* if and only if for any set X and element A, if XRA then YRA for some finite subset Y of X.

THEOREM 4   If L is a radical presuppositional language with $\mathbf{C}$ and $\mathbf{N}$ finitary, then $X \Vdash A$ in L if and only if A belongs to $\mathbf{Cn}(X)$.

For in that case, $\mathbf{Cn}(X)$ is the smallest set containing X which is closed under $\mathbf{C}$ and $\mathbf{N}$.

The reason for considering the general case (THEOREM 3) is that there are important consequence relations which are not finitary. An example important to the logic of singular terms is the *substitution interpretation of the quantifiers*. This interpretation is given by: if $a_1, \ldots, a_k, \ldots$ are the substituends for the variable x, $(x)Fx$ is true if and only if all of $Fa_1, \ldots, Fa_k, \ldots$ are true. This yields immediately the example: $(x)Fx$ is a consequence of the infinite set $\{Fa_1, \ldots, Fa_k, \ldots\}$ but not of any of its finite subsets. For the usual (*referential*) interpretation of the quantifier, however, the consequence relation is finitary.

Turning now to the conservative policy, we must first provide it with a precise definition. The policy has at least the assumptions that all presuppositions of a given sentence are reflected in **N**, and if all these presuppositions are satisfied, the sentence is either true or false. It would seem reasonable therefore to stipulate that a saturated set G induces an admissible supervaluation only if it satisfies the condition

(17) if all the presuppositions of A in L belongs to G, so does either A or $\neg A$.

This supposes that the language L contains choice negation. That supposition concerns specifically the syntax and classical valuations of L, and we prefer here to be neutral on those features as far as possible.

There is however a more serious objection to the course of taking condition (17) as defining the conservative policy. When we first introduced this policy, we said that it assumed also that the reasons for which a sentence can lack a truth-value are all reflected in **N**. That the present proposed precization does not fulfill this assumption is seen when we ask the question: if G satisfies condition (17), how could it fail to be maximal among the saturated sets satisfied by a given valuation v?

Suppose that G satisfies (17) but is not maximal in this sense; that is that v satisfies a saturated set G' of which G is a proper subset. Let A_1 belong to G' but not to G. Then neither A_1 nor $\daleth A_1$ belongs to G. So A_1 must have a presupposition A_2 which does not belong to G. It belongs to G', however, because A_1 does. Now A_2 belongs to G' but not G; hence A_2 has a presupposition A_3 which does not belong to G. But A_3 belongs to G', because A_2 does... ; and so on. Thus we obtain an infinite chain $A_1, A_2, \ldots, A_k, \ldots$, such that for each i, A_1 is neither true nor false because it presupposes A_{i+1}, and A_{i+1} is neither true nor false. Could this be because the whole set $\{A_1, \ldots, A_k, \ldots\}$ has a presupposition B? Certainly not, for then B belongs to G', hence its negation does not belong to G (and so on). The fact that a truth-value gap occurs is never explained in terms of $\mathbf{N}$, but always in terms of $\mathbf{N}$ and some further truth-value gap. If we deny this possibility, we arrive at the conclusion that G must be maximal after all. This gives us the correct definition of the conservative policy.

> (18) A presuppositional language L is *conservative* if the supervaluation induced by a saturated set G is an admissible valuation if and only if for some classical valuation v, G is maximal among the saturated sets satisfied by v.

This means that to show that X does not semantically entail A, we must show that X can be embedded in a maximal saturated set not containing A. The obvious tool to use is therefore Zorn's lemma; and it is not easy to see how it could be applied except under the assumption that $\mathbf{C}$ and $\mathbf{N}$ are finitary.[10]

THEOREM 5   If L is a conservative presuppositional language with $\mathbf{C}$ and $\mathbf{N}$ finitary, and $X \Vdash A$ in L, then A belongs to $\mathbf{C}n(X)$.

10. Zorn's lemma (equivalent to the axiom of choice) states: if every chain in a partially ordered set P has an upper bound in P, then P contains a maximal element.

In this case the proof is a little bit more complicated. Let us suppose that A does not belong to $Cn(X)$. Since $Cn(X)$ is closed under C, it follows that A is not a classical consequence of $Cn(X)$. Hence there must be a classical valuation v, which assigns T to every member of $Cn(X)$, but assigns F to A. We must now show that from this it follows that there is an admissible supervaluation which satisfies $Cn(X)$ but not A.

Well, $Cn(X)$ is a saturated set satisfied by v. Let F be the family of all saturated sets which contain $Cn(X)$ and are satisfied by v. This family is partially ordered by set inclusion. Consider the chain

$$C_1 \subseteq C_2 \subseteq \ldots \subseteq C_k \subseteq \ldots$$

of elements of F. The union of all the sets C_i is again satisfied by v. This union is closed under C and N because each of the sets C_i is and these are finitary relations. So this union also belongs to the family F: it is an upper bound of that chain in F. The argument being general, we conclude that each chain in F has an upper bound in F. Therefore, by Zorn's lemma, F has a maximal element M. This set M must also be maximal among the saturated sets satisfied by v, for any larger such set would contain M, and hence $Cn(X)$, and hence belong again to F. So M induces an admissible supervaluation. This supervaluation satisfies M, and hence $Cn(X)$, but cannot assign T to A: for v does not assign T to A, so A cannot belong to M. Thus we have found the desired counterexample.

THEOREM 6   If L is a conservative presuppositional language, with C finitary and N both finitary and normal, then every sentence valid in L is classically valid in L.

This is proved by an application of THEOREM 5 to the case in which X is empty; note that then, if N is normal, $Cn(X) = C(X)$.

Thus if **C** and **N** are finitary, the set of valid arguments of *L* is the same whether the radical or the conservative policy is adopted; if in addition **N** is normal, the set of valid sentences is the same whether or not **N** is disregarded. These results have obvious implications for soundness and completeness questions concerning logical systems. Whether or not this leads to interesting new logical systems, however, depends on whether **N** can be specified through axioms or rules. There is the rub: can **N** be both interesting and recursive?

THE CONSEQUENCE RELATION IN PRESUPPOSITIONAL LANGUAGES

The preceding section has shown in part that classically valid sentences and arguments remain valid when presuppositions are countenanced. A caveat is here in order, however: much reasoning, both philosophical and mathematical, cannot be appraised simply through considerations of validity in the language used to formulate its premises and conclusions.

At first sight this may seem paradoxical. To make it clearer, let us first have a look at the well-known fact that mere considerations of validity of sentences is not enough. This may be illustrated from the history of logic. Nonstandard logics seem to owe their origin mainly to the occurrence of paradoxes in standard logic: intuitionist logic, to the paradoxes of set theory, modal logic, to the paradoxes of material implication, and free logic, to the paradox that existence follows from a logical truth. Accordingly each of these systems was first formulated as a fragment of standard logic. In the case of modal and free logic, these systems can also be formulated as extensions of standard logic. Can this be done for intuitionistic logic? The answer to this question will illustrate our point.

In 1933 Gödel published a result which has been described as showing "that the classical logic can be interpreted in the intuitionistic one."[11] More precisely, he showed that the two systems have exactly the same theorems among those sentences in which the only logical signs are occurrences of & and ⅂. Since in the classical logic, the other connectives can be defined in terms of these, the result can be stated as: every classical theorem of (propositional) logic is a theorem of intuitionistic logic.[12]

The temptation is now to say that, from the point of view of the intuitionist, the classical logician managed to develop the correct logic of & and ⅂ (though not of the other connectives), and that classical logic can be regarded as a fragment of intuitionistic logic. The reason that surrendering to this temptation would lead us into error is that the result concerns only valid sentences and not valid arguments. The classical logician accepts as valid the argument "⅂⅂A, hence A", and the intuitionist does not. What makes possible this divergence on the subject of deduction after complete agreement on theorems? The answer is that the intuitionist does not accept the following classical principle concerning statements and inferences:

> (19) The argument from A to B is valid if and only if the sentence ⅂(A & ⅂B) is valid.

Hence the appraisal of reasoning requires attention to more than just the question of which sentences are valid.

In my opening paragraph, however, I claimed that it requires more even than attention to the question of which sentences and which arguments are valid. That this is so follows from a careful consideration of the effect of countenancing

11. A. Mostowski, *Thirty Years of Foundational Studies* (New York, Barnes & Noble, 1966), p. 13.

12. For the extension to the quantifiers, and a stronger result concerning deducibility, see S. Kleene, *Introduction to Metamathematics* (Amsterdam, North Holland, 1952).

presuppositions. We have seen that this does *not* lead to a tightening of logical connections *in* the language. But it leads to a tightening of logical connections in discourse *about* that language.[13] Thus the analogue of *Modus Tollens* for $\Vdash$, namely

(20) $\dfrac{A \Vdash B}{\neg B \Vdash \neg A}$

is classically valid, but not valid for presuppositional languages. For $A \Vdash B$ holds if B is a presupposition of A; but then if $\neg B$ is true, neither A nor $\neg A$ is true. Principles of the form of (20) are used in Gentzen and natural deduction formulations of logic; and there is general agreement that those formulations of logic show a good deal of agreement with the actual structure of reasoning. In so far as such a system is used merely to catalogue the set of classically valid sentences and arguments, it does not go wrong even after the countenancing of presuppositions of course. But such a rule as (20), if used indiscriminately (that is, with premises not representing classically valid arguments) leads to false conclusions.

What is the status of (20)? It is an argument about arguments; or it may be regarded as a statement about the consequence relation $\Vdash$ in L. It is not correct, unlike for example

(21) $\dfrac{X \Vdash A ; Y,A \Vdash B}{X,Y \Vdash B}$

which corresponds to Gentzen's famous rule *Cut*, and expresses the transitivity of $\Vdash$. There are other principles of this form which remain valid for presuppositional languages. For example, if the classical valuations of L are as usual, then (21) and

(22) $A, \neg A \Vdash B$

---

13. It is due to this that the *Liar* and similar semantic paradoxes can be disarmed by pointing to their presuppositions; see van Fraassen, "Presupposition," section IV.

hold and together "justify" (in an obvious way)

$$(23) \quad \frac{X \Vdash A}{X, \neg A \Vdash B}$$

but not (20).

My intention is now to show that arguments about arguments in a presuppositional language L are valid *only if* they are justified by the transitivity of $\Vdash$ and the validity of some argument in L [in the way that (21) and (22) justify (23)]. To demonstrate this, we must first give a certain amount of precision to the theory of the consequence-relation in presuppositional languages.[14]

We use X, Y to denote sets of sentences, and A, B sentences, of a presuppositional language L, in each case with or without subscripts. Adapting some terminology introduced by Curry, we call

$$(24) \quad X \Vdash A$$

an epistatement with antecedent X and consequent A. This epistatement is *true in L* if and only if the argument from X to A is valid in L. We use E, with or without subscripts, to range over epistatements.

An *epitheoretic argument* is an argument whose premises and conclusion are epistatements. A minimal sense of *validity* for such an argument in a language L would be: either not all its premises are true in L or its conclusion is true in L. However, the notion of validity is not interesting when we are considering only one interpretation of the premises and conclusion; validity is an interesting notion only in the presence of a certain degree of abstraction. In the present context, it is most relevant to abstract from the content of N. If L and L' are both

14. In doing so I was much helped by reading N. D. Belnap and R. H. Thomason, "A Rule-Completeness Theorem," *Notre Dame Journal of Formal Logic, 4* (1963), 39–43.

radical or both conservative languages, we shall call L' a *necessitation-extension* of L if and only if L' and L have the same syntax and class of classical valuations, but the relation N' of nonclassical necessitation of L' contains the corresponding relation N of L.

(25) The epitheoretic argument

$$\frac{E_1; \dots; E_k; \dots}{E}$$

is *valid* in a radical or conservative presuppositional language L if and only if for every necessitation-extension L' of L, either E is true in L' or not all of $E_1; \dots; E_k; \dots$ are true in L'.

We wish now to characterize the set of epistatements $X \Vdash A$ which can be deduced from a set K of epistatements by means of the rule *Cut* [(21)—the transitivity of $\Vdash$]. It is necessary to take into account the infinitary case; $A \Vdash (x)Fx$ should be considered a consequence of

$$A \Vdash Fx_1; \dots; A \Vdash Fx_k; \dots$$

(where $x_1, \dots, x_k, \dots$ are all the substituends for x) under the substitution interpretation of the quantifier, although no finite number of applications of *Cut* could lead to this conclusion. (We do limit ourselves to at most countable sets of epistatements, although this makes little difference to our argument.) Hence we define:

(27) $CONL(X,K)$ is the smallest set Y satisfying
  (a) X is contained in Y
  (b) if for every member A of X_i, $Y \Vdash A$ is true in L and $X_i \Vdash B$ is either true in L or a member of K, then B is in Y.

Note that Y is closed under $\Vdash$, and hence under **C** and **N**.

THEOREM 7   If L is a radical or conservative presuppositional
language, and A belongs to $CONL(X,K)$, then
the epitheoretic argument from K to $X \Vdash A$ is
valid in L.

It is clear that if every member of K is true in L', then any
admissible valuation for L' which satisfies X will satisfy every
member of $CONL(X)$—for if $Y \Vdash A$ in L, then $Y \Vdash A$ in L'—for
every necessitation-extension L' of L. This proves the theorem.

THEOREM 8   If L is a radical presuppositional language, and
A does not belong to $CONL(X,K)$, then the
epitheoretic argument from K to $X \Vdash A$ is not
valid in L.

To show that 'K, hence $X \Vdash A$' is not valid in L we must find a
necessitation-extension L' of L in which every member of K,
but not $X \Vdash A$, is true. We construct L' by setting $Y \mathbf{N}'B$ if YNB,
and also if $Y \Vdash B$ is a member of K. Note that $CONL'(X,K) =
CONL(X,K)$; the extension of $\mathbf{N}$ to $\mathbf{N}'$ is chosen so as
not to increase the set of sentences semantically entailed by
$CONL(X,K)$. So $CONL'(X,K)$ is a saturated set of L' not
containing A. Thus $X \Vdash A$ is not true in L'; but clearly, each
member of K is true in L'. This finishes the proof.

THEOREM 9   If L is a conservative presuppositional language
with $\mathbf{C}$ and $\mathbf{N}$ finitary, and A does not belong to
$CONL(X,K)$, then the epitheoretical argument
from K to $X \Vdash A$ is not valid in L.

In this case we must take care, in our construction of L', to
keep $\mathbf{N}'$ finitary. We begin with the stipulation that $Y \mathbf{N}'B$ if
YNB, and also if Y is finite and $Y \Vdash B$ belongs to K. If $Y \Vdash B$
belongs to K and Y is not finite, there are two cases to be
considered. If Y is included in $CONL(X,K)$ we choose alphabetically the first sentence in Y, say D, and set $\{D\}\mathbf{N}'B$ (if Y is

empty let D be alphabetically the first valid sentence of L).
If Y is not included in $CONL(X,K)$ we choose alphabetically
the first sentence of Y which does not belong to $CONL(X,K)$,
say D, and set $\{D\}N'B$. Now each member of K is true in L';
yet $CONL'(X,K) = CONL(X,K)$. So now $CONL(X,K)$ is a
saturated set of L' not containing A; as in the proof of THEOREM
5 it can be extended into a maximal saturated set not containing A. Thus $X \Vdash A$ is not true in L'.

Neither in THEOREM 8 nor in THEOREM 9 can we modify the
construction of L' in such a way that N' will necessarily be
normal. The reason is that K may include a member of form
$\Lambda \Vdash B$.

It may be instructive to consider some examples. Using
p,q,r to denote atomic sentences of the language L of the
propositional calculus, with N void, the instance

$$\frac{p \Vdash q}{\neg q \Vdash \neg p}$$

of (20) is refuted by setting $\{p\}N'q$ in L' (which may be taken as
radical or as conservative). Similarly

$$\frac{p \Vdash r \,;\, q \Vdash r}{p \vee q \Vdash r}$$

is refuted by setting $\{p\}N'r$ and $\{q\}N'r$—from which it does not
follow that $\{p \vee q\}N'r$ nor that $p \vee q \Vdash r$. Another instance of
the same rule ("disjunction introduction on the left") is

$$\frac{p \Vdash r \,;\, \neg p \Vdash r}{\Vdash r}$$

which is therefore refuted by taking r as a presupposition of p.
Finally

$$\frac{p \Vdash \neg p \,;\, \neg p \Vdash p}{q \Vdash r}$$

is refuted by making p a sentence which cannot possibly have a truth-value; that is, by setting $\{p\}N'$ ($\daleth p$) and $\{\daleth p\}N'p$, in which case p presupposes (p & $\daleth p$).

APPLICATION TO FREE LOGIC

The method of supervaluations has been applied to several distinct subjects: free logic,[15] quantum logic,[16] future contingencies, truth,[17] the semantic paradoxes[18] and, of course, presuppositions. This last application is of central importance, being somehow involved in all the others. Historically, however, the application to free logic was the first; I would like to take this opportunity to review my work in free logic and show how it relates to the theory of presuppositional languages.

In free logic we deal with the language of quantification theory, with the additional stipulation that the singular terms in the language may fail to refer. The interpretation of the language follows the usual pattern: a certain class of objects is chosen to be the domain of discourse. A statement of form $(x)Fx$ is interpreted to mean that every element of this domain satisfies the formula Fx. A singular term b may or may not denote an element of this domain; if it does not, then Fb clearly does not follow from $(x)Fx$.

15. R. Meyer and K. Lambert, "Universally Free Logic and Standard Quantification Theory," *Journal of Symbolic Logic*, *33* (1968), 8–20. B. C. van Fraassen, "The Completeness of Free Logic," *Zeitschrift für mathematische Logik und Grundlagen der Mathematik*, *12* (1966), 219–34; "Singular Terms, Truth-value Gaps, and Free Logic," *Journal of Philosophy*, *63* (1966), 481–95.

16. K. Lambert, "Logical Truth and Microphysics," this volume pp. 93–117.

17. Lambert, ibid.; van Fraassen, "Singular Terms," section VIII; van Fraassen, "Presupposition, Implication," section III.

18. B. Skyrms, "Return of the Liar," commentary on J. Pollock's "The Truth about Truth," APA (Western Division), Chicago, May 1967. van Fraassen, "Presupposition, Implication," section IV.

Accordingly, Leonard and his immediate successors in the area constructed the relevant logical systems by, in effect, eliminating the theorem

(27) $\vdash (x)Fx \supset Fb$

from a more familiar system of logic.

From Quine's writings, it appeared clear to me that quantification theory is essentially independent of the theory of singular terms. The arguments of Karel Lambert convinced me that the various ways in which quantification theory had been extended to deal with singular terms, had on the whole been adopted *faute de mieux*, for lack of an adequate theory. These two complementary convictions led me to reformulate free logic as an *extension*, rather than a *fragment* of standard logic.[19] In retrospect this was rather a simple matter; the key was the decision to reserve the variables of quantification solely for the job of referring to elements of the domain of discourse.

This decision is directly concerned not with the nature of the logical system, but with the semantic structure of the language. It is therefore perhaps not surprising that the logical system was reformulated in this manner in the course of a semantic completeness proof for free logic.[20] This was a weak completeness proof, that is, it concerned only the validity of statements and of arguments with at most finitely many premises. A strong completeness proof (for a slightly different semantics) was given soon after by Leblanc and Thomason,[21] using the Henkin method. I extended my own result to the

19. Exactly what fragment is described in the earlier formulations was shown precisely by Meyer and Lambert, "Universally Free Logic."

20. van Fraassen, "The Completeness of Free Logic."

21. H. Leblanc and R. H. Thomason, "Completeness Theorems for Some Presupposition-Free Logics," *Fundamenta Mathematica* (1968), forthcoming; abstract in *Journal of Symbolic Logic, 63* (1966), 699–700.

infinitary case about a year later, adapting Beth's topological methods.[22]

In all the results I have mentioned, the semantic analysis of free logic followed the guidelines laid down by Leonard, specifically in accepting bivalence. Concurrently with my weak completeness proof I pointed out that the set of valid statements need not be affected by the decision to reject bivalence. This was connected with an attempt to take Strawson's critique of the standard theory of singular statements into account—but only in an informal, not at all rigorous fashion. The remainder of this section exhibits that connection, with the precision made possible by our semantic analysis of the notion of presupposition.

Although Hintikka[23] used the term "existential presupposition" in connection with the elimination of (27), it is clear that we should read "free logic" with Lambert as an abbreviation for "logic free of existence-assumptions with respect to its terms (singular or general)." For what is eliminated is the assumption that b refers, without which the inference from $(x)Fx$ to Fb is not valid. On the other hand, it is true that in the older systems, $E!b$ (b exists) is a presupposition of Fb, in the precise sense that both of

(28a) Fb, hence $E!b$
        and
(28b) $\neg Fb$, hence $E!b$

are valid. But this was trivially so, since $E!b$ was itself a valid sentence. If we are truly to countenance $E!b$ as a presupposition of Fb, we must retain (28a) and (28b) as valid inferences, while

22. van Fraassen, "A Topological Proof of the Lowenheim-Skolem, Compactness, and Strong Completeness Theorems for Free Logic," *Zeitschrift für mathematische Logik und Grundlagen der Mathematik*, forthcoming.

23. J. Hintikka, "Existential Presuppositions and Existential Commitments," *Journal of Philosophy*, 56 (1959), 125–37.

rejecting the validity of $E!b$. We now know that this can be done in any number of ways, by adjoining any relation N satisfying at least $Fb N E!b$ and $(\daleth Fb)N E!b$ for relevant sentences Fb. At the time I followed what was ostensively a different procedure, and I wish now first to point out that the earlier procedure is but a special case of the present one.

A given (possible) situation involves a set D of individuals, furnishing the domain of discourse for a corresponding interpretation of the language. Each n-ary predicate P has an extension $f(P)$: the set of n-tuples of members of D which satisfy P; some constants b have a denotation $f(b)$ in D. Together D and f represent all the facts about this situation which can be described in the language: we call $\langle f,D \rangle$ a *model*. The model divides the classical valuations into those which correctly represent this situation, and those which do not. Each classical valuation representing the situation does something more; it assigns T or F to sentences which are not just about the individuals in D (sentences containing nonreferring terms). A sentence is true in that situation (in that model) if it is assigned T by all the classical valuations representing it. Should we add "and only if"? The answer is *yes* if we have no information about nonexistents; the possibility is, however, that we do have such information (Zeus was worshipped by the Greeks; Hamlet is a character created by Shakespeare). Such information may eliminate as incorrect some of the classical valuations agreeing with the model. What is left is a set of classical valuations V, determining a supervaluation s which is defined by

(29) $s(A) = $ T(F) if for all v in V, $v(A) = $ T(F).

But this is just the supervaluation induced by the set $\{A : v(A) = $ T for every v in $V\}$. Let us call this set $G(M)$ where M is the model in question. If we now define XNA by $X \Vdash A$ but not XCA, then we see that every such set $G(M)$ is saturated.

So every admissible valuation is a supervaluation induced by a saturated set: the language is a presuppositional language.

This result has no interest beyond the obvious: the earlier procedure is a special instance of our present procedure. The definition of **N** certainly gives us no further insight into which arguments become valid beyond the obvious (28a) and (28b). This will depend of course on the nature of the set $G(M)$, which can be just the set of sentences assigned T by all classical valuations agreeing with M (infimum) or the set of sentences assigned T by a single such valuation (supremum), or anywhere between.

It might be thought that the infimum is somehow the "correct" case: that an atomic sentence must be such that it presupposes the existence of the individuals which it names. This is of course simply a misapprehension, at one time furthered by the ideal-language philosophers, who tended to conceive of atomic sentences as corresponding to an especially simple kind of sentence in a natural language. But the symbolization of a sentence as $Pt_1 \ldots t_n$ indicates only the extent to which its internal structure has been analyzed; and the depth of the analysis need only be sufficient unto the purposes thereof.

The symbol '$=$' is a predicate constant, and is given a definite interpretation: numerical identity. It might therefore be thought that a definite commitment is in order concerning the presuppositions of a statement of form $t = t'$. In the case which I have called the infimum, $t = t'$ presupposes $(E!t \lor E!t')$. It is my opinion that this is not correct in general, but only for certain (kinds of) terms. It would be hard to make a case for the view that either of the assertions

$$\text{Allah} = \text{the god of Islam}$$
$$\text{Zeus} \neq \text{the god of Islam}$$

carries an existential commitment.

Finally, the earlier procedure was based on the assumption that if a sentence contains no nonreferring terms, then it has no fallible presuppositions. This is the main reason why I consider it now of rather limited interest. I should add, however, that in a particular application, where the atomic sentences have a definite interpretation of a certain kind, the earlier approach might be intuitively correct.

5. Logical Truth and Microphysics[1]

Karel Lambert

My main purpose is to show that certain microphysical statements can be construed as neither true nor false, while yet retaining the classical codification of statement logic. The major philosophical implication of this thesis is that whether microphysics requires a nonclassical codification of statement logic is independent of the question of what truth-value, if any, is to be assigned to certain microphysical statements. This matter will be discussed later.

The existence of such a possibility depends upon a revision in the prevailing explication of logical truth, a revision which is more harmonious (if that is the right word) with the idea of argument validity as merely truth-preserving. The revision in question, in turn, depends upon Bas van Fraassen's[2] investigations into the semantical foundations of my system of free logic,

1. This essay is a much revised version of an address originally given to the department of the history and philosophy of sciences at the University of Indiana in January of 1967. I profited from the helpful comments of Michael Scriven, Milton Fisk, Wesley Salmon, and Stephen Körner. Special thanks are due to Bas van Fraassen for his many constructive critical comments. My greatest debt, however, is to my dear friend and teacher Henry Leonard. Indeed it was he who turned my scientific bias against "philosophical" questions into a deep appreciation of their importance, especially in logic—of all places.

2. Bas C. van Fraassen, "The Completeness of Free Logic," *Zeitschrift für mathematische Logik und Grundlagen der Mathematik, 12* (1966), 219–34.

a species of logical system whose philosophical significance was first made plain in Henry Leonard's pioneering study of 1956, entitled "The Logic of Existence."[3] So the preliminary parts of this essay consist in an application of van Fraassen's semantical insights to the problem of logical truth. Before turning to the problem of logical truth let me ask for a pair of understandings.

First, the word 'statement' refers to the sort of thing which can occupy positions where it would be coherent to use a placeholder like $p, q, r \ldots$, to purloin Quine's limpid phraseology. More accurately, a statement is a formula without free variables of the sort found in the simple languages studied in elementary logic. Examples are:

(a) Mr. King was happy to meet Mrs. Queen.
(b) No one is king for a day.
(c) There was a Swedish king who admired Jim Thorpe.

Secondly, the simple languages in question are first-order languages. First-order languages do not contain statements like 'There is a property had by everything' or 'Every property Jim has, the king has.' The first-order languages I have in mind have a vocabulary consisting of variables, connectives, quantifiers, predicates, and both referential singular terms (e.g. 'Jim Thorpe') and nonreferential singular terms (e.g. 'the Queen of the U.S.'). It will not be too misleading to think of them as certain restricted fragments of English.

LOGICAL TRUTH AND TRUTH-VALUELESS STATEMENTS

A feeling familiar to teachers of beginning logic is the frustration evoked by students who steadfastly refuse to accept an argument as valid unless all of the component statements are *in fact* true. At the peak of frustration, these instructors are

3. H. Leonard, "The Logic of Existence," *Philosophical Studies*, 7 (1956), 49–64.

apt to say something like the following; "Now look! The validity of an argument has to do with its *form* alone. So to say that an argument is valid is to say *only* that if its premises *were* true its conclusion *would* also be true!" Notice that according to this plea not only is the argument from the pair of false statements 'Jim Thorpe was Russian' and 'if Jim Thorpe was Russian, he was a bolshevik' to the false statement 'Jim Thorpe was a bolshevik' valid, but so is the argument from the pair of (allegedly) truth-valueless statements 'The Queen of the United States dreamed she was being led down a bridal path by a gorilla' and 'If the Queen of the United States dreamed she was being led down a bridal path by a gorilla then she desires to marry a man named 'Harry'' to the (allegedly) truth-valueless statement 'The Queen of the United States desires to marry a man named 'Harry''.[4] In other words, the semantical characterization of validity as merely truth-preserving does not imply that the constituent statements of an argument are true nor even that they have any truth-value at all—despite one's philosophical beliefs about whether there are or are not any truth-valueless statements. Why this should be embarrassing, given the dominant account of logical truth, is not hard to explain. Customarily logical truth is taken to be a measure of validity; an argument is valid if and only if the conditional, which has the premises of the argument as antecedent and the conclusion of the argument as consequent, is logically true. But, even if interest is restricted to the classical logic of statements, the prevailing version of logical truth excludes truth-valueless statements. I say this even though that statement of logical truth, viz., truth under all assignments of truth-values to the atomic components, does not, on the face of it, exclude the possibility that *no* assignments to the atomic components are made—that the atomic components have no truth-values!

4. The ultimate responsibility for this example falls on Professor Wesley Salmon; it was he who first revealed this shocking news about the good queen.

To bolster the point, recall that classical two-valued state-ment logic recognizes statements other than conditionals as logically true. For example, any statement of the form '*p* or not *q*' is logically true. The prevailing explication of logical truth thus is framed to include statements like 'Jim Thorpe is an athlete or he is not' as logical truths. However, it is an easy matter to show, given the Tarski truth-criterion, that if such statements are regarded as logically true, then truth-valueless statements must be excluded.

For suppose otherwise; assume that '*A* or not *A*' is logically true, but that '*A*' is truth-valueless. If '*A* or not *A*' is logically true, it is true. By the Tarski truth-criterion, therefore, we have *A* or not *A*. Further, the Tarski truth-criterion, and the con-vention that '*A* is false' means '(not *A*) is true' yields the conditional that if *A* or not *A*, then '*A*' is true or '*A*' is false. But we already have *A* or not *A*. Hence, the consequence that '*A*' is true or '*A*' is false follows immediately by *Modus Ponens*, a consequence which contradicts the assumption that '*A*' is truth-valueless.

To sum up, the notion of validity as merely truth-preserving inclines one toward a conception of logical truth which pre-supposes nothing about the truth-values of statements. On the other hand, the classical codification of logical truths plus the Tarski truth-criterion demand acceptance of an account of log-ical truth which definitely excludes truth-valueless statements.

I doubt whether the conflict just described comes as a surprise to many. But reaction to it runs the gamut from the philosophical concern it produces in those neutralists who believe that logic should not prejudge philosophical questions to the ho-hum response of those who have "adjusted" to the facts of logical life. Such disparity of reactions is, I suppose, evidence again that, in philosophy, one man's obsession is another man's sedative.

One way out of the present conflict would be to reject, or at least to modify, the Tarski truth-criterion.[5] To my knowledge, this course has had few if any takers, probably because most philosopher-logicians are inclined to believe, quite independently of the Tarski truth-criterion, that an adequate semantics for classical statement logic which allows for truth-valueless statements simply is not possible. It is not hard to find cases. For example, one finds the attitude expressed by Wesley Salmon in his recent essay, "Verifiability and Logic."[6]

In an argument designed to show the question-begging character of Ayer's account of cognitive meaningfulness, Salmon writes:[7]

> Very briefly, the situation is this. Cognitive statements are taken to be just those statements which are either true or false. Statements which are either true or false are the admissible substituends for the variables of truth-functional logic. But, for those statements which are neither analytic nor selfcontradictory, a statement is cognitive if and only if it is empirically verifiable. The test for empirical verifiability involves using a statement as a substituend for a truth-functional variable (or larger expression involving variables) in the premise of a deductive argument. *This procedure is logically permissible only if the statement in question is either true or false, which is precisely the question at issue.*

Van Fraassen's recent semantical investigations, however, provide a way of characterizing logical truth which does not do violence to the conception of validity as merely truth-

5. Bas C. van Fraassen, "Singular Terms, Truth-Value Gaps, and Free Logic," *Journal of Philosophy, 63* (1966), 481–95.

6. W. Salmon, "Verifiability and Logic," in P. Feyerabend and G. Maxwell, eds., *Mind, Matter, and Method: Essays in Philosophy and Science in Honor of Herbert Feigl* (Minneapolis, University of Minnesota Press, 1967), p.359.

7. Wesley Salmon kindly brought this passage to my attention. *Italics added.*

preserving—that is, truth-valueless statements are not excluded
—while yet retaining the classical codification of statement
logic. The implication of this ingenious discovery is that the
classical logic of statements is neutral with respect to whether
there are or are not truth-valueless statements; for whether
there are or are not, the codification of statement logic nevertheless remains the classical one. To be sure, some ideas must
be modified, the major one being a modification of Tarski's
truth-criterion. That this move is not as drastic as might
appear at first glance will be made plain shortly.

A REVISED ACCOUNT OF LOGICAL TRUTH

The objective of this section is to capture the merely truth-
preserving character of validity in the notion of logical truth.
Another way to look at the goal is this: how can the account
of logical truth (qua statement logic) be freed from the commitment to assignments to the atomic components? For recall,
'logical truth (qua statement logic)' means 'true for all assignments of truth-values to the atomic components.' This
statement of logical truth is perfectly acceptable, provided it
can be construed as not having existential import—as not
implying the existence of such assignments. Still another way
of looking at the matter might be more helpful. How can the
notion of logical truth (qua statement logic) be made to
conform to what is expressed (roughly) by the subjunctive
statement, "*Were* the atomic components of a statement to be
assigned truth-values, no matter what assignments be made,
the statement in question *would* be true"?

In contemporary formal semantics, the notion of logical
truth is explicated with the help of the notion of a model.
Typically a model contains a set of objects—called a domain
of discourse—and various rules which associate the predicates
of a language with classes of objects in the domain of discourse,
and some or all of the singular terms of the language with the

objects in the domain of discourse. For examples, suppose the language is some fragment of English containing the predicate 'is an athlete' and the name 'Jim Thorpe,' and suppose the domain of discourse is the domain of physical objects. Then typically the model associates the predicate 'is an athlete' with some class, say, the class of athletes, and the name 'Jim Thorpe' with some physical object.

Given the assignments of expressions to things, one can now say what it means for a statement to be true in the model, to be false in the model, and even, if one wishes, to have some other value in the model. The characterization of truth-value assignments is called a *valuation*. Classical valuations entertain only two kinds of truth-value, True and False. In general a classical valuation assigns True or False to each statement in steps; first, to the atomic statements and, second, to the compound statements (like 'Jim Thorpe is an athlete or he isn't'), in terms of the assignments to the atomic components and the truth-functional characterization of the connectives.

It is important to notice that the criterion for truth or falsity of atomic statements may be such that all of the statements of the language have a determined truth-value, or only that some do. For example, we might say that an atomic statement ('Jim Thorpe is an athlete') is true when its subject term ('Jim Thorpe') designates a physical object which is a member of the class of things associated with its predicate ('is an athlete'); that an atomic statement ('Jim Thorpe is a Russian') is false if its subject term ('Jim Thorpe') designates a physical object which is not a member of the class associated with its predicate ('is a Russian'). If the language contains only referential singular terms, then all of the statements of the language will have a determined truth-value. On the other hand, suppose the language contains nonreferential singular terms, singular terms which are not associated with any object in the domain of discourse. Then, given the present characterizations of truth and falsity in the model, some of the statements of the language—for example, the statement 'The Queen of the United States is an athlete'—would not have a determined truth-value. This does not mean that they would not have a truth-value—a classical valuation requires that they have one—but only that their particular truth-value would not be determined in the model. When we have a subclass of statements of a language whose truth-value is not determined according to some criterion, we have, in effect, a class of statements which one could say are the classical surrogates of the truth-valueless statements of the user of that language. The intuitive idea here is that if a statement is regarded as truth-valueless, then if it were to be assigned a truth-value in a classical valuation, the assignment would be arbitrary; it could, with equal justification, be assigned True or be assigned False.

This situation can be represented graphically as follows: suppose we have a language which consists of only two atomic statements, 'A' and 'B.' Let 'A' be a statement with the determined truth-value True; 'B' be a truthvalueless candidate; '⌐' be the classical 'not' and 'v' the classical 'or.' Then there are two possible classical valuations in the model with respect to these two statements.

	C_1	C_2
A	T	T
⌐A	F	F
B	T	F
⌐B	F	T
A v ⌐A	T	T
⋮	⋮	⋮
B v ⌐B	T	T

In this tabular representation we have a general procedure for describing, in classical terms, which statements a person takes as truthvalueless, if any—given a statement of his standard for truth-value assignments to the atomic statements. Consider now the following valuation.

	S_1
A	T
$\neg A$	F
B	–
$\neg B$	–
$A \vee \neg A$	T
⋮	⋮
$B \vee \neg B$	T

S_1 is an example of what van Fraassen calls a *supervaluation*.[8] A supervaluation tells us which truth-value assignments to make—true, false, or none at all—given the classical valuations. In general it represents a truth-value-assignment rule obeying the principle that all and only those statements assigned True (or False) in all the classical valuations over the model are to be assigned True (or False). Accordingly the supervaluation S_1 represents what the classical valuations C_1 and C_2 have *in common*.

Notice that in the supervaluation S_1, the statement 'A' is assigned T(rue), its negate is assigned F(alse), 'B' and its negate are assigned nothing, i.e. are truth-valueless, and finally '$A \vee \neg A$', *and* '$B \vee \neg B$' are assigned T(rue). The reason the compound '$B \vee \neg B$' is assigned True is that no matter which truth-value 'B' were to get in the classical valuations, it always

8. "Singular Terms, Truth-Value Gaps, and Free Logic," p. 486.

turns out true; its truth-value is determined in the classical valuations. So it cannot be construed as truth-valueless, according to the intuitive idea that the truth-valueless statements are those whose truth-values are undetermined in classical valuations; supervaluations give us a way of representing both the assignment of truth-values and the nonassignment of truth-values.

It is important to realize that supervaluations are not classical valuations because they tolerate cases where no truth-value assignment is made. Yet one can *use* classical valuations to determine which statements of the language have truth-value assignments and which do not. Lest one think this procedure terribly mysterious, one need only remember that it bears a striking resemblance to Quine's attitude toward truth valueless statements in his *Methods of Logic*.[9]

The concept of a supervaluation provides the means for explicating logical truth in conformity with the requirements listed at the beginning of this section. Customarily 'logical truth' is defined as 'true in all classical valuations over all models.' In other words, no matter what domain of discourse and which associations between words and things is chosen, if a statement is logically true, it will be assigned True by any classical valuation. Now consider supervaluations. Remember there are cases where no truth-value assignments are made. So 'logical truth' can now be defined as 'true in all supervaluations over all models,' with the assurance that the logical truths will be the conventional ones, and without the presumption that the atomic components actually have truth-values. For example, though 'A v $\neg A$' is logically true, it does *not* follow that 'A' is true or 'A' is false.

Let me illustrate further. Consider, for example, 'B v $\neg B$.' In the supervaluation listed above, it is assigned true, but its component 'B' is assigned nothing. Notice how this conforms

9. W. V. O. Quine, *Methods of Logic* (rev. ed., New York, Holt, 1959), p. 220.

to the previously stated mark of adequacy. The reason '$B \lor \neg B$' is true, while 'B' is truth-valueless in the super-valuation is because it is true no matter what truth-value 'B' is assigned, *were* it to be assigned one—as can be proved by looking at the corresponding classical valuations. I hope it is clear that no matter how the model is varied, the same relation-ship between the classical valuations and supervaluations containing '$B \lor \neg B$' will obtain. Hence '$B \lor \neg B$' is logically true. I conclude that, in the precise explication of logical truth as true in all supervaluations over all models, we have captured a sense of logical truth which corresponds rather closely to argument validity as *merely* truth-preserving.

Before turning to the implications of these developments for the logic of microphysics, I want to discuss two items briefly; the first has to do with the question, raised earlier, of the philosophical neutrality of the classical codification of statement logic, and the second, with Tarski's truth-criterion.

Van Fraassen's definition of logical truth—what he calls SL truth—is neutral on the question of whether or not the atomic components have a truth-value. For it has already been shown that '$B \lor \neg B$' is logically true while 'B' is truth-valueless. But, as one can easily see by checking the supervaluation listed above, '$A \lor \neg A$' is also true, yet 'A' is assigned True. This situation holds in all supervaluations. Hence '$A \lor \neg A$' is logically true no matter what truth-value 'A' has—and, by hypothesis, it has one. Accordingly, the present explication of logical truth is neutral with respect to the question of whether or not there are truth-valueless statements. Now it is provable that if a formula is SL true it is a theorem of classical statement logic, and vice versa. It follows that the classical codification of logic is neutral with respect to the question of whether there are or are not truth-valueless statements.

There is a proviso to this latter claim; Tarski's truth-criterion must be modified. For recall that it was by means of

Tarski's criterion that any statement of the form '$p \vee \daleth p$' was shown to imply that its component of the form 'p' is true or is false. Perhaps the most profound philosophical implication of a notion of logical truth which conforms to the notion of validity as merely truth-preserving is that it requires a modification of Tarski's truth-criterion, *if* one wishes to retain the classical codification of statement logic. This implication should not cause undue alarm; it would be more accurate to view the present analysis as revealing a presupposition of Tarski's truth-criterion rather than as requiring a drastic alteration in our notion of truth. For all this analysis demands is that, however one discriminates between the truth-valueless and the truth-valued, the Tarski criterion holds for any statement which meets the standard for being truth-valued. For example in van Fraassen's own treatment, every atomic nonidentity statement containing a nondesignating singular term is taken to be truth-valueless. So, in these cases, the truth-criterion might be modified thusly : If A is an atomic nonidentity statement containing a singular term 'a' then ('A' is true if and only if A) *provided* $(\exists y)(y = a)$ where '$(\exists y)(y = a)$' is the object language correlate of '"a' designates.'

Incidentally, the claim that the Tarski truth-criterion presupposes that statements are truth-valued is provable under one recent interpretation of 'presupposition.' A statement A presupposes a statement B if and only if whenever A is true, B is true and whenever $\daleth A$ is true, B is true. It turns out that 'presupposition' so construed bears a striking resemblance to Strawson's view.

If A is imagined to be the following version of the Tarski truth-criterion, namely, ' 'S' is true $\equiv S$,' and B is imagined to be ' 'S' is true or 'S' is false,' then A presupposes B; for whenever ' 'S' is true $\equiv S$' is true then ' 'S' is true or 'S' is false' is true, and whenever '$\daleth$('S' is true $\equiv S$)' is true, then ' 'S' is true or 'S' is false' is true. The reader can verify this result by examining the semantical development in the first part of van Fraassen's contribution to this volume. On the other hand, as the reader also can verify, it is not the case that "'S' is true ≡ S" presupposes 'S.'

TRUTH-VALUELESS MICROPHYSICAL STATEMENTS

Throughout this discussion certain statements usually have been termed truth-valueless rather than neither true nor false. There are very good reasons for this.

First, the expression 'is neither true nor false' is prima facie ambiguous, but that prima facie ambiguity could not be appreciated fully until now. Its use may mean that there is a third truth-value—some call it the value Middle, others the value Meaningless or Absurd—or merely that there are truth-valueless statements. The difference, semantically speaking, is that between assigning something to a statement and not assigning anything.

Secondly, the more conventional interpretation of the expression 'is neither true nor false' is perhaps that which has it representing a third truthvalue. Hence, usually the expression 'is neither true nor false' is associated with a nonclassical codification of statement logic of the sort, often called simply "three-valued logic." Thus, Goddard in his very interesting and provocative work on formal theories of meaningfulness, construes Ryle's assertion that category mistakes are neither true nor false, as implying a three-valued logic of significance.[10] Surely it is the proclivity to think of the label 'is neither true nor false' as representing a third truth-value which has persuaded many conservative philosophers that a language allowing statements which are neither true nor false will be very unconventional. On this matter, van Fraassen's work,

10. L. Goddard, "Predicates, relations and categories," *Australasian Journal of Philosophy, 44* (1966), 139–71.

therefore, can be seen as valuable in two respects. First, it shows that the interpretation of 'is neither true nor false' as meaning 'no truth-value assignment is made' is prima facie distinct from the usual three-valued interpretation which construes 'is neither true nor false' as a truth-value distinct from the truth-values 'true' and 'false.' Indeed one might think of the expression "no truth-value assignment is made" as the formal counterpart of Strawson's informal aphorism "the question concerning the truth-value of the statement does not arise." Secondly, the fact that van Fraassen's interpretation of 'is neither true nor false' as truth-valueless does not require a nonclassical codification of statement logic should quell the uneasy feelings of those who suspect the unconventional.

It ought to be mentioned, however, that nothing said so far prohibits one from interpreting 'is neither true nor false' as another truth-value and attempting to develop valuation rules that have the effect of supervaluations. For example, the logician, Robert Meyer, who sees the world through many-valued glasses, prefers this tack. But a policy which condones the pullulation of philosophical entities of any kind shows too little regard for the distinction between what is needed and what is possible.

The issue of how to interpret the expression 'is neither true nor false' has implications for the problem of the logic of microphysics. In 1957, Hilary Putnam[11] argued that the expression 'is neither true nor false' could be applied gainfully to certain physical statements of the form 'Object b has position such and such at time t.' He construed 'is neither true nor false' as representing a third truth-value, called "Middle," and laid down truth rules for it. The consequent three-valued logic, he claimed, had at least one profound effect in microphysics: it allowed one, as Reichenbach had previously noted,

11. H. Putnam, "Three-Valued Logic," *Philosophical Studies*, 5 (1957): 73–80.

to hold consistently both to the laws of quantum physics and to the principle that there is no velocity greater than the speed of light. By contrast, given the meaningfulness of all statements of the form 'Object b has position such and such at time t,' in classical two-valued logic, the principle that there is no velocity greater than the speed of light is incompatible with the laws of quantum mechanics.

Isaac Levi[12] and Paul Feyerabend[13] have raised vigorous objections to Putnam's position and have recommended that we dispense with the middleman in the logic of microphysics. Levi complains that there is no real choice between a two-valued logic which recognizes unknown or undecidable truths and the three-valued analogue which assigns to exactly the same statements a third truth-value, namely Middle.[14] It ought to be noticed that if Putnam's allegation of incompatibility holds, then the two-valued analogue entertained by Levi would have to be nonclassical, e.g. like intuitionistic statement-logic.

Feyerabend's objections are quite different. He does not challenge Putnam's belief that the truth-value Middle can be given a distinct meaning, but he rejects Putnam's three-valued proposal as being but the most modern of "the sly procedures which have been invented for the purpose of saving an incorrect theory in the face of refuting evidence."[15] For the statement that there is no velocity greater than the velocity of light "is a well-corroborated statement of physics."[16] Secondly, he rejects Putnam's allegation of an incompatibility

12. I. Levi, "Putnam's Three Truth Values," *Philosophical Studies, 5* (1959), 65–69.

13. P. Feyerabend, "Reichenbach's Interpretation of Quantum-Mechanics," *Philosophical Studies, 4* (1958) 49–59.

14. "Putnam's Three Truth Values," p. 68.

15. "Reichenbach's Interpretation of Quantum-Mechanics," p. 50.

16. Ibid.

in classical two-valued logic between the laws of quantum mechanics and the principle that no velocity exceeds that of the speed of light. However, says Feyerabend, Putnam's three-valued proposal does have implications for the following supposed incompatibility: the laws of quantum mechanics are incompatible with the principle that every entity possesses always one property out of each of the set of mutually exclusive classical categories,[17] a principle which implies that every entity has both a well-defined position and a well-defined momentum. But then, Feyerabend complains, acceptance of Putnam's proposal would require us to acknowledge the propriety of the *false* principle that every entity always has one out of every pair of mutually exclusive classical properties.[18]

Feyerabend also takes both Putnam and Reichenbach to task on their claim that the three-valued way out of the difficulties occasioned by the physics of the minute is superior to Bohr's proposal to treat the offensive statements as "meaningless." Thus, among other things, he accuses Putnam and Reichenbach of apriorism in their assertion that the statements Bohr calls "meaningless" indeed "have a very clear cognitive use." He further argues that the Putnam–Reichenbach proposal fails to satisfy the Reichenbach standard of adequacy that "every law of quantum mechanics should have either the truth-value True or the truth-value False, but never the truth-value Indeterminate."[19] Specifically, Feyerabend presents an important argument to show that, given the Putnam–Reichenbach three-valued proposal, "every quantum-mechanical statement containing noncommuting operators can only possess the truth-value [Middle]."[20]

17. Ibid., p. 53.
18. Ibid., p. 51.
19. Ibid., p. 53.
20. Ibid., p. 54.

I shall not deal here with Feyerabend's objection that quantum-mechanical statements containing noncommuting operators get the truth-value Middle in the Putnam–Reichenbach scheme except to say that his argument is questionable, and that even if legitimate as a counter to the Putnam–Reichenbach position, it is *not* a legitimate counter to the position that certain elementary quantum mechanical statements are truth-valueless as opposed to Middle. The justification for these assertions will be found in van Fraassen's paper, "The Labyrinth of Quantum Logic."[21] But the remarks which I shall make in the rest of this section will indeed bear on the remaining Levi and Feyerabend objections.

Consider the following pair of statements: first, "There are mountains on the other side of the moon," and second, "The Queen of the United States wants to marry a man named 'Harry'." Before rocketships et al., the first statement was a standard philosophical example of a statement that had a truth-value, but whose particular truth-value was unknown. Still its truth (or falsity) was potentially verifiable (or falsifiable). However, the second statement, it has been urged, is different. It is neither potentially verifiable nor potentially falsifiable, and thus it would be misleading to say that its truth-value is unknown. Now Putnam's remarks about the truth-value Middle seem to point to some such distinction, for he says that it does not mean "unknown truth-value".[22] Further, he suggests that, under certain conditions, we can know, by virtue of a physical law and certain observational data, that a statement like 'Object b has position such and such at time t' can never be falsified or verified. This would seem to put statements about an object's position, under certain conditions, in the same group as statements about the Queen of the

21. B. van Fraassen, "The Labyrinth of Quantum Logic" (forthcoming).
22. Putnam, "Three-Valued Logic," p. 75.

United States—with respect to verifiability and hence truth-valuehood. This of course does not mean that there is no distinction at all between statements about the Queen of the United States and object *b*.

Suppose now we construe the expression 'is neither true nor false' as meaning 'truth-valueless.' Then it does not follow that to call certain physical statements neither true nor false requires a nonclassical codification of statement logic. For those like Putnam and Reichenbach, who find sense in such statements, this approach to certain microphysical statements would clearly be more palatable than the Bohr approach which, in effect, excludes such statements as legitimate instances of classical two-valued schemata.

Let me amplify these cryptic claims. First, recall the developments of the previous section. The conditions there under which an atomic statement was assigned true, false, or nothing in the supervaluation S_1 may be summed up as follows:

Let '*Fa*' represent an arbitrary atomic nonidentity statement containing '*a*' as singular term. Then we have:

   (i) '*Fa*' is true if *a* is an existent which is a member of the class of things which are F.
  (ii) '*Fa*' is false if *a* is an existent which is not a member of the class of things which are F.
 (iii) '*Fa*' is truth-valueless if *a* is not an existent.

For when *a* is an existent and is a member of the class of things which are F, '*Fa*' is true in all valuations, hence true in the supervaluation, S_1. Similarly, when *a* is an existent but is not a member of the class of things which are *F*, '*Fa*' is false in all valuations, hence false in the supervaluation, S_1. Finally, when *a* does not exist, '*Fa*' is false in some valuations and true in others, hence truth-valueless in the supervaluation, S_1.

In analogous fashion we can lay down the truth-conditions for elementary microphysical statements and thus tell which statements will be assigned True, False, or nothing in a given supervaluation. Thus let 'Gb' be short for 'b has position G at time t.' Then we can lay down the truth-conditions for statements of this form as follows:

(i) 'Gb' is true if b has position G at time t.

(ii) 'Gb' is false if b has some position other than G at time t.

(iii) 'Gb' is truth-valueless if b has a property (e.g. momentum M) which is quantum theoretically incompatible with having a definite position at time t.

Now care must be taken to distinguish between

(1) $\Vdash$ '$Gb \lor \neg Gb$' is true,

and

(2) $\Vdash$ 'Gb' is true or '$\neg Gb$' is true.

(1) is shorthand for: it is always the case that 'b has position G at time t or some other position at that time' is true, whereas (2) abbreviates something very different: it is always the case that 'b has position G at time t' is true, or that 'b has some position other than G at time t' is true. From the discussion above it ought to be plain that, under the present interpretation of elementary microphysical statements, (1) does **not** imply (2). And **in fact** (2) is false, for example, when b has a definite momentum at time t; that is, under such circumstances, neither 'Gb' nor '$\neg Gb$' is true. This fact is captured in (iii) of the above set of truth-conditions for 'Gb'.

Consider now the classical principle C, the principle that "each entity possesses *always* one property out of each [classical] category."[23] C implies (1). But Reichenbach thought

23. Feyerabend, "Reichenbach's Interpretation of Quantum-Mechanics," p. 51.

that it must also imply (2), apparently because of the belief that (1) must inevitably imply (2). Thus he was led to what surgeons call the "heroic treatment" of rejecting the classical codification of statement logic. I share Feyerabend's suspicion of such drastic philosophical treatments. But it is simply unwarranted to assume that C must imply (2), that is, that C must imply, for example, that an "electron always possesses a well-defined position and a well-defined momentum."[24] For, under the present interpretation of elementary microphysical statements, (1) need not and does not imply (2).

In the previous paragraph I mentioned Reichenbach's apparent belief that (1) implied (2). The word "apparent" is to be taken seriously. I don't wish to discount the possibility that Reichenbach so construed the principle C that (2) is a direct consequence of it. Indeed, then Feyerabend's objection would be a telling one against Reichenbach's (and, derivately, Putnam's) acceptance both of C and of the laws of quantum mechanics. As a matter of fact, I believe Feyerabend's objection to Reichenbach's approach could have been put even more strongly. Thus, given Reichenbach's rejection of both (1) and (2), it is hard to see how Reichenbach could retain the classical principle C in any sense. Accordingly, the most that is claimed for the present interpretation of elementary microphysical statements is that it represents a reasonable reconstruction of Reichenbach's position, given his desire to maintain C.

The present reconstruction of the Reichenbach–Putnam position on elementary microphysical statements will perhaps be congenial to those who find Bohr's approach, as interpreted by Reichenbach, unacceptable. Besides having a definite "if-it-offends-thee-pluck-it-out" aura about it, the Bohr approach à la Reichenbach is in some respects more extreme than the Reichenbach–Putnam adoption of a three-valued logic for elementary microphysical statements. Bohr's position

24. Ibid., p. 51.

is that a sentence like '*b* has position *G* at time *t*' is "meaning-ful" only if certain physical conditions are realized. The upshot is that elementary microphysical statements are allowed to be substituends for the schematic letters in the schemata of classical statement logic only if certain physical conditions (e.g. measurement conditions) are realized. (Note the striking similarity here to the attitude of those who deny the conditional 'If Pegasus does not exist then there is something which doesn't exist' the status of a counterexample to the validity of the logical schema called Particularization on the ground that 'Pegasus does not exist' is "ill formed" or "meaningless.") But surely this is the counsel of the ostrich. It amounts to burying one's head in the sand in the face of a threat to a longstanding theory. Indeed, it is an attitude which would be disastrous in science. For it suggests that no new theories or explanations are ever necessary because there would be no conflicting instances to the old theory to explain ; the purported counterexamples to the old theories turn out to be merely nonsensical.

Nor is Feyerabend's cry of "Apriorism!" to Putnam's assertion that such sentences as '*b* has position *G* at time *t*' have a clear cognitive use very convincing. Indeed Feyerabend's claim that "in our search for better theories we frequently discover that situations we thought would obtain universally do in fact exist only under special conditions, which implies that the properties of these situations are applicable in those conditions only"[25] is disputable. In fact, often it is the case that an assertion containing a property word, made in a context where the appropriate special conditions are not realized, is meaningful but false, or at least not true.

Consider again Levi's objection to Putnam's third truth-value, Middle. Roughly it is that there is no distinctive answer to the question: What is this thing called Middle?—to para-

25. Ibid., p. 56.

phrase the popular song. But Levi's argument loses its force, by default if you will, with respect to the expression 'truth-valueless' there being no "thing" which a statement is assigned when it is said to be truth-valueless. Accordingly the present reconstruction of the Putnam–Reichenbach position is not vitiated by Levi's forceful arguments against three-valued logic.

I shall end this penultimate section with a brief remark on what I believe to be the most important philosophical implication of the present enterprise, an implication whose acceptability depends only upon the present reconstruction of Reichenbach's interpretation of elementary microphysical statements as a possible interpretation of same. The implication in question is this: which truth-value, if any, is to be assigned to certain elementary microphysical statements is independent of the question of whether microphysics requires a nonclassical logic. For even if no truth-value is assigned to certain microphysical statements it is still possible to define 'valid,' etc., in such a way that all classically valid arguments and statements remain valid. This implication runs against the grain of the historical tradition which teaches that classical logic dictates a particular interpretation of microphysical statements, and insofar as the required interpretation runs afoul of the laws governing the physics of the minute, classical logic is wanting. The force of the present reconstruction of Reichenbach's position has been rather that classical logic is neutral with respect to the interpretation of elementary microphysical statements. It is no more incompatible with rejection of the principle that every entity always has a determinate position than it is with acceptance of that principle. At the semantic level, this shows up in the fact that the truth of (2) is independent of the truth of (1). Nor is this reading of the independence of (2) and (1) any more farfetched than taking the nonsemantical statement '$a = b$' to be false when the semantical statement "Everything which term 'a' designates, term 'b' designates" is false.

SOME OBJECTIONS

In this final section I should like to discuss some objections to the present treatment of elementary microphysical statements.

The first objection might be put as follows. Intuitively it is not the case that every statement of the form $Fa \lor \neg Fa$, where F is any predicate and a is some nondesignating singular term, is true let alone logically true. Michael Scriven has suggested to me that 'The greatest natural number is prime or it is not' is such a nontruth. So, in this respect at least, the present reconstruction of Reichenbach's position is inferior to Reichenbach's original approach via three-valued logic. For in Reichenbach's original approach Scriven's example would not be logically true and could indeed be assigned the value Middle consistent with ordinary intuitions.

Three replies come to mind. First, intuition is a questionable guide in these matters. Thus recall that the characterization of logical truth I gave earlier was motivated by a certain basic intuitive consideration explained in the second section of this essay. And *that* intuitive guide does yield the result that a statement like 'The greatest natural number is prime or it is not' is logically true. Thus we are put in the position of asking which intuition to trust. But I know of no final intuitive answer to this question.

Secondly, it is not necessarily the case that adoption of a logic in which Excluded Middle fails for atomic statements containing a nondesignating singular term requires adoption of such a logic in microphysics. For, in the latter case, presumably 'b' in 'b has G at time t' is a designating term. Hence the reasons for calling it truth-valueless will be quite different.

In the third place, even granting the intuitive nontruth of (1), who is to say that subsequent developments in microphysics and in its logic might not dictate an alteration in our intuitions more in line with the present interpretation of elementary microphysical statements? The success of Newtonian physics, after all, required an alteration in ordinary (Aristotelian) intuitions about the behavior of physical objects, an analogy brought to my attention by Stephen Körner.

Milton Fisk, and independently Wesley Salmon, have suggested to me that logical laws can be regarded as truth-valueless when they have truth-valueless components, without thereby having to abandon the classical codification of statement logic. The trick is to interpret 'logically true' as meaning simply 'is never assigned false.' Then, for example, any statement of the form '$p \lor \neg p$' will be logically true, though there will be instances of this schema which are assigned no truth-value i.e. are truth-valueless. Fisk suggests that this latter approach would be more acceptable to those, including himself, who do not find the subjunctive, "Ignoring existence presuppositions, if the components of a statement '$A \lor \neg A$' were assigned truth-values, it would be true" an adequate basis for assigning True to '$A \lor \neg A$' where 'A' is in fact truth-valueless.

To this remark I have two replies. First, Fisk's suggestion has the following unpalatable consequence. Assuming logical truth as a measure of validity, Fisk's alteration in the concept of logical truth requires a similar alteration in the concept of validity; validity must now be construed as 'nonfalsehood preserving.' Now Fisk's suggestion has the effect of letting certain conditionals be logical truths which though not always assigned True nevertheless are never assigned False. But then there may be valid arguments with, say, true premises and a truth-valueless conclusion. Surely this destroys the usefulness of deductive procedures in the sense that inference can no longer be thought of as an instrument of proof where 'proof' means 'establishing the truth of some claim.'

Secondly, a closely related point is the following: it is not true that the Fisk interpretation of logical truth necessarily yields the classical codification of statement logic. The rule of *Modus Ponens*, a crucial rule in classical statement logic, is truth preserving, but it is not nonfalsehood preserving in the present semantical development. Thus, let '*A*' be truth-valueless and let '*B*' be assigned False. Then '*A*' is nonfalse and '*A* ⊃ *B*' is nonfalse, but '*B*' is False.

Finally, there is the objection that the present reconstruction of Reichenbach's approach to elementary microphysical statements succeeds only at the expense of trivializing certain consequences of the classical principle *C*. This objection is haunted by the ghost of the analytic–synthetic distinction. To be sure, the classical principle *C* has certain consequences which are logically true under the present interpretation of elementary microphysical statements, but it is not obvious that therefore they are physically trivial, that is, nonempirical. Even so, the present interpretation of the classical principle *C* avoids a dilemma which many have felt in the wake of quantum physics. For, given the present interpretation of *C*, it is not the case that the classical principle *C* is an inextricable part of classical physics—to put it paradoxically. (Parenthetically, this would be true even if the classical principle *C*, interpreted as implying (2), were abandoned. For if classical physics were axiomatized, then it would probably be capable of an interpretation in which (2) fails but (1) holds.) So those who have wanted to acknowledge the facts of microphysics can now do so without feeling that they do so only at the expense of making the conventional notion of "physical object" unintelligible.

6. Modal Logic and Metaphysics[1]

Richmond H. Thomason

1. In recent years, the research of many logicians has converged toward a solution of the problem of quantification into modal contexts, and in the last decade a new level of understanding has been achieved in this area.[2] Of course, problems still remain; but these can now be treated within the context of a well-articulated logical theory. In this paper I wish to discuss in an informal way some of my own contributions to this development; these consist primarily of semantical completeness theorems for some systems of modal logic with quantifiers.

Perhaps the simplest example of a theorem of this sort is the one obtained by Post in the 1920s for the familiar sentential calculus. Post showed that every formula provable in this system was tautologous, and conversely that every tautology was a theorem: thereby establishing that a notion of *validity* for such formulas coincides with a notion of *provability*. Such a theorem was obtained for the predicate calculus of first order with identity in 1930 by Gödel. A stronger result holding for

1. The research described in this paper was supported in part under National Science Foundation grant GS-1567.
2. For a brief history of this research, see Bibliographical Note below, pp. 144–45.

sets of formulas of the predicate calculus was obtained by Henkin in 1947.

My own results are analogues of Henkin's theorem for certain modal systems. There are many systems for which such results have been obtained, but in this presentation I will confine myself to three systems which seem of particular interest—two of them with completeness theorems. (The other results can, for the most part, be obtained from these two by minor changes.) The theorems themselves are mathematical in character, and are proved by algebraic techniques resembling those used in representation theorems. But when discussed in an informal way these results, so far from appearing technical, take on a metaphysical character. The reason for this is that the heuristic notions arising in the semantical interpretation of quantified modal logic are concepts of traditional philosophic concern; and so, in much the same way that a mathematician explaining his work might refer to space and its characteristics, I will be speaking of existence, substances, and accidents.

2. The central task of this paper is to provide an adequate semantical account of a sufficiently rich formal system of modal logic.

By an *adequate* semantical account, I mean one that is intuitively plausible (and hence, will provide an informally satisfying explanation of what modality is about), as well as technically acceptable. A crucial technical test of adequacy is the establishment of a semantical completeness theorem of the sort described above; but symbolic logic, being a well-articulated discipline, also imposes numerous criteria which any well-made logical theory must meet. So, as well as shaping logical work in the light of heuristic philosophical considerations, I have often found myself modifying metaphysical preconceptions in the light of technical considerations.

By a *sufficiently rich* formal system of modal logic I mean, for present purposes, something quite specific; the system must contain formal apparatus sufficient to express the following:

> Truth-functional connectives,
> Modal connectives,
> Identity,
> Universal quantification over individuals,
> Definite descriptions.

As we will see, profound difficulties are involved in handling all of these simultaneously, which cannot be settled on a piecemeal basis; for instance, one might possess a satisfactory semantics for all of the above notions except for identity, and yet have no idea of how the theory could be satisfactorily extended to account for identity.

Accordingly, our formal language will include individual variables x, y, z, ...; individual constants a, b, c, ...; i-ary ($i \geq 0$) predicate letters P, Q, ...; and sentential connectives $\supset$, $\sim$, and $\square$. We may also construct identity-formulas $s = t$, universal quantifications $(x)A$, and descriptions $\imath_x A$. *Terms t* and *formulas A* are defined inductively as usual. By means of these primitives, we can then define disjunction, conjunction, equivalence, possibility, existential quantification, and unique-existential quantification ($\vee$, $\wedge$, $\equiv$, $\diamondsuit$, $\exists$, $\exists!$). We also use the following definitions:

$$E t =_{df} (\exists x) x = t$$

$$E\square t =_{df} (\exists x)\square(x = t).$$

The next three sections discuss some familiar ways of handling the sentential connectives, identity, and universal quantification. I will assume that the reader is familiar with these topics, and will be very brief.

3. For definiteness, let's choose a simple axiomatization of classical sentential logic, consisting of the three axiom-

schemes
$$A \supset (B \supset A)$$
$$(A \supset (B \supset C)) \supset ((A \supset B) \supset (A \supset C))$$
$$(\sim A \supset \sim B) \supset (B \supset A),$$

and the rule *Modus Ponens*.

$$\frac{A \quad A \supset B}{B}$$

All of the systems considered below will possess these axiom-schemes and this rule in unrestricted form.[3]

The connectives $\sim$ and $\supset$ have the usual two-valued truth-functional semantics, which is characteristic for the above axiomatization; i.e. there is semantical completeness here.

The connective $\square$ will be interpreted according to Kripke's semantics. A *model structure* consists of a nonempty set $\mathscr{K}$ (of "possible worlds") and a binary relation $\mathscr{R}$ (of "alternativeness" or "relative possibility") on $\mathscr{K}$. A formula $\square A$ takes the value T in a member α of $\mathscr{K}$ if and only if A takes the value T in all members β of $\mathscr{K}$ such that $\alpha \mathscr{R} \beta$. By imposing various conditions on $\mathscr{R}$, we obtain interpretations corresponding to various kinds of modality: e.g., if $\mathscr{R}$ is assumed reflexive and transitive, the semantics corresponds to Lewis' **S4**.

For definiteness, the modality of **S4** will be paradigmatic in this paper; thus, I will posit the axiom-schemes

$$\square(A \supset B) \supset (\square A \supset \square B)$$

$$\square A \supset A$$

$$\square A \supset \square \square A,$$

and the rule of necessitation,

$$\frac{A}{\square A}$$

3. One exception: the alternative to Russell's theory of descriptions mentioned in n. 8 would involve certain restrictions on the use of sentential axioms containing descriptions. But this alternative is only mentioned in passing.

in unrestricted form in the systems considered below. But the results of this paper will not depend on our choice of **S4**; they hold for most familiar systems of sentential modality.

I will refer to the axioms and rules of this section as sentential axioms and rules.

4. For the semantical interpretation of identity we introduce the notion of a *domain* of individuals; terms are assigned values in this (nonempty) domain, and $s = t$ takes the value T if and only if s and t are assigned the same member of the domain.

Let $A^s/\!/t$ be any result of replacing any number of free occurrences of t in A by occurrences of s (relettering bound variables, if necessary, to avoid binding a free variable in A). Then the two schemes

$$t = t \qquad\qquad \text{(SId)}$$
$$s = t \supset (A \supset As/\!/t) \qquad \text{(InId)}$$

yield an axiomatic basis for the classical theory of identity. (The second scheme will be restricted in some of the systems presented below.)

5. According to the classical theory of universality a formula $(x)A$ takes the value T if A is true of all members of the domain. This can be made suitably precise by speaking of an *interpretation* I on a domain D; such an interpretation assigns values $I(x)$ and $I(a)$ in D to individual variables and constants x and a, and relations $I(P)$ on D to predicate letters P. Where d is a member of D, let I^d/x be the interpretation like I except that $I^d/x(x) = d$. Then:

$$I((x)A) = \text{T iff for all } d \in D \ I^d/x(A) = \text{T}.$$

Corresponding to this semantics, we have axiom-schemes

$$(x)(A \supset B) \supset ((x)A \supset (x)B) \qquad \text{(Dist)}$$
$$(x)A \supset A^t/x \qquad\qquad\qquad \text{(Inst)}$$

where A^t/x is the result of replacing all free occurrences of x

in A by occurrences of t (again, relettering if necessary), and a rule of *conditional universalization,*

$$\frac{A \supset B}{A \supset (x)B}$$

where x does not occur free in A.

6. We have not yet considered the theory of descriptions, but let us adopt for the time being Russell's theory. According to this way of handling descriptions, expressions $\imath_x A$ are not part of the primitive notation of the language; hence, the only terms are individual variables and constants. Descriptions are introduced by means of a contextual definition, of which the following is an instance:

$$P(\imath_x Q(x)) = {}_{\mathrm{df}} (\exists x)((y)(Q(y) \equiv y = x) \wedge P(x)).$$

Since descriptions are defined, they may be neglected in formulating a semantics for the language, leaving truth-functions, modality, identity, and universality to be considered.

By a **Q1**-*model structure* (**Q1**ms), we will understand a system $\langle \mathcal{K}, \mathcal{R}, \mathcal{D} \rangle$, where $\langle \mathcal{K}, \mathcal{R} \rangle$ is an **S4**-model structure and $\mathcal{D}$ a nonempty domain. A **Q1**-*interpretation* I assigns a value $\mathrm{I}(a)$ or $\mathrm{I}(x)$ in $\mathcal{D}$ to each individual constant or variable, respectively, of the language, and to each n-ary predicate letter P a subset $\mathrm{I}_\alpha(P)$ of $\mathcal{D}^n$ for each $\alpha \in \mathcal{K}$ (if $n = 0$, $\mathrm{I}_\alpha(P)$ is one of the values T and F). Where I is a **Q1**-interpretation on $\langle \mathcal{K}, \mathcal{R}, \mathcal{D} \rangle$ and $\mathrm{d} \in \mathcal{D}$, let I^d/x be the **Q1**-interpretation which assigns x the value d and in other respects is just like I.

The truth-value $\mathrm{I}_\alpha(A)$ of A in α under a **Q1**-interpretation I on a **Q1**ms $\langle \mathcal{K}, \mathcal{R}, \mathcal{D} \rangle$ (where $\alpha \in \mathcal{K}$), is defined inductively as follows:

(1) $\mathrm{I}_\alpha(P(t_1 \ldots t_n)) = \mathrm{T}$ if $\langle \mathrm{I}(t_1), \ldots, \mathrm{I}(t_n) \rangle \in \mathrm{I}_\alpha(P)$,
   $\mathrm{I}_\alpha(P(t_1 \ldots t_n)) = \mathrm{F}$ otherwise;
(2) $\mathrm{I}_\alpha(s = t) = \mathrm{T}$ if $\mathrm{I}(s) = \mathrm{I}(t)$,
   $\mathrm{I}_\alpha(s = t) = \mathrm{F}$ otherwise;

(3) $I_\alpha(A \supset B) = T$ if $I_\alpha(A) = F$ or $I_\alpha(B) = T$,
$I_\alpha(A \supset B) = F$ otherwise;
(4) $I_\alpha(\sim A) = T$ if $I_\alpha(A) = F$,
$I_\alpha(\sim A) = F$ otherwise;
(5) $I_\alpha(\Box A) = T$ if for all $\beta \in \mathcal{K}$ such that $\alpha \mathcal{R} \beta$, $I_\beta(A) = T$,
$I_\alpha(\Box A) = F$ otherwise;
(6) $I_\alpha((x)A) = T$ if for all $d \in \mathcal{D}$, $I^d/x_\alpha(A) = T$,
$I_\alpha((x)A) = F$ otherwise.

(Clauses 3, 4, and 5, of this definition are standard, and will not be repeated in later definitions of satisfaction.)

This definition determines in the usual way notions of *satisfiability, validity, simultaneous satisfiability,* and *implication,* which we will term **Q1**-*satisfiability,* etc.

The question now arises, how to axiomatize the notion of **Q1**-validity. First, it is readily confirmed that all of the axioms we have presented above for truth-functional and modal connectives, for identity and for quantifiers, are **Q1**-valid; also, that all the rules presented above preserve **Q1**-validity. It therefore seems reasonable to choose at least these axioms and rules: namely, the sentential axioms and rules, together with SId, InId, Dist, Inst, and the rule of conditional universalization. These axioms and rules, however, turn out to be **Q1**-incomplete. First, although

$$\Box(x)A \supset (x)\Box A \qquad (\text{CvBP})^4$$

can be obtained from them, the **Q1**-valid formula

$$(x)\Box P(x) \supset \Box(x)P(x)$$

cannot be thus obtained. Therefore, we must adopt another

4. A note on nomenclature: 'BP' is for 'Barcan Principle,' and 'CvBP' for 'Converse Barcan Principle.' NecId asserts that identicals are *nec*essarily *id*entical, and NecDif that different things are *nec*essarily *dif*ferent.

axiom-scheme,

$$(x)\Box A \supset \Box(x)A \qquad (BP).^5$$

Second, though

$$s = t \supset \Box s = t \qquad (NecId)$$

can be obtained from InId and the other axioms, the **Q1**-valid formula

$$\Diamond a = b \supset a = b$$

cannot be thus obtained, and we therefore require still another axiom-scheme,

$$\Diamond s = t \supset s = t \qquad (NecDif).^6$$

We will call the system constituted by these axioms and rules **Q1** (in a wider context, the name '**S4Q1**' would be more appropriate). In the usual way, notions of **Q1**-*theoremhood*, **Q1**-*deducibility*, and **Q1**-*consistency* are determined by the system. As it turns out, these syntactically defined concepts are equivalent in extension to the corresponding semantical concepts; we thus have semantic completeness for **Q1**, in the strong as well as the weak sense.

7. The ontology corresponding to **Q1** is reminiscent of Leibniz. The world consists of a number of substances (the members of $\mathscr{D}$) which persist through changes (conceiving of the relation $\mathscr{R}$, for the time being, as temporal), in which they may exchange attributes. These substances are never generated

5. As we will see, the import of BP is that nothing comes into existence; the import of CvBP is that nothing passes out of existence.

6. Intuitively, the content of NecDif is that things which are distinct in a given situation can never become identical. This suggests a way of interpreting identity so that NecDif would not be valid, by providing for the "merging" of distinct individuals (but *without* permitting the "separation" of identicals). If carried out, this yields a completeness theorem for the remaining axioms and rules, besides establishing the independence of NecDif.

or destroyed; their number is fixed and immutable. When, on the other hand, $\mathscr{R}$ is taken to be a relation of *metaphysical* possibility[7] (and the members of $\mathscr{K}$ are, accordingly, metaphysically possible worlds rather than temporal stages), this corresponds to the two principles that every possible object is existent, and that every existent object is necessarily existent.[8] When possibility is understood in this way, Leibniz holds that there are possible objects that do not exist in all worlds; in fact, he asserts that there are no possible objects which exist in more than one world. **Q1** may therefore be regarded as corresponding to Leibniz' notion of temporal possibility, though not to his notion of metaphysical possibility.

More generally, **Q1** is reminiscent of any atomistic ontology (ancient or modern), in which "atom" is construed in the strict sense: no atom can be generated or destroyed. The various possible worlds in $\mathscr{K}$ will correspond in this case to possible configurations of atoms; here, **S5** would be a more appropriate sentential modality, unless $\mathscr{R}$ is understood temporally and

7. I should mention at this point that I am conceiving of the notion of a model structure (and hence of a possible world), as used in the semantics of modal logic, as an abstract or structural concept having a number of kinds of realizations. (This is true in general of semantical notions—e.g. of the concept of a domain in classical quantification theory; but the abstractness is rather trivial in this case since domains have no structure.) For instance, possible worlds may be interpreted temporally, metaphysically, linguistically (as "state descriptions") or probabilistically (as sample points in a probability space). In the present paper, I will appeal mostly to the temporal interpretation, since it is the one which seems to be most valuable heuristically where quantification theory is concerned; we have some idea of how to identify individuals across temporal worlds, since we have an idea of what temporal change is like. But "metaphysical change" is more problematic.

8. The reason for this is that CvBP guarantees that since necessarily everything (i.e. every *existing* thing) exists, everything necessarily exists; while BP guarantees that if everything necessarily has a property, then nothing can come into being which does not have that property. For further information on this point, see the discussion of **Q3** below, sections **14** ff.

physical laws are not required to be symmetric with regard to time.

Further insights into **Q1** are gained by considering the solution which it affords to the following stock modal paradox:

> $\square(2 < 3)$
> $3 = $ the number of living Presidents
> $\therefore \square(2 < $ the number of living Presidents).

In general, there are a number of ways of handling such a paradox: denying either of the premises, denying the validity of the inference but holding that the conclusion (though apparently false) is innocuous, or holding that any of the statements in the argument is meaningless. **Q1** takes the third course; though it sanctions the inference, the conclusion, once formalized according to the Russellian theory of descriptions, has the form

$$(\exists x)[(y)(\mathrm{NP}(y) \equiv x = y) \wedge \square\, 2 < x],$$

which is harmlessly true. The paradox is thus *explained away*, since despite appearances the conclusion does not turn out to be a statement of necessity.

8. Two objections to **Q1** are suggested by the above considerations: first, that **Q1** supposes that the same individuals are found in all possible worlds, and second, that **Q1** must employ Russell's theory of descriptions. Perhaps more should be said at this point concerning the second of these objections, since all we have claimed so far is that this theory explains away our Presidential paradox; but surely, explaining away is not in itself objectionable. Quite apart from this, however, it seems to me that the Russellian theory is infected with inelegancies and inadequacies. The inelegancies result from the unperspicuous notation and awkward considerations of scope arising from the contextual definition of descriptions. An inadequacy closely related to this is that the formalization of sentences from natural languages is *artificial* in many cases; e.g. 'The largest prime number is even or not even' is formalized not as an instance of excluded middle, but as an existential quantification. Another inadequacy is that it is plausible to regard some sentences about nonexistents as true; e.g. sentences asserting their nonexistence.[9] All of these objections to the Russellian theory are interrelated in such a way that a proponent of Russell's theory can meet them by making distinctions of scope; but a dialogue of this sort soon shows that this theory results in strained relationships to natural language. The Russellian must eventually cut his moorings and claim that natural language is inherently "confused" or "vague."

It is significant that both of the above sources of dissatisfaction with **Q1** point in the same direction: to a revision of classical quantification theory as regards existential presuppositions. In particular, the principle called into question is Inst; when contraposed, this yields the principle

$$A^t/x \supset (\exists x)A \qquad \text{(CvInst)}.$$

And the special case

$$t = t \supset Et$$

guarantees that every term will refer. But this is clearly incompatible with allowing names to designate objects not in the actual world (e.g. objects which did exist, but don't at this time), as well as with allowing descriptions to be primitive. Both modifications force us to give up the assumption that individual terms always refer.

Now, systems of quantification theory modified in this way have been proposed and investigated during the past ten years

9. The first two difficulties can be resolved by allowing descriptions to be primitive, and assigning any formula the value F if it contains a description not meeting the unique-existence condition; if the condition is met, the description is assigned the obvious designatum. This semantical theory of descriptions is readily axiomatized and proved complete; but this involves revising classical sentential logic, and does not meet our third objection to the Russellian theory.

or so by a number of logicians,[10] and their semantical and
syntactical characteristics disclosed. As far as the predicate
calculus without modality and descriptions is concerned, at
least two semantical interpretations have been proposed: one
by van Fraassen, and one by Leblanc and myself. Although
van Fraassen's theory is better adapted to description theory,
I will confine my remarks here to the latter of these interpretations, which is easier to formulate. According to this
interpretation there are *two* (disjoint) domains: a nonempty
"inner" domain D and an "outer" domain D'. Individual
terms are assigned values in either domain, and predicate
letters assigned relations on the union of the domains; thus
$P(a)$, e.g. will be either true or false under any interpretation
even if a is assigned a "nonexistent" value, in the outer domain.
Bound variables are construed as ranging over the inner
domain, so that $I((x)A) = T$ if for all $d \in D$, $I^d/x(A) = T$.

Syntactically, the formulas valid under this interpretation
may be characterized by axioms and rules sufficient to generate
all tautologies, together with the rule of conditional universal
generalization, the axiom-schemes InId, SId, Dist, and the
following axiom-schemes:

$$(x)A \supset (Et \supset A^t/x) \qquad \text{(EInst)}$$
$$(\exists x)Ex \qquad \text{(NEm)}$$
$$(x)Ex \qquad \text{(EU)}.$$

Following Lambert's terminology, we call this logic *free*
quantification theory; the system determined by the above
axioms and rules will be called **F**.

9. Free quantification theory is to be used as the basis of a
more natural theory of descriptions, and of a modal semantics
allowing the generation and destruction of individuals. I will
first turn to the theory of descriptions. The account I will

10. Lambert, Hintikka, Hailperin and Leblanc, van Fraassen, and myself,
among others.

describe is similar to one due to van Fraassen; he and Lambert also have a completeness theorem for it.[11] According to this theory, the value $I(\imath_x A)$ assigned by I to $\imath_x A$ is the unique member d of the inner domain, such that $I^d/x(A) = T$, if there exists such a unique member; otherwise, $I(\imath_x A)$ is an arbitrary member of the outer domain (in description theory, then, we must assume the outer domain to be nonempty).

It turns out that only two simple and plausible axioms are needed to suit this interpretation; these, in conjunction, of course, with **F**, yield a *minimal* kind of description theory.

$$E\imath_x A \supset (\exists!x)A \qquad \text{(DE)}$$
$$(x)[(y)[A^y/x \equiv x = y] \supset x = \imath_x A] \qquad \text{(DI)}$$

DI is subject to the restriction that y have no free occurrences in A.

10. We may now proceed to sketch a semantical interpretation of the whole language: truth-functions, modality, universal quantification, identity, and descriptions. The resulting theory **Q2** will play a dialectical role in the present paper, serving to introduce problems which (I shall claim) are resolved by the theory **Q3**. Anyone who tries to verify whether particular formulas are valid in **Q2** will soon find that this notion of validity is very complicated. As it turns out, this complexity is more than just apparent; David Kaplan has informed me that there is no axiomatization of **Q2**—the set of **Q2**-valid formulas is not recursively enumerable. (This result is unpublished, and depends on work which appears in Kaplan's dissertation.) With this in mind, let's turn to a semantical characterization (which, of course, will be infinitistic) of **Q2**.

11. Clearly, our semantical interpretation will involve a system of possible worlds, each with a domain. Besides these,

11. They differ from the ones given in my "Some Completeness Results for Modal Predicate Calculi," Proceedings of the 1968 Irvine Philosophy Colloquium, forthcoming.

we will want still another set to serve as an outer domain, since otherwise every singular term (including, e.g. $\imath_x(P \wedge \sim P)$) would perforce be assigned an individual existing in some possible world.

Individual terms are assigned values in the domains of these possible worlds. When we did this in connection with **Q2**, we assigned each term a value which was fixed beforehand for all worlds; the value assigned to a in α was the same as the value assigned to a in β. This procedure seemed natural at the time, because we had supposed that the same domain was associated with all worlds; but this assumption glosses over the problem of *identifying individuals across worlds*.

In the present more general case, then, we define a **Q2**-*model structure* $\langle \mathcal{K}, \mathcal{R}, \mathcal{D}, \mathcal{D}' \rangle$ in such a way that the component $\mathcal{D}$, rather than being a fixed domain, is a *function* taking worlds α into nonempty domains $\mathcal{D}_\alpha$. $\mathcal{D}'$ is a nonempty domain serving as a "limbo" for individuals not existing in any world in $\mathcal{K}$. As before, we suppose that $\langle \mathcal{K}, \mathcal{R} \rangle$ is an **S4** model structure.

Before determining how to assign values to terms in general, let us consider a description: say, 'the thing in place p.' We fix the designation of this term in a given world according to whether there is a unique individual in the domain of that world having the property of being in place p in that world; if there is, we assign that thing to the term. But individuals can change position, and in general the designatum of $\imath_x P(x)$ in world α and the designatum of $\imath_x P(x)$ in world β will not be the same.

Applying this idea to terms in general, let us regard a **Q2**-interpretation, I, on a **Q2** ms $\langle \mathcal{K}, \mathcal{R}, \mathcal{D}, \mathcal{D}' \rangle$ as assigning for each $\alpha \in \mathcal{K}$ a value $I_\alpha(t)$ in $\mathcal{D}' \cup \bigcup_{\alpha \in \mathcal{K}} \mathcal{D}_\alpha$ to each individual variable or individual constant t; and to each description $\imath_x A$ a value $I_\alpha(\imath_x A) = d$, where if there is a unique member e of $\mathscr{D}_\alpha$ such that[12] $I^e/x(A) = T$, then d $=$ e, and if there is no such member, then d $\notin \mathscr{D}_\alpha$; and finally, to each n-ary predicate letter P a relation $I_\alpha(P)$ on $\mathscr{D}' \cup \bigcup_{\alpha \in \mathscr{K}} \mathscr{D}_\alpha$. Predicate letters, then, are assumed to be defined for all individuals: those in $\mathscr{D}'$, as well as those in the domains of the possible worlds. In this way, excluded middle is preserved.

The definition of **Q2**-*satisfaction* is straightforward in the case of atomic formulas:

(1) $I_\alpha(P(t_1 \ldots t_n)) = T$ if $\langle I_\alpha(t_1), \ldots, I_\alpha(t_1) \rangle \in I_\alpha(P)$,
$I_\alpha(P(t_1 \ldots t_n)) = F$ otherwise;
(2) $I_\alpha(s=t) = T$ if $I_\alpha(s) = I_\alpha(t)$,
$I_\alpha(s=t) = F$ otherwise.

An atomic formula, e.g. $P(a)$, is true in a possible world if and only if the relation assigned to P in that world holds of the individual assigned to a in that world.

Cases (3), (4), and (5) of the definition are treated as on p. 125, above. Using only these clauses of the definition, it may be seen that

$$s=t \supset (A \supset A^s/\!\!/t)$$

is valid provided that no occurrence of t in A at which an occurrence of s appears in $A^s /\!\!/ t$ is within the scope of a modal operator (in other words, provided that s is substituted for t only in *transparent* contexts). Let us call this qualified form of InId "RInId" ("Restricted Indiscernability of Identicals"). Although RInId is **Q2**-valid, InId is not. E.g. let $\mathscr{D}_\alpha = \mathscr{D}_\beta = \{0,1\}$, where $\alpha \neq \beta$, and $\alpha \mathscr{R} \beta$, and let $I_\alpha(a) = I_\alpha(b) = 0$ and $I_\beta(a) = 0$, $I_\beta(b) = 1$. Then $I_\alpha(a=b \supset (\square a=a \supset \square a=b)) = F$ (and $I_\alpha(a=b \supset \square a=b) = F$ as well). The principle

$$\square s=t \supset (A \supset A^s/\!\!/t) \qquad (\text{In}\square\text{Id}),$$

12. Strictly speaking, this is sloppy. Actually, **Q2**-*interpretation* and *truth-value under a* **Q2**-*interpretation* should be defined by a simultaneous induction.

however, is **Q2**-valid. It is clear, therefore, that in **Q2** the Presidential paradox (above, p. 128) is solved by denying the validity of the argument, which depends on the principle InId. The force of the paradox may then be ascribed to the failure to distinguish identity from necessary identity, with resultant confusion of InId with In□Id.

All of this may be seen without completing the definition of satisfaction; at some point, however, we must determine the truth-conditions of universal formulas. When A contains no modal operators, it is clear that $I_\alpha((x)A)$ should be T if and only if for all d in $\mathcal{D}_\alpha$, $I'_\alpha((x)A) = $ T for all interpretations I' differing from I at most in the value assigned to x in α, and such that $I'_\alpha(x) \in \mathcal{D}_\alpha$. But, e.g. in the case of $(x)\Diamond P(x)$, the truth-value in α will depend in general not only on the interpretation of x in α, but on the values assigned to x in other worlds as well. How, then, are we to define the truth-value in such cases?

There are some radical approaches to this problem which merit brief discussion. First, one could restrict the language in such a way that well-formed formulas do not involve any quantification into modal contexts. When bolstered by philosophic arguments, this approach may appear plausible, but at bottom these arguments simply restate the fact that there is a problem. Thus, this seems to me to be more a suppression than a solution of the difficulty; certainly, if this technique were generally applied to areas in which difficult problems arise, life would be rather dull.

Another solution[13] would be to interpret quantification as having to do with the substitution of names; we could then say that $I_\alpha((x)A) = $ T if for all terms t of the language, $I_\alpha(A^t/x) = $ T. This proposal raises a host of technical difficulties. Obviously, it conflicts with the decisions made above concerning existence,

---

13. This has been suggested by R. Barcan Marcus.

since Inst is valid under this interpretation. Even if this and related difficulties were solved, a more vexing problem would arise, concerning descriptions. The definition of satisfaction under this interpretation of quantification presupposes that the truth values of *all* identities are fixed beforehand, but the definition of identities involving descriptions presupposes in turn the definition of satisfaction. This circularity is *vicious*: the usual sort of inductive definition breaks down, and there is no straightforward way of guaranteeing that a satisfaction function I exists, given an assignment of values to atomic formulas and atomic terms. Of course, this problem could be solved by appealing to Russell's theory of descriptions or a similar theory; but this limitation is surely a defect. Further technical difficulties arise concerning the definition of implication, since under the substitution interpretation the rule of complete induction is valid. It therefore follows from Gödel's incompleteness theorem (or, equally well, from Tarski's theorem) that any effective formulation of this quantification theory will be incomplete as to consequences, since all of the truths, e.g. of first-order arithmetic, would be implied by the usual axioms; but the class of arithmetic truths is not effectively enumerable. To top these difficulties, there is the more philosophical objection that the substitution interpretation is plausible as an interpretation of *quantification* only if everything has a name. But this last condition is not always met, and there does not seem to be any good reason to suppose in logic that it is. For these reasons, though I feel that the substitution interpretation (i.e. the rule of complete induction) is worthy of investigation in its own right, it does not seem to me that substitution is a satisfactory surrogate for quantification over individuals.

The most attractive remaining alternative—certainly, the one most in harmony with the semantic approach of this paper—is the one in which formulas of the sort $(x)A$ are interpreted universally with respect to *all* ways of identifying the value of x. We make this more precise by letting a *world-line* d on a **Q2**-model structure $\langle \mathscr{K}, \mathscr{R}, \mathscr{D}, \mathscr{D}' \rangle$ be any function from $\mathscr{K}$ into $\mathscr{D}'' \cup \bigcup_{\alpha \in \mathscr{K}} \mathscr{D}_\alpha$. Also, let I^d/x differ from I in that for all $\alpha \in \mathscr{K}$, $\mathrm{I}^d/x_\alpha(x) = d_\alpha$. The final clause of **Q2**-*satisfaction* then reads as follows:

> (6) $\mathrm{I}_\alpha((x)A) = \mathrm{T}$ if for all world-lines d on $\langle \mathscr{K}, \mathscr{R}, \mathscr{D}, \mathscr{D}' \rangle$
> such that $d_\alpha \in \mathscr{D}_\alpha$, $\mathrm{I}^d/x_\alpha(A) = \mathrm{T}$,
> $\mathrm{I}_\alpha((x)A) = \mathrm{F}$ otherwise.

The only technical difficulty with this definition is that the class of world-lines may be nondenumerably infinite, even in cases where $\mathscr{D}'$ and the $\mathscr{D}_\alpha$ are denumerable; but this will seem a glaring defect only to those who do not countenance nondenumerable infinities. More problematic is the fact that certain rather counterintuitive theses turn out to be validated in **Q2**. An example of this sort is

$$(\exists x)\square Ex;$$

this ontologically tantalizing conclusion follows from the more general principle

$$\square(\exists x)A \supset (\exists x)\square A,$$

where no free occurrence of x in A falls within the scope of a modal operator—which also is **Q2**-valid.

12. Though I believe **Q2** and related logics to be worthy of further investigation, I take these results to be symptomatic of a deeper infirmity, having to do with the notion of *substance*. Recall that above, when we were motivating the sort of reference involved in **Q2**, we used descriptions as a paradigm. The effect of this was to suggest that the fundamental way of identifying individuals across worlds was by means of *properties* (e.g. we identify the thing in place p by means of a distinguishing property), and this in turn suggested that all world-lines are semantically on a par. When all such identifications are subsumed under this paradigm, one is led to the conclusion that, e.g. Socrates-at-t_1 is identified with Socrates-at-t_2 (i.e. shares with Socrates-at-t_2 a world line which is a value of a variable), because the properties of the one are like the properties of the other. And the slipperiness of this "likeness" soon suggests that it is arbitrary or conventional that these are given the same name: any world-line is, in reality, as worthy to be the value of a variable as any other.

In contrast to the view sketched in the above paragraph, it seems to me that we do—at least, in temporal cases—identify individuals across worlds in a way more absolute than that taken into account by **Q2**. Thus, I am inclined to take the sort of reference in which a name ('Socrates') is assigned *one thing* (Socrates) *which is the same in many possible worlds,* as primary or paradigmatic. The defect, then, of **Q2**, is that it does not allow for this unity: for preferred world-lines which may be regarded as single things remaining fixed through a change. In a word, **Q2** lacks a concept of *substance.*

13. Before formulating a system **Q3** in accordance with these suggestions, it may be appropriate to support the above opinions by a philosophical consideration or two. It may be that those who held views similar to those motivating **Q2** were led to do so by the impression that identification of *properties* across worlds is somehow less problematic than identification of *individuals* across worlds; this, certainly, would be a reason to attempt the elimination in modal logic of singular terms in favor of distinguishing properties. But there is, so far as I can see, absolutely no reason to suppose that this is the case: if anything, the identification of properties is *more* problematic. How can properties be identified across worlds (without, of course, appealing to substances)?

Certainly, not by means of their extension, for this presupposes identification of individuals. Perhaps, then, by means of properties of properties; but this obviously leads to an infinite regress. If there is reason to cut this regress anywhere in order to allow a foundation for the whole series, it is at the very beginning: namely, with identification of individuals. Finally, perhaps by intensional criteria; but these would have to be explicated. If the explication were to involve the notion of alternative situations or possible worlds, the problem would remain unsolved; but it is hard to imagine an adequate explication that would not involve this notion in some form.[14]

These arguments are not without double edges. For instance, if I were pressed as to how individuals are identified and give any sensible answer (say, "by continuity"), I could be led in similar circles. But I do feel that such arguments can legitimately be used to remove prejudices or misconceptions that may stand in the way of **Q3**.

14. As in the case of **Q2**, a **Q3**-*model structure* is a quadruple $\langle \mathcal{K},\mathcal{R},\mathcal{D},\mathcal{D}'\rangle$. Now however, we will construe overlaps of the $\mathcal{D}_\alpha$ as indicative of substances; i.e. we regard an individual as existing in both α and β if it is a member of $\mathcal{D}_\alpha \cap \mathcal{D}_\beta$. More precisely, we will regard all individuals in $\mathcal{D}' \cup \bigcup_{\alpha\in\mathcal{K}}\mathcal{D}_\alpha$ as *already* identified across worlds; any individual d of a **Q3**ms is the same with respect to all worlds of the model structure. We will construe individual variables as ranging over substances, and thus will take seriously the classical doctrine that

---

14. To give this argument some content, imagine a world possible to this one in which everyone calls a horse's tail a leg. What we identify in that world with the property of being a horse's leg will depend on whether we go on the principle that "calling a tail a leg makes it one," or the principle that "a tail isn't a leg, whatever you call it." (I have been told that this elegant example goes back to Buridan, but have not verified the reference.)

Strictly speaking, the problem of identifying properties across worlds does not arise explicitly until one attempts to provide a semantics for *second-order* modal logic. Nevertheless, I would claim that it is present implicitly in the modal notion of *property*.

only substances are "beings" in the fullest sense of the word. In practice, this means that if an individual variable is assigned a value in world α, it is automatically assigned the same value in every other world β (whether or not it is in the domains of these worlds). Thus, so far as the interpretation of individual variables goes, we are reverting to the sort of reference we had in **Q1**.

As regards descriptions, however, we will retain the treatment of **Q2**; this means that descriptions may refer to non-substances, even though the individual variables range in **Q3** over substances; there is thus a major difference in the way **Q3** treats individual variables, on the one hand, and descriptions, on the other. But this is precisely the distinction that is wanted, and creates no difficulties since the underlying quantification theory is free; descriptions need not designate values of individual variables.

The question of how to handle individual constants is delicate. Most uses of proper names seem to be of the sort in which substances are intended; e.g.

$$(x)(x = \text{Socrates} \supset \Box x = \text{Socrates})$$
$$\text{and } (x)(x = \text{Texas} \supset \Box x = \text{Texas})$$

have a ring of truth. This would suggest that in **Q3** individual constants should be treated like individual variables. There are, however, some uses of proper names (roughly classifiable as *titulary* uses) which do not meet this condition. For example, if we call anyone holding a certain political office "Caesar," then various people may be Caesar in different possible worlds, and

$$(x)(x = \text{Caesar} \supset \Box x = \text{Caesar}),$$

or equivalently,

$$E \Box \text{Caesar}$$

is false. Similarly with "Miss America," and other cases in which a name is *won*. "Coriolanus" is perhaps a borderline case. It seems rather artificial to make a *syntactical* distinction between these and other sorts of namings, and therefore in **Q3** I will treat individual constants more like descriptions than individual variables; any world-line may be assigned to an individual constant. The supposition that an individual constant refers to a substance can, however, always be made explicitly, by means of assertions of the sort

$$E \Box a.$$

15. A **Q3**-*interpretation* on a **Q3ms** $\langle \mathcal{K}, \mathcal{R}, \mathcal{D}, \mathcal{D}' \rangle$, then, is an assignment I of members of $\mathcal{D}' \cup \bigcup_{\alpha \in \mathcal{K}} \mathcal{D}_\alpha$ to individual variables, world-lines on $\langle \mathcal{K}, \mathcal{R}, \mathcal{D}, \mathcal{D}' \rangle$ to individual constants, and relations on $\mathcal{D}' \cup \bigcup_{\alpha \in \mathcal{K}} \mathcal{D}_\alpha$ to predicate letters (one for each world in $\mathcal{K}$). This may be summarized by saying that a **Q3**-interpretation is a **Q2**-interpretation, except that for all individual variables x and all $\alpha, \beta \in \mathcal{K}$, $I_\alpha(x) = I_\beta(x)$. Descriptions are handled precisely as in **Q2**.

Let I^d/x differ from I at most in that for all $\alpha \in \mathcal{K}$, $I^d/x_\alpha(x) = d$. Then the most important clauses of the definition of **Q3**-satisfaction are:

(1) $I_\alpha(P(t_1 \ldots t_n)) = T$ if $\langle I_\alpha(t_1), \ldots, I_\alpha(t_n) \rangle \in I_\alpha(P)$,
    $I_\alpha(P(t_1 \ldots t_n)) = F$ otherwise;
(2) $I_\alpha(s=t) = T$ if $I_\alpha(s) = I_\alpha(t)$,
    $I_\alpha(s=t) = F$ otherwise;
(6) $I_\alpha((x)A) = T$ if for all $d \in \mathcal{D}_\alpha$, $I^d/x_\alpha(A) = T$,
    $I_\alpha((x)A) = F$ otherwise.

16. In seeking an axiomatization of **Q3**, we must first note that the principle EInst is **Q3**-invalid. To **Q3**-satisfy, e.g. the negation of

$$(x) \Box Ex \supset (Ea \supset \Box Ea)$$

(an instance of EInst), let $\mathcal{D}' = \{0\}$, and $\mathcal{D}_\alpha = \mathcal{D}_\beta = \{1\}$, where $\alpha \neq \beta$ and $\alpha \mathcal{R} \beta$. Then let $I_\alpha(a) = 1$ and $I_\beta(a) = 0$. Now,

$I_\alpha((x)\Box Ex) = T$ (because $\mathscr{D}_\alpha \subseteq \mathscr{D}_\beta$), and $I_\alpha(Ea) = T$; but $I_\beta(Ea) = F$, and so $I_\alpha(\Box Ea) = F$. The reason for this failure of EInst in **Q3** is clear; the variables of **Q3** range over *substances*: i.e. over objects identified across worlds. Thus, terms which fail to refer to the same object in all worlds, as well as terms not referring to existents, may not instantiate such variables. This diagnosis indicates how to remedy the difficulty; in **Q3**, we posit the axiom-scheme

$$(x)A \supset (E\Box t \supset A^t/x) \qquad \text{(SInst)}.$$

Besides SInst, we will incorporate in **Q3** the sentential axioms and rules, Dist, NEm, and EU;[15] also the principles DI and DE, and SId and RInId. Our treatment of free individual variables renders two further axiom-schemes indispensible:

$$x = y \supset \Box x = y, \text{ and } \Diamond x = y \supset x = y,$$

where x and y are individual variables.[16]

15. The system **Q3Em** obtained by dropping the Axiom-scheme EM from **Q3** is characterized semantically by relaxing the restriction on **Q3** model structures $\langle \mathscr{K},\mathscr{R},\mathscr{D},\mathscr{D}' \rangle$ that $\mathscr{D}_\alpha$ be nonempty for all $\alpha \in \mathscr{K}$.

16. In the proof of semantical completeness given in my "Some Completeness Results for Modal Predicate Calculi," five additional rules must be incorporated in **Q3**.

$$\frac{A \supset B}{A \supset (x)B}, \qquad \text{where } x \text{ is not free in } A.$$

$$\frac{A \supset \Box B}{A \supset \Box(x)B}, \qquad \text{where } x \text{ is not free in } A.$$

$$\frac{A \supset .. B_1 \prec .... \prec . B_n \prec \Box C}{A \supset . B_1 \prec .... \prec . B_n \prec \Box(x)C}, \qquad \begin{array}{l}\text{where } x \text{ is not free in} \\ A, B_1, \ldots, \text{ or } B_n.\end{array}$$

$$\frac{A \supset \sim t = x}{\sim A}, \qquad \text{where } x \text{ is not free in } A \text{ or in } t.$$

$$\frac{A \supset . B_1 \prec .... \prec . B_n \prec \sim t = x}{A \supset . B_1 \prec .... \prec . \Box \sim B_n}, \qquad \begin{array}{l}\text{where } x \text{ is not free in} \\ A, B_1, \ldots, B_n, \text{ or } t.\end{array}$$

It is not known at present whether or not these rules are redundant.

The system **Q3** given by these axioms and rules is semantically complete, in both the weak and strong senses.

17. The above list of axioms and rules, and the definition of **Q3**-validity, in all likelihood will provide the reader with only a rough idea of what the system **Q3** is like. It may be helpful at this point to list some **Q3**-valid, **Q3**-invalid, and **Q3**-satisfiable formulas. Of course, every substitution-instance of a sentential theorem of **S4** is **Q3**-valid; so also is any substitution-instance of a theorem of classical quantification theory *without free individual terms*. E.g. any formula of the kind $(x)((y)A \supset A^x/y)$ is **Q3**-valid. Besides these, all formulas of the following sorts are **Q3**-valid:

$$E\imath_x P(x) \supset P(\imath_x P(x)),$$
$$(y)(y = \imath_x P(x) \equiv (P(y) \wedge (x)(P(x) \equiv x = y))),$$
$$\square(\exists x)E\square x,$$
$$\square(x)E\square x, \text{ and}$$
$$(x)(y)(x = y \supset (A \supset A^x/y)) \quad \text{InIdS}).$$

The following formulas, however, are **Q3**-invalid:

$$(x)\square P(x) \supset \square(x)P(x) \qquad\qquad (1),$$
$$\square(x)P(x) \supset (x)\square P(x) \qquad\qquad (2),$$
$$\diamondsuit(x)P(x) \supset (x)\diamondsuit P(x) \quad \text{and} \qquad (3),$$
$$a = \imath_x P(x) \supset (\square Q(a) \supset \square Q(\imath_x P(x))) \qquad (4).$$

The first three of these formulas may be falsified in a **Q3**-model structure with only two worlds α and β, where $\alpha\mathcal{R}\beta$. To falsify (1), let $\mathscr{D}_\alpha = \{0\}$ and $\mathscr{D}_\beta = \{0,1\}$, and let $I_\alpha(P) = \{0\}$ and $I_\beta(P) = \{0\}$. Then $I_\alpha((x)\square P(x)) = T$, but $I_\beta((x)P(x)) = F$, and hence (1) is false. (Note that this is a case of *coming to be*.) To falsify (2), let $\mathscr{D}_\alpha = \{0,1\}$ and $\mathscr{D}_\beta = \{0\}$, and let $I_\alpha(P) = \{0,1\}$ and $I_\beta(P) = \{0\}$. Since $I^1/x_\beta(P(x)) = F$, $I^1/x_\alpha(\square P(x)) = F$ and hence $I_\alpha((x)\square P(x)) = F$, since $1 \in \mathscr{D}$. But, $I_\alpha(\square(x)P(x)) = T$, and hence (2) is false. (Note that this is a case of *passing away*.) Finally, to falsify (3), let $\mathscr{D}_\alpha = \{0,1\}$ and $\mathscr{D}_\beta = \{0\}$, and

$I_\alpha(P) = \{0\}$ and $I_\beta(P) = \{0\}$. Now, $I^1/x_\alpha(P(x)) = F$ and $I^1/x_\beta(P(x)) = F$, so $I^1/x_\alpha(\diamond P(x)) = F$ and hence $I_\alpha((x)\diamond P(x)) = F$, since $1 \in \mathscr{D}_\alpha$. But $I_\beta((x)P(x)) = T$, so $I_\alpha(\diamond(x)P(x)) = T$; hence (3) is false.

The duals of (1)–(3) are, of course, also invalid.

The formula $(x)\diamond \sim Ex$ is **Q3**-satisfiable, as well as the slightly more gloomy formula $(x)\square\diamond \sim Ex$. It therefore is consistent in **Q3** to suppose that everything is perishable, or even that everything is *necessarily* perishable. (It would, of course, be **Q3**-inconsistent though to assert that everything is *simultaneously* perishable.)

18. Finally, it will be worthwhile to discuss the way in which **Q3** solves the presidential paradox; like **Q2**, the system **Q3** renders the argument of the paradox—which has the form

$$a = \imath_x P(x)$$
$$\square Q(a)$$
$$\therefore \ \square Q(\imath_x P(x))$$

and is thus an instance of (4), above—invalid, and so blocks the paradoxical inference. But besides providing a well-articulated semantical theory in which the argument is invalidated, **Q3** disarms the paradox in a deeper and more significant sense, by at once explaining why the argument of the paradox is seductive, and at the same time fortifying our resistance to those seductions.

The argument of the paradox is plausible because it is an instantiation of InIdS (i.e. of $(x)(y)(x = y \supset (A \supset Ay/x))$), which is **Q3** *valid*. But the semantical theory of **Q3** makes it clear that the universality of InIdS applies only to *substances*, not to nonsubstantial world-lines. It is therefore a conflation of substance and accident that makes the paradox plausible; and in retrospect it is not surprising that if this conflation is made, one should be able to generate modal paradoxes. The difficulty of this puzzle was compounded by the uncritical acceptance during the first half of our century of the principle Inst; thus, the crucial step in loosening this modal *aporia* must be credited to Leonard, Lambert, Hintikka, Leblanc, Hailperin, and other workers in the logical analysis of existence.

19. Some readers may feel that the present paper has been long on logic and short on metaphysics. It would have been possible to render the above material more philosophical and less technical, but it is my feeling that, at the present stage of philosophic inquiry into these topics, what is most needed is a firmer technical foundation; and this I have tried to provide. I hope, though, that the relevance of this discussion to traditional metaphysical concepts is clear. And—though I have not made this explicit either—its relevance to modern philosophical treatments of logical problems concerned with modality, reference, and existence will be apparent to anyone familiar with the literature on this topic.

BIBLIOGRAPHY

Bibliographical Note: The first semantical account of modality known to me is that of Carnap [1]; this paper includes a treatment of quantifiers, which may be regarded as a special case of the theory **Q1** formulated in the present paper. During the 1950s the semantics of sentential modality was developed by several researchers, including Montague, Kanger, and Kripke. The most detailed presentation of this theory is in Kripke's article [7]; references to other semantical theories of modality (e.g. the algebraic interpretation of McKinsey and Tarski) are also given there. During this period, all of the above three authors were developing or had developed a semantical theory of quantification as well; quantification is treated explicitly in Kanger[5] and Kripke [6], and a quite sophisticated theory is sketched in Montague [11]. In the 1960s these ideas have crystalized and developed into general, rigorous semantical theories of modal languages with quantifiers. Much of this recent research is still unpublished, and to my knowledge, the mathematical details of a general theory have not yet appeared in print. But expositions of such theories have been published during the past six years; among the most important of these are Hintikka [2] and [3], and Kripke [8].

This account is far from being historically complete; other logicians who have contributed to the subject are Dana Scott, David Kaplan, and Arthur Prior, and many more. Research in this area seems to a remarkable extent to have developed independently; my own work, though inspired by Kripke's early papers, has also developed without much influence from the above sources.

References

[1] CARNAP, R., "Modalities and Quantification," *Journal of Symbolic Logic, 11* (1946), 33–64.

[2] HINTIKKA, J., "Modality as Referential Opacity," *Ajatus, 20* (1957), 49–63.

[3] HINTIKKA, J., *Knowledge and Belief* (Ithaca, Cornell University Press, 1962).

[4] HINTIKKA, J., "Studies in the Logic of Existence and Necessity: I. Existence," *The Monist, 50* (1966), 55–76.

[5] KANGER, S., *Provability in Logic* (Stockholm, Almqvist and Wiksell, 1957).

[6] KRIPKE, S., "A Completeness Theorem in Modal Logic," *Journal of Symbolic Logic, 24* (1959), 1–14.

[7] KRIPKE, S., "Semantical Analysis of Modal Logic I: Normal Propositional Calculi," *Zeitschrift für mathematische Logik und Grundlagen der Mathematik, 9* (1963), 67–96.

[8] KRIPKE, S., "Semantical Considerations on Modal Logic," *Acta Philosophica Fennica, 16* (1963), 83–94.

[9] LEBLANC, H. and T. HAILPERIN, "Nondesignating Singular Terms," *Philosophical Review*, *68* (1959), 239–43.

[10] LEONARD, H., "The Logic of Existence," *Philosophical Studies*, *7* (1956), 49–64.

[11] MONTAGUE, R., "Logical Necessity, Physical Necessity, Ethics, and Quantifiers," *Inquiry*, *4* (1960), 259–69.

[12] RESCHER, N., "On the Logic of Existence and Denotation," *Philosophical Review*, *68* (1959), 157–80.

[13] THOMASON, R., "Some Completeness Results for Modal Predicate Calculi," *Proceedings of the 1968 Irvine Philosophy Colloquium*, forthcoming.

[14] THOMASON, R., and H. LEBLANC, "Completeness Theorems for Some Presupposition-Free Logics," *Fundamenta Mathematicae*, *62* (1968), 123–164.

[15] VAN FRAASSEN, B., "The Completeness of Free Logic," *Zeitschrift für mathematische Logik und Grundlagen der Mathematik*, *12* (1966), 219–34.

[16] VAN FRAASSEN, B., and K. LAMBERT, "On Free Description Theory," *Zeitschrift für mathematische Logik und Grundlagen der Mathematik*, *13* (1967), 225–40.

7. A Modal Analogue of Free Logic[1]

Milton Fisk

I shall try to show that in modal logic there is a difficulty parallel to the one in quantificational logic, which ultimately led to free logic. The parallel between the difficulties suggests an attempt to resolve the difficulty in modal logic by adopting a modal logic free of certain presuppositions. However, my conclusion will be that such a "free" modal logic only partially resolves the difficulty. A full resolution can be effected within the context of traditional modal logic by adopting a new semantics for modalities, one I shall label the semantics of strength.

THE PRECRITICAL INTERPRETATION

The analogy between modalities and quantifiers is obvious at the syntactical level. The quantifiers in:

(1) $(x)A \supset At/x$ QInst
(2) $At/x \supset (\exists x)A$ QGen

1. This paper was read at the Michigan State University Symposium on Free Logic, June 9 and 10, 1967. Suggestions and criticisms made by J. Canty, B. van Fraassen, K. Lambert, H. Leblanc, T. Scharle, and S. Sudik have been the source of important improvements.

occupy the same positions as the modalities in:

(3) $\Box A \supset A$ MInst
(4) $A \supset \Diamond A.$ MGen

And apart from quantifiers and modalities these laws are otherwise alike. (In respect to (1) and (2), the usual assumption is made here that t is not bound when it occupies a place in A at which x was free.) The analogy just described is also found between the definitions:

(5) '$(\exists x)A$' for '$\sim(x) \sim A$'
(6) '$\Diamond A$' for '$\sim \Box \sim A$'.

In view of this analogy between basic laws and definitions, the corresponding modalities and quantifiers—(x) and $\Box$, $(\exists x)$ and $\Diamond$—can themselves be said to be syntactically analogous.

But the analogy also has a semantical basis. This is true at least for what I shall call the "precritical" interpretation of modalities and quantifiers and for the more adequate interpretation to be developed toward the end of this paper. The precritical interpretation has common-sense plausibility. I shall elaborate it first informally and then more precisely, calling attention to the semantical analogy between modalities and quantifiers only in connection with the more precise formulation.

It is commonsensical to hold that a universal sentence is true only if it is not false of any individual of the specified domain. When a domain contains individuals of several types, such as physical objects and numbers, a universal sentence is not held false simply because it has no truth-value in connection with individuals of one of those types. But if no instance of a universal sentence had a truth-value, there would be common-sense plausibility to the suggestion that it has no truth-value itself. Such would be the case for '$(x)(x$ is blue)' when the domain is limited to numbers, since all instances, such as '7 is blue' are category mistakes. Whether inadvertently or by design, common sense places no restrictions on what the specified domain may be. So the empty domain is not excluded. Further, since it makes sense to say that certain individuals do not exist, names are not limited to names of existents. Nonexistents are simply individuals outside the chosen domain.

On the precritical interpretation, the nonmodal connectives have their usual meanings when they operate on sentences with truth-values. But for it, a compound sentence is deprived of a truth-value by having a truth-valueless component. This requirement is based on the view that compounds are assertions about the truth-values of truth-valued sentences. Thus, for example, $A \vee B$ says that at least one of the following, each of which has a truth-value, is true: A,B. If A is true and B lacks a truth-value, then the presupposition that both A and B have truth-values fails, and $A \vee B$ is itself without a truth-value. This view would seem more plausible to common sense than the view that compounds are assertions about the truth-values of sentences, with or without truth-values. Just as it is appropriate to respond to 'Harry Truman's assassin is a Republican' with 'But Harry Truman was not assassinated' rather than with 'That's false', so too it is appropriate to respond to 'Harry Truman's assassin is a Republican $\vee$ Harry Truman was president' in exactly the same way rather than with 'That's true', indicating thereby a failure of the presupposition that the disjuncts have truth-values.

A more precise formulation[2] of the precritical semantics will reveal the semantical analogy between quantifiers and modalities. An ordered triple $\langle K,R,D \rangle$ is to be called a "model structure" when K is a nonempty set, R is a reflexive relation with K as its field, and D is a function, with sets as values, of

2. This formulation is suggested by the following works: Saul A. Kripke, "Semantical Considerations on Modal Logic," *Acta Philosophica Fennica, 16* (1963), 83–94, and Jaakko Hintikka, "Modality and Quantification," *Theoria, 27* (1961), 119–28.

members of K. Since we are interested in interpreting modalities, K can be thought of as the set of all possible worlds. R can then be thought of as the relation holding from one world to a world "possible relative to" it. Where H and H' are members of K, H' is possible relative to H, that is, HRH', when any sentence which is necessary in H is not false in H'. Finally, $D(H)$ can be thought of as the domain of individuals of the world H.[3] Now let a "model" ϕ on a model structure $\langle K,R,D \rangle$ be a binary function assigning a truth-value, T or F, or the one non-truth-value, an arbitrarily chosen entity which we designate by 'U', to every atomic sentence in respect to every world of K. (When a sentence is T, F, or U in respect to that member of K which is the actual world, the sentence can be said, without explicit relativization to a world, to be T, F, or U.) The precritical interpretation can then be embodied in the following rules of evaluation for molecular sentences:

(I) (a) $\phi(\sim A,H) = $ T iff $\phi(A,H) = $ F,
     (b) $\phi(\sim A,H) = $ F iff $\phi(A,H) = $ T,
     (c) $\phi(\sim A,H) = $ U otherwise, that is, iff $\phi(A,H) = $ U.

(II) (a) $\phi(A \supset B,H) = $ T iff either $\phi(A,H) = $ F and
          $\phi(B,H) = $ T or F, or $\phi(B,H) = $ T and
          $\phi(A,H) = $ T or F,
     (b) $\phi(A \supset B,H) = $ F iff $\phi(A,H) = $ T and $\phi(B,H) = $ F,
     (c) $\phi(A \supset B,H) = $ U otherwise.

3. Here it will not in general be the case that $D(H) = D(H')$. This contradicts Wittgenstein's influential stricture of 2.022–2.023 of his *Tractatus*: "However different from the real one an imagined world may be, it must have something —a form—in common with the real world. This fixed form consists of the objects." The familar argument for identifying the domains of possible worlds is that thereby "No new entity is spawned in a possible world" (R. Barcan Marcus, "Modalities and Intensional Languages," in I. M. Copi and J. A. Gould, eds., *Contemporary Readings in Logical Theory* [New York, Macmillan, 1967], pp. 278–93). But this metaphysical attitude should not prevent the consideration in logical theory of worlds with individuals not contained in the actual world. For, no more is implied about the ontological status of such worlds by such a consideration than that they can be thought of.

(III) (a) $\phi((x)A,H) = $ T iff for any t if t belongs to the domain, $D(H)$, of H, then $\phi(At/x, H) = $ T or, if there is a t of $D(H)$ such that $\phi(At/x, H) = $ U, then there is no t of $D(H)$ such that $\phi(At/x, H) = $ F, and there is a t of $D(H)$ such that $\phi(At/x, H) = $ T,

    (b) $\phi((x)A,H) = $ F iff there is a t such that t belongs to $D(H)$ and $\phi(At/x, H) = $ F,

    (c) $\phi((x)A,H) = $ U otherwise, that is, iff for any t if t belongs to $D(H)$ then $\phi(At/x, H) = $ U.

The complex condition expressed in (IIIa) allows '$(x)(x$ is wood $\supset x$ will burn)' to be true, even though '7 is wood $\supset 7$ will burn' is truth-valueless. Undoubtedly, more qualifications are built into (III) than commonsense would immediately recognize as required. In the case of necessity, on the other hand, I intend to work only gradually toward the proper qualifications. So the following rule for necessity does not stand at as high a level of refinement as (III). But the analogy between the two will, in important respects, increase, rather than decrease, as refinements are added to (IV). At this point the semantical analogy consists chiefly in the fact that just as universality concerns all members of the domain of a given world, so too necessity concerns all worlds possible relative to a given world. Further, just as universality does not require truth but allows for the mere absence of falsity in respect to members of the domain, so too necessity requires only the absence of falsity in respect to possible worlds. There are, to be sure, obvious disanalogies, but the analogy is strong enough to suggest meeting the difficulties for quantificational and modal laws, to be set forth in the following section, in a parallel fashion. Here then is the rule for necessity:

(IV) (a) $\phi(\Box A,H) = $ T iff for any H' if H' is possible relative to H, that is if HRH', then it is not the case that $\phi(A,H') = $ F, that is, $\phi(A,H') \neq $ F,

    (b) $\phi(\Box A,H) = $ F otherwise.

Some sentences that we shall want to regard as valid can, by these rules, be truth-valueless. So validity here should not mean being always true. Among the possible alternatives, the following definition of validity seems most in keeping with the spirit of the above treatment of truth-valuelessness.

Sentence A is defined as "valid" if and only if for any model structure $\langle K,R,D \rangle$, any model ϕ on that model structure, and any member H of the K of that model structure, (i) $\phi(A,H) \neq$ F and (ii), when $\phi(A,H) =$ U, $\phi^*(A,H) =$ T. Now, as will be explained in detail below, $\phi^*(A,H) =$ T if $\phi(A,H) =$ U can be changed to $\phi(A,H) =$ T by certain reassignments of values. Roughly, a reassignment of the kind in question assigns any combination of truth-values to those occurrences of truth-valueless atomic parts of A which do not occur within segments of A with truth-values, and it assigns the original values to all other occurrences of atomic parts of A.

Sentential expression B is defined as "atomic" if and only if B is a sentence or open sentence lacking sentential connectives, modal operators, and quantifiers. By an "open sentence" I mean an expression with free individual variables that becomes a sentence by binding those variables with quantifiers. An expression, C, may occur several times within a sentence, A, and thus I shall speak of its "occurrences," $c_1, c_2, \ldots, c_k$, within A. Whatever value ϕ assigns to C, in respect to H, it assigns the same value to any occurrence c_i of C within A.

Now an occurrence b_i of B is defined as a "U-occurrence" within A in respect to ϕ and H if and only if (i) B is an atomic sentential expression, (ii) b_i occurs in A but in no segment C of A such that $\phi(C,H) =$ T or F, and (iii) if B is a sentence $\phi(B, H) =$ U, whereas if B is an n-place open sentence $\phi((x_1)(x_2)\ldots(x_n)A,H) =$ U. So a U-occurrence in A is an atomic occurrence that occurs in no truth-valued part of A and is itself truth-valueless or has a truth-valueless closure.

Finally, before defining ϕ^*, I shall define a set of functions—the F-functions—that act as auxiliaries to the model function ϕ. Let $a_1, a_2, \ldots, a_m$ be all the U-occurrences within A in respect to ϕ and H. Now f is an "F-function" for A in respect to ϕ and H if and only if (i) f assigns a truth-value to every sentence-occurrence and every instance associated with every open-sentence occurrence among $a_1, a_2, \ldots, a_m$, subject to the condition that the same value is assigned to all occurrences of the same expression, and (ii) f assigns the same truth-value assigned by ϕ, in respect to H, to every sentence-occurrence and every instance associated with every open-sentence occurrence among the atomic non-U-occurrences of A. (It should be explained that if a_k is an occurrence of, for example, a one-place open sentence then for any t of $D(H)$ $a_k t/x$ is to be called an "instance associated with the open-sentence occurrence" a_k.)

Now I say that $\phi^*(A,H) = T$ if and only if (i) $\phi(A,H) = T$, or (ii) $\phi(A,H) = U$ yet if, in the calculation of $\phi(A,H)$, the values given to the atomic occurrences, or instances of them, of A by any F-function for A in respect to ϕ and H replace the values they are given by ϕ, then the calculation yields the value T. On the other hand, $\phi^*(A,H) = U$ if and only if $\phi(A,H) = U$ and the described replacement of ϕ-values with F-values yields the value T for some F-function and the value F for some other F-function. Finally, $\phi^*(A,H) = F$ if and only if (i) $\phi(A,H) = F$, or (ii) $\phi(A,H) = U$, yet the described replacement of ϕ-values with F-values yields the value F for every F-function. We can then define A as "self-contradictory" when it is always the case that (i) $\phi(A,H) \neq T$ and (ii), when $\phi(A,H) = U$, $\phi^*(A,H) = F$.

Despite the third value, U, the laws of the classical propositional calculus are valid. For example, though $\phi(A \vee \sim A, H) = U$ when $\phi(A,H) = U$, $\phi^*(A \vee \sim A) = T$ since replacing the value U for A with either the value T or the value F yields the value T.[4] However, as I shall show in the next section, not all laws of classical quantificational logic are valid. Furthermore, there are failures among the modal analogues of the classical quantificational laws that fail. These analogues are laws of Lewis' system Sl.[5]

THE BREAKDOWNS

Using definition (5), a simple derivation leads from the above rules of evaluation to:

(V) (a) $\phi((\exists x)A,H) = T$ iff there is a t such that t belongs to $D(H)$ and $\phi(At/x,H) = T$,

　　(b) $\phi((\exists x)A,H) = F$ iff for any t if t belongs to $D(H)$ then $\phi(At/x,H) = F$ or, if there is a t of $D(H)$ such that $\phi(At/x,H) = U$, then there is no t of $D(H)$ such that $\phi(At/x,H) = T$ and there is a t of $D(H)$ such that $\phi(At/x,H) = F$,

　　(c) $\phi((\exists x)A,H) = U$ otherwise, that is, iff for any t if t belongs to $D(H)$ then $\phi(At/x,H) = U$.

4. Cf. Bas C. van Fraassen, "Singular Terms, Truth-Value Gaps, and Free Logic," *Journal of Philosophy, 63* (1966), 481–95. The rules of evaluation (I) and (II) and the above definition of validity allow that a valid sentence, such as $A \vee \sim A$, may have the value U. On the other hand, van Fraassen, who also preserves the validity of the laws of the classical propositional calculus while countenancing truth-valuelessness, employs the standard notion of validity, which requires that valid sentences always be true. Thus even when A is U, $A \vee \sim A$ must, for van Fraassen, be true. He meets this requirement by using the notion of a "supervaluation." A supervaluation assigns a truth-value to a sentence with a truth-valueless component only if, for a given set of truth-values for all other components of the sentence, the sentence has the same truth-value when its truth-valueless component is considered true as when it is considered false. This common truth-value is the one assigned by the supervaluation to the sentence as a whole. The analogue to a supervaluation in my account is ϕ^*, but ϕ^* is used to determine validity, not to determine truth-values. It seems to me an undesirable feature of van Fraassen's semantics that a sentence can be true or false when, as with $A \vee \sim A$, its only component is truth-valueless.

5. Cf. C. I. Lewis and C. H. Langford, *Symbolic Logic* (2nd ed. New York, Dover, 1959), Appendix II, pp. 492–502.

Using definition (6), a simple derivation also leads from the rules of evaluation of the last section to:

(VI) (a) $\phi(\diamond A,H) = $ T iff there is an H' such that HRH' and $\phi(A,H') = $ T,

(b) $\phi(\diamond A,H) = $ F otherwise.

It might have seemed, on the basis of (IV), that A would be possible when it is merely not false in some world. But that truth in some world is really required for possibility is clear from this derivation:

1 $\phi(\diamond A,H) = $ T iff $\phi(\sim \square \sim A,H) = $ T   by (6)

2 $\phi(\sim \square \sim A,H) = $ T iff $\phi(\square \sim A,H) = $ F   by (Ia)

3 $\phi(\square \sim A,H) = $ F iff there is an H' such that both HRH' and it is not the case that $\phi(\sim A,H') \neq $ F   by (IVb)

4 It is not the case that $\phi(\sim A,H') \neq $ F iff $\phi(\sim A,H') = $ F   by double negation

5 $\phi(\sim A,H') = $ F iff $\phi(A,H') = $ T   by (Ib)

$\therefore$ 6 $\phi(\diamond A,H) = $ T iff there is an H' such that HRH' and $\phi(A,H') = $ T   from 1–5

The derivation of (VIb) follows similar lines.

Now the following laws are no longer valid under the above semantics:

(7) $(x)A \supset (\exists x)A$ QPartic

(8) $\square A \supset \diamond A$.   MPartic

QPartic fails for the case of the empty world. In this case the antecedent of QPartic is, by (IIIa), true since there is no t in $D(H)$ to make At/x false or neither true nor false. But the consequent is, by (Vb), false since there is no t in $D(H)$ to make At/x true or neither true nor false. To see that MPartic also fails, choose a model structure $\langle K,R,D \rangle$ with the following features. (A specific example will be given at the end of this section in connection with sentence (S1).) There will be a world, H, of K such that no world possible relative to H contains a counterexample to A. At the same time, there will be no world possible relative to H in which A is true or false. Thus, by (IVa), A is necessary relative to H, but by (VIb), A is not possible relative to H. For A to be possible relative to H, there must be some world possible relative to H in respect to which it is true, but it is neither true nor false in respect to any world possible relative to H.

So far, our interpretation has treated atomic sentences without explicitly considering their components. But to give a rationale for a model's assigning the non-truth-value U to well-formed sentences, the semantics of the parts of these sentences must be considered. The atomic sentence Pa may have the non-truth-value U in respect to a world H because:

  (i) the name a is uninterpreted in respect to H,

 (ii) the predicate P is uninterpreted in respect to H,

(iii) a and P are both interpreted in respect to H but the type of the individual named by a is such that the property signified by P is not an appropriate property of that individual, or

(iv) a and P are both interpreted in respect to H but the individual named by a is not a member of $D(H)$, whereas the extension of P is limited to individuals from $D(H)$ without P's signifying the property of belonging to the domain of the world in question.[6]

6. The Frege–Strawson theory of nondesignating singular terms does not seem to distinguish case (i) from case (iv); nor does it distinguish between case (iv) and the case which is like (iv) except that the extension of P is not limited to individuals from the domain in question. Thus on that theory both 'Zeus is more powerful than anyone in this room' and 'Zeus is thinkable' are without truth-value, whereas on the theory presented here, only the first is without a truth-value. Cf. G. Frege, "On Sense and Reference," in *The Philosophical Writings of Gottlob Frege*, ed. and trans. P. Geach and M. Black (Oxford, Blackwell, 1952), pp. 56–78, and P. F. Strawson, "On Referring," *Mind, 59* (1950), 320–44.

To elucidate these divisions I wish to contrast the idea of a predicate's being uninterpreted in respect to a world with the idea of its being uninterpreted simpliciter. If a predicate is uninterpreted simpliciter it signifies no property. A predicate which signifies a property, and is thus interpreted simpliciter, does not signify that property merely relative to a certain possible world. But an extension is something a predicate has relative to a possible world. A predicate is interpreted in respect to a possible world H if in respect to H it has the null or a nonnull extension.[7] Many predicates, such as 'red' and 'powerful' have different extensions in respect to different worlds. In respect to the actual world the extension of the

7. But why not treat a property as a class of extensions, each containing members from a different member of K, and such that there is an extension corresponding to every member of K in respect to which the relevant predicate is interpreted? If we did, the simpliciter interpretation would be reducible to a derivative sort of interpretation. But there is a basis for the heuristic Platonism espoused here. Suppose I ask whether the entity named by a, which has the property signified by P, *could* also have the property signified by Q. On the view that a property is a class of extensions from possible worlds, it seems that the answer must always be affirmative. Whatever the extensions of the predicates P and Q in the actual world, there is no reason on this view why their extensions should not overlap, with the entity named by a as a common member, in a possible world. The reply that any world in which they overlap might be impossible can be made only if it is allowed that it might be impossible precisely because of what the predicates P and Q might signify. Thus the notion that an entity named by a, which has the property signified by P, could not have the property signified by Q ceases to be an intelligible notion on the class-of-extensions view of properties. (A view akin to this extensional one of properties was developed by Richard Montague, in his paper, "The Nature of Certain Philosophical Entities," at the APA, Chicago, May 1967. C. I. Lewis distinguished the "denotation" of a term, which is the class of actual things to which it applies, from its "comprehension," which is made up of all possible things to which it could be correctly applied. But, as in the present paper, he does not identify the comprehension with what he calls the "signification" of a term, which is the property in things making the term applicable. Cf. C. I. Lewis, *An Analysis of Knowledge and Valuation* [La Salle, Illinois, Open Court, 1946], p. 39.)

predicate 'powerful' does not include Zeus, though in respect to some mythological world it may well include Zeus. The extension of 'object of thought', however, even in respect to the actual world, includes Zeus. Now the predicate 'red' is uninterpreted in respect to a world of numbers, since redness is not an appropriate property of individuals of that world and thus the predicate has neither the null nor a nonnull extension in respect to that world. On the other hand, 'mythical' will be interpreted in respect to such a world if, in K, there is also a world containing mythical objects. Thus a predicate like 'mythical' is uninterpreted in respect to a world only if being mythical is not an appropriate property of individuals in any world of K.

Frequently we are more interested in the intersection of a predicate's extension with respect to a world with the domain of that world than we are in its extension with respect to that world. Thus I introduce the notion of a predicate's being interpreted in respect to a world *on that world*. A predicate, P, is uninterpreted in respect to a world, H, "on H" if the property signified by P is not an appropriate one of individuals of H. Otherwise, P is interpreted in respect to H on H. Then P is said to have an extension in respect to H on H. That extension is the intersection of its extension with respect to H with $D(H)$. If there is in addition to a world of numbers also a world of mythical objects and both are members of K, then 'mythical' is interpreted even in respect to the world of numbers. But it is uninterpreted in respect to the world of numbers on that world. By contrast, 'red' is uninterpreted in both senses for the world of numbers. In respect to the actual world, 'nonactual' has the null extension on the actual world, but in respect to the actual world, it has a nonnull extension on some nonempty, nonactual world.

To bring these matters within the precritical interpretation, let us begin anew with different model structures and models.

The model structures will now be ordered quintuples, $\langle K,R,D,U,S \rangle$, where U is an entity belonging to the domain of no member of K and S is a set of properties. A model on a model structure will now assign values to names and predicates rather than to sentences. A model ϕ on a model structure $\langle K,R,D,U,S \rangle$ is a binary function which assigns the value $\phi(a,H)$ to the name a in respect to the world H, the value $\phi(P,H)$ to the predicate P in respect to the world H, and the value $\phi(P,P)$ to the predicate P in respect to itself. Either $\phi(a,H)$ is an individual from the domain of some member of K, not necessarily from $D(H)$, or it is U, in which case we say a is uninterpreted in respect to H. For example, in respect to the actual world 'Zeus' and 'Harry Truman's assassin' might designate beings who exist only in possible worlds in which Greek gods exist or the thirty-third president of the United States was assassinated. For the n-adic predicate P, either $\phi(P,H)$ is the null class or a nonnull class of ordered n-tuples, which in either case we call the extension of the n-adic predicate P in respect to H, or it is U and we say P is uninterpreted in respect to H. In general, an n-tuple which is a member of $\phi(P,H)$ is a member of the n-th Cartesian product of the union of the domains of all members of K with itself and not necessarily a member of the n-th Cartesian product of $D(H)$ with itself. However, an n-tuple which is a member of the extension of P with respect to H *on* H will belong to the n-th Cartesian product of $D(H)$ with itself. $\phi(P,P)$ is a member of S; it is the property which, for the model in question, is signified by P. It will be assumed that every predicate signifies a property, that is, that no predicate is uninterpreted simpliciter.

Now we add to (I)–(IV) the following rule for evaluating atomic sentences:

(VII)   (a) $\phi(Pa_1 \ldots a_n,H) = T$ iff $\langle \phi(a_1,H), \ldots, \phi(a_n,H) \rangle$ is a member of $\phi(P,H)$,

(b) $\phi(Pa_1 \ldots a_n, H) = F$ iff $\langle \phi(a_1, H), \ldots, \phi(a_n, H) \rangle$ is not a member of $\phi(P, H)$ but its type is such that $\phi(P, P)$ is an appropriate property of it,

(c) $\phi(Pa_1 \ldots a_n, H) = U$ otherwise, that is, iff either

   (i) there is an i such that $1 \leq i \leq n$ and $\phi(a_i, H) = U$,

   (ii) $\phi(P, H) = U$,

   (iii) neither (i) nor (ii) is the case but $\{\phi(a_1, H), \ldots, \phi(a_n, H)\}$ belongs to a type such that $\phi(P, P)$ is not an appropriate property of it, or

   (iv) neither (i) nor (ii) is the case but, though there is an i such that $1 \leq i \leq n$ and $\phi(a_i, H)$ is not a member of $D(H)$, any member of any n-tuple of $\phi(P, H)$ is a member of $D(H)$ but $\phi(P, P)$ is not the property of belonging to the domain of the world in question.[8]

8. Two things must be noted about condition (iv). First, one and the same shape can, in one context, be a predicate whose extension goes beyond a given world and, in another context, be a predicate whose extension is limited to that world. In respect to the actual world, 'The Emerald City of Oz is green' is true only if the extension of 'green' in respect to the actual world includes the nonactual Emerald City of Oz. However, in respect to the actual world, 'My neighbor Jones is green' is false only if 'green' is equivalent to 'green in this world' and hence its extension in respect to the actual world includes only members of the actual world, for surely there is a possible world in which Jones is green. (We could, of course, say the extensions of 'green' are the same in the two cases but the copula changes significance. Then simply write the predicate as 'is green' and the original point applies.) Thus when I say, on the basis of (iv), that, for example, 'Harry Truman's assassin is a Republican' is truth-valueless, 'a Republican' is to be understood as equivalent to 'a Republican in this world' (or 'is a Republican' to 'is Republican in this world'). Second, in view of the penetrating analysis of Keith S. Donnellan ("Reference and Definite Descriptions," *Philosophical Review, 75* [1966], 281–304), condition (iv) for truth-valuelessness can be seen to need a pragmatic qualification. If $\phi(a, H)$ is not a member of $D(H)$ then $\phi(Pa, H) = U$ only if a is used "attributively," rather than "referentially," in Pa. 'The killer of Smith is tall' will have a truth-value, even though Smith died of natural causes, if in it 'the killer of

As indicated earlier, it is helpful to have the notion of the extension of P in respect to H on H. To bring this notion within reach of our symbolism, I define $\phi(P,H)_H$ as follows:

(D1) $\phi(P,H)_H$ = the intersection of $\phi(P,H)$ with the n-th Cartesian product of $D(H)$ with itself, or if no n-tuple of the n-th Cartesian product of $D(H)$ with itself is of a type such that $\phi(P,P)$ is an appropriate property of it, then $\phi(P,H)_H = $ U, but not both.

When $\phi(P,H)_H = $ U, I say P is uninterpreted in respect to H on H. Otherwise, $\phi(P,H)_H$ is to be called the extension of P in respect to H on H.

I shall now apply the precritical semantics by means of a few simple examples. Let K be a set of worlds containing only abstract individuals. Thus 'anguished', when interpreted simpliciter to signify the property of being anguished, must be uninterpreted in respect to every H of K. At least, it must be uninterpreted in respect to every H of K if category mistakes are to be truth-valueless. Should the predicate be given the null extension in respect to some H, then, in respect to H, it would be false that any individual of the domain of this member of K is anguished. For example, it might be false that 3 is anguished. But, as I shall argue shortly, category mistakes are best viewed as truth-valueless. So, though there are no counterexamples to:

(S1) $(x)(x$ is anguished $\supset x$ experiences a psychic phenomenon)

Smith' is used referentially, that is, to pick out, say, the suspected but innocent Jones. If, however, 'the killer of Smith' is used attributively, that is, not to pick out anyone in particular other than someone whom the description fits, then since Smith was not killed, the sentence is neither true nor false. Adopting condition (iv) amounts to the assumption that any name which happens to be a description is limited to its attributive use.

in any H of K, neither is it true in any H of K, for from (VIIcii), (IIc), and (IIIc) it follows that (s1) is truth-valueless in every H of K. But then by (IVa), we must regard (s1) as necessary in respect to any H of K, even though it is true in respect to no H of K.

Since QPartic and MPartic are not valid, we should expect that the laws (1)–(4) are also not valid. Consideration of:

(s2)   Santa Claus does not exist $\supset$ $(\exists x)(x$ does not exist)

makes clear that on the precritical interpretation QGen is not valid. Assume that 'Santa Claus' is interpreted in respect to the actual world. This is possible since we have allowed that a name can be interpreted in respect to a world when it is assigned a designatum outside that world. Since 'Santa Claus' does designate an individual outside of the actual world, the antecedent is true. However, by (Vb), the consequent of (s2) is false; for there to be a nonexistent individual it would have to belong to the domain of the actual world and hence exist.

But QGen and QInst also fail where truth-valuelessness becomes relevant. In respect to a world, H, of blue things, '$(x)(x$ is blue)' is T and '7 is blue' is U. But $\phi^*($'$(x)(x$ is blue) $\supset$ 7 is blue', $H) \neq$ T. For, when an F-function assigns F to '7 is blue', it leaves '$(x)(x$ is blue)' T, since '$(x$ is blue)' is not a U-occurrence here.

That MInst and MGen are not valid can be seen from considering:

(s3) $\square(3$ is anguished) $\supset$ 3 is anguished.

By (VIIciii), it is clear that the consequent of (s3) has the value U in any possible world. But then by (IVa) the antecedent is true. Since it is true, the occurrence in the antecedent of '3 is anguished' is not a U-occurrence, though its occurrence in the consequent is. Thus when an F-function assigns F to the consequent, it leaves the truth-value, T, of the antecedent unchanged. We then have $\phi^*((s3),H) \neq T$, for any H. So (s3), though never false, is not valid.

Notice that MPartic was shown to be nonvalid by reference to (s1) without reliance on the capacity of an F-function to assign different values to occurrences of the same expression. In the case of (s3) we saw that since only one occurrence of '3 is anguished' is a U-occurrence, F-functions assign the different occurrences of this expression different values. This capacity of an F-function was essential in showing MInst and MGen nonvalid. Now MPartic follows from MInst and MGen by the transitivity of the $\supset$. Short of abandoning this property of the $\supset$, that capacity of an F-function must play a vital role in the definition of validity. Analogously, '$(x)(x$ is blue) $\supset$ $(\exists x)(x$ is blue)' can be shown to be nonvalid, if the empty world is allowed, without reliance on the mentioned capacity of an F-function; but it clearly follows from '$(x)(x$ is blue) $\supset$ 7 is blue' and '7 is blue $\supset (\exists x)(x$ is blue)'. And the invalidity of these two rests on the possibility of assigning, by F-functions, '7 is blue' F and T respectively, while leaving the quantified sentences T and F respectively. This possibility rests on the fact that the occurrences of '7 is blue' are U-occurrences, whereas those of 'x is blue' are not.

THE CLASSICAL SOLUTION

Classically, two steps have been taken to avoid these breakdowns in quantification logic:

(A)   The notion of validity is changed so as to require that a sentence not be false in nonempty worlds rather than in nonempty worlds and the empty world;

(B)   Names are restricted to those which designate members of the domain of the actual world.

Since (A) limits our interest to nonempty worlds, it is natural, once (A) is accepted, to limit the range of the variable H of (III) to nonempty worlds. If H is not so limited, then QPartic will be false in the case of some H even though, by (A), it will be valid. If H is so limited, the validity of QPartic will correspond to its not being false in respect to any H. As regards names, there are several alternatives for the treatment of 'Santa Claus' of (s2) above. (a) There is the Quine–Russell theory of descriptions, according to which the antecedent of (s2) is equivalent to '$\sim (\exists y)(x)\,(x\,\text{santa-clausizes} \equiv (x = y))$'. But then (s2) is not an instance of QGen. In view of objections of the sort raised by Strawson[9] is is doubtful whether proper names and definite descriptions are eliminable in the manner prescribed by this theory. In the absence of arguments which establish any more than convenience for an elimination of proper names and definite descriptions, it will be assumed hereafter that both are ineliminable and behave as genuine singular terms. (b) There is the view that 'Santa Claus' is noneliminable as a name but, at the same time, not allowable, in view of (B), in sentences. For, ϕ('Santa Claus,'H) is not a member of $D(H)$, where H is this world. Not being an allowable sentence, (s2) is not a counterexample to QGen. But (B) is clearly objectionable. It deprives us of any means of denying existence of individuals picked out by names. And it leads to circularity in deciding what names are allowable: 'Smith' is an allowable name only if 'Smith exists' is true; the latter is true only if a sentence; it is a sentence only if 'Smith' is an allowable name.

The two steps, (A) and (B), have characterized most thinking in quantificational logic. The view that all well-formed sentences are true or false—the theory of bivalency—has equally characterized most thinking in all branches of symbolic logic. Thus I lump those steps and that view together under

9. Cf. W. V. O. Quine, *Methods of Logic* (rev. ed. New York, Holt, 1959), pp. 218–22. P. F. Strawson, "On Referring"; "Singular Terms, Ontology, and Identity," *Mind*, 65 (1956), 433–54.

the heading "the classical solution." The above breakdowns in modal logic disappear if all well-formed sentences are given truth-values. But since a sentence cannot have a truth-value unless it is fully interpreted, the requirement of bivalency is to be enforced by assigning designata and extensions to previously uninterpreted names and predicates. So the classical solution for modal logic comes about by requiring that (i) there be no a and H for which $\phi(a,H) = U$, (ii) there be no P and H for which $\phi(P,H) = U$, (iii) there be a truth-value assigned to sentences which by (VIIciii) are assigned U, that is, to category mistakes, and (iv) there be a truth-value assigned to sentences which by (VIIciv) are assigned U, that is, to sentences which suffer from a failure of existential presupposition. Under these requirements the cases demanding (c) of (VII) do not arise. Thus a considerable simplification of the precritical semantics results from bivalency.

Now requirements (i) and (ii) can be satisfied in various ways. One way would be simply to eliminate from the language names and predicates uninterpreted in respect to given worlds. This would be an extreme step, at least in the case of predicates; all psychological predicates, whatever their form, would be eliminated if a world without organic beings were possible. Another way would be to contrive interpretations, however artificial, for expressions uninterpreted in respect to given worlds. Thus we would introduce an "outside" domain, which contains neither U nor any member of $D(H)$ for any H of K, and we would locate the designata of, say, 'the integer between 2 and 3' and 'Thomas J. Inequality' in this outside domain.[10] Further, in respect to a world of numbers, we might choose the null class to be the extension of 'anguished'.

Due to (i), any name will designate an individual in the domain of some possible world or in the outside domain.

10. Cp. R. H. Thomason, "Modal Logic and Metaphysics," this volume, pp. 119–46.

Will there still be names which are empty in the narrower sense of not designating actualities that is, members of the actual domain? If we adopt (B) of the classical solution in quantificational logic, there will be no names that are empty in this narrower sense either. However, (B) must be regarded as overly restrictive for modal logic, where there is not a single domain but many domains corresponding to many possible worlds. We want to be able to consider Santa Claus coming down a chimney as a true state of affairs in respect to some possible world. Thus we do not want to banish the name 'Santa Claus' simply because it does not designate an entity in the actual world. But even if we were to proceed independently of (B) and hence with a modified classical solution, trouble would confront us in connection with nonexistential names. Apart from (B), 'Harry Truman's assassin is a Republican' is an allowable sentence and, because of the requirement of bivalency, either true or false. But such an assignment of a truth-value is surely objectionable where the failure of existential presupposition naturally requires truth-valuelessness.

But the objection to the classical solution most relevant here is its insensitivity to type violations. When, on the precritical interpretation, $\phi(P,H) = U$, this lack of interpretation is associated with the fact that $\phi(P,P)$ is not appropriate to members of the domain of the given world H or to n-tuples of the n-th Cartesian product of the domain of the world H with itself. But by (ii), $\phi(P,H)$ cannot be U. Either $\phi(P,P)$ is changed when P is given an extension in respect to H, or P is given the extension without changing $\phi(P,P)$, with the result that violations of type restrictions and hence category mistakes are introduced. But even if the classical solution does not introduce category mistakes in this way, it does so through requirement (iii).

My reason for thinking that category mistakes are truth-valueless is that they involve a failure of presupposition which, like a failure of existential presupposition, destroys the possibility of a truth-value. Suppose P, Q, and R are a complete set of "characteristic" predicates relative to a predicate C. That is, suppose, first, that, relative to any H of K, the extensions of P, Q, and R are mutually exclusive and exhaustive subsets of the extension of C and, second, the principle or principles by which individuals are differentiated as between the three subsets are not exemplified outside of the extension of C. In saying Pa, it is presupposed, since P is a characteristic predicate relative to C, that the designatum, relative to the given H, of a has a property, namely that signified by C, relative to which the property signified by P can be regarded as one of the alternative specifications. For clearly, in its informative use, Pa would be used to state what color the entity named by a is if P happens to be a characteristic predicate relative to 'color', and thus it is presupposed, when Pa is so used, that the entity named by a has a color. If, however, a is such that its designatum is of a type excluded from the extension of C, the presupposition fails and Pa is neither true nor false. We say that Pa is a category mistake since P is an appropriate predicate only for individuals of a type not excluded from the category indicated by C.

Apparent denials of category mistakes, such as '7 is not blue', are often something quite different. If the use of '7 is not blue' is such that it is presupposed that 7 is a colored object and the force of the 'not' is to deny that blue is the right alternative among colors, then '7 is not blue' is neither true nor false. This is the traditional finite negation. Suppose, however, '7 is not blue' is used to make the categorial statement that, whatever the type of 7, that type is excluded from the category in respect to which one of the characteristic predicates signifies being blue. Then, '7 is not blue' is true, but it is not by any means the denial of an atomic sentence. This is one interpretation of the traditional infinite negation. Any temptation there is to assign truth-values to category mistakes and their denials can only arise from a confusion of them with their counterparts that affirm or deny the inclusion of types of individuals in categories corresponding to certain characteristic predicates.[11]

THE FREE LOGIC SOLUTION

In regard to quantification, the advocate of free logic would applaud the precritical interpretation for its avoidance of the two presuppositions that there are individuals and that all individuals exist. It avoids the first presupposition by allowing the variable H to range over both empty and nonempty worlds. It avoids the second by allowing names to which models assign designata outside the given domain. Free logic comes about by the recognition that in the absence of these presuppositions the laws of quantificational logic stand in need of revision.[12] So instead of QInst and QGen we are to have:

(9) $(x)A \supset (E!t \supset At/x)$ RQInst
(10) $At/x \supset (E!t \supset (\exists x)A)$.   RQGen

QPartic is not then derivable, and like QInst and QGen, it is not valid, since the semantics is that of the precritical interpretation. The interpretation for 'E!t', which symbolizes 't exists', is:

(VIII)   (a) $\phi(E!t,H) = T$ iff $\phi(t,H)$ is a member of $D(H)$,

11. This statement can be applied to the view of F. Summers that "Category mistakes ['The equator is clean'] are false statements whose denials ['The equator is unclean (or not clean)'] are also false," but whose negations ['It is not the case that the equator is clean'] are true ("Predicability," in M. Black, ed., *Philosophy in America* [London, Allen and Unwin, 1965], pp. 262–81).

12. Cf. the pioneering work in free logic by Henry S. Leonard, "The Logic of Existence," *Philosophical Studies*, 7 (1956), 49–54. See also, Karel Lambert, "Existential Import Revisited," *Notre Dame Journal of Formal Logic*, 4 (1963), 288–92, and B. C. van Fraassen, "The Completeness of Free Logic," *Zeitschrift für mathematische Logik und Grundlagen der Mathematik*, 12 (1966), 219–34.

(b) $\phi(E!t,H) = F$ iff $\phi(t,H)$ is not a member of $D(H)$
but $\phi(t,H) \neq U$,
(c) $\phi(E!t,H) = U$ otherwise.

By making existence-claims minor premisses in instantiation and generalization, names for nonexistents can be used with impunity in such reasonings. Still, bound variables range only over existents. If there were an identity predicate and the usual semantics for it were supplemented by the condition that an identity sentence with an uninterpreted name is U, 'E!' could then be defined as follows:

(11) 'E!t' for '$(\exists x)(x = t)$'.

Free modal logic also sets out from the precritical interpretation. Modal operators can then operate on truth-valueless sentences. There is no restriction, as in the classical solution, to bivalency. Some worlds may then be "semantically incomplete" in one of various senses. There may be names and predicates that are uninterpreted in respect to those worlds *on those worlds*; or there may be names and predicates that are uninterpreted in respect to those worlds; or there may be only names which are uninterpreted in one of these ways; and so on. Free modal logic comes about by the recognition that, under the precritical interpretation, a modification of traditional modal laws is required. So in place of MInst and MGen we are to have:

(12) $\Box A \supset (S!A \supset A)$ RMInst
(13) $A \supset (S!A \supset \Diamond A)$.   RMGen

The interpretation for 'S!A', which symbolizes 'A has a truth-value', is:

(IX)   (a) $\phi(S!A,H) = T$ iff $\phi(A,H) = T$ or F,
        (b) $\phi(S!A,H) = F$ otherwise.

Now MInst was seen not to be valid by a consideration of (s3).

However, there is no corresponding counterexample to RMInst, for 'S!(3 is anguished)' is, by (IXb), false.

Suppose one introduces propositional quantifiers and interprets a claim beginning with a universal propositional quantifier as true when it holds for all propositions with truth-values. One can then define 'S!', as understood by (IX), as follows:

(14) 'S!A' for '$(\exists p)(p \equiv A)$',

which parallels the definition for 'E!'.[13]

THE CATEGORY SOLUTION

Perhaps free quantificational logic is the only satisfactory way to avoid the double difficulty of the classical solution that logical validity becomes something less than holding in all worlds including the empty one and that the only individuals that can be talked about by name are existents. But is free modal logic—where by 'free' I mean free of the presupposition that sentences have truth-values—unavoidable? The classical solution in modal logic led to the violation of type-restrictions. Can the classical solution be modified to avoid this, while at the same time preserving the traditional laws MInst, MGen, and MPartic of modal logic, as free modal logic does not?

13. One can easily prove E!$t \supset (\exists x)(x = t)$ using (9) and $t = t$. Similarly, S!$A \supset (\exists p)(p \equiv A)$ is provable from $(p)A \supset (S!B \supset AB/p)$ and $A \equiv A$. The converses are, as K. Lambert has pointed out to me, provable from, on the one hand, $(x)E!x$ and (i) $t = u \supset (E!u \supset E!t)$ and, on the other hand, $(p)S!p$ and (ii) $A \equiv B \supset (S!B \supset S!A)$. However, though (i) is valid, (ii) is not, for when S!B is true and S!A is false the antecedent of (ii) is truth-valueless and the consequent false, and there is an F-function which makes the antecedent true and leaves the consequent false. Thus, though the biconditional corresponding to definition (11) is provable in a valid system in which 'E!' is primitive, there is no precisely parallel proof of that corresponding to (14) in a valid system with 'S!' primitive. Nonetheless, from (IX) and the indicated semantics for propositional quantifiers, it is clear that $(\exists p)(p \equiv A) \supset$ S!A is valid.

Like the classical solution, the solution I shall now consider —to be called the category solution—requires bivalency. But it realizes this requirement in a different way. It does not assign truth-values to sentences which would be assigned U. Rather sentences which would otherwise be assigned U are assigned no value at all; only sentences which would have truth-values on the precritical interpretation can now be arguments in a model-function. The point of this is not to have to bother with sentences violating type-restrictions or manifesting a failure of existential presupposition. On the category solution, a predicate, P, uninterpreted in respect to a world, H, remains uninterpreted in respect to H. To give P an extension in respect to H without changing the property signified by P would be pointless. For, sentences formed with P and names of individuals would not be evaluated, since they would be category mistakes.

What, on this view, is to be understood by necessity? Suppose that, in respect to some H, P is uninterpreted on H. Even if a names an individual in that H, Pa is not assigned a value in respect to that H since it is a category mistake. But then (IV) becomes inadequate for the semantics of necessity; it cannot tell us whether Pa is necessary, for it is presupposed by (IV) that, in respect to every H, Pa is assigned T, F, or U. It is natural to modify (IV) by expanding 'for any H'' to read 'for any H' in respect to which A is evaluated by the model ϕ'. Will this do?

Does this revised interpretation of necessity weaken the notion beyond all recognition? How can we claim to have necessity unless consideration is given to the value of the sentence in question in respect to all possible worlds? Here we have left out of consideration (a) all those possible worlds in respect to which the predicate of the sentence is uninterpreted on those worlds and, a fortiori, all those in respect to which it is uninterpreted, and (b) all those possible worlds in respect to which the predicate is interpreted on those worlds and yet the sentence is a category mistake. (Henceforth I drop the question of uninterpreted and nonexistential names, since the new problems to be encountered concern predicates.)

Suppose we consider only the weaker form of this objection which leaves out of account what might happen by not considering possible worlds (b). The following is a plausible defense of the category solution against this weaker objection. Let H be a possible world in respect to which P is uninterpreted on H, that is, $\phi(P,H)_H = U$. It seems there should be a possible world, H', such that not only is P interpreted in respect to H' on H', that is, $\phi(P,H')_H \neq U$ but also H is imbedded in H'. I say that:

(D2)   World W is *imbedded* in world W' iff for any atomic sentence A if $\phi(A,W) = T$ then $\phi(A,W') = T$, and if $\phi(A,W) = F$ then $\phi(A,W') = F$.

The claim that any possible world, H, in respect to which some predicate, P, is uninterpreted on H is imbeddable in a possible world, H', in respect to which P has an interpretation on H' I shall call the Imbedding Postulate. This postulate tells us that, if the restriction on (IV) called for by the category solution leaves out only possible worlds (a), it does not really weaken the notion of necessity. For, the possible worlds which are thereby not considered—namely, those in which the sentence is not evaluated because the predicate is uninterpreted in respect to that world on that world—are, if the postulate is correct, imbedded in possible worlds which are not left out. Suppose then there were an obstacle to the necessity of the sentence hidden in a possible world which possible world is left out because the predicate of the sentence in question has no interpretation in respect to that possible world on that possible world. Then this obstacle would show up in a possible world in respect to which these predicates are interpreted on it and in which the former world is imbedded.

Suppose W is imbedded in W' and that $\phi(P,W)_W = U$ but that $\phi(P,W')_{W'} \neq U$. Then there are individuals in $D(W')$ which are not of the same type as individuals in $D(W)$. This need not mean that $D(W') \neq D(W)$. For, the same individuals can be of different types in different possible worlds. The same individual, a, which in W is a psychic phenomenon may be a brain state in W'. Thus in respect to W, it is a category mistake to say a is a motion, but not in respect to W'. This does not imply a rejection of "essentialism," according to which individuals have necessary properties, but only that the type of an individual need not be a necessary property of it.

ANALYTIC CONTINGENCIES

I shall now show that the Imbedding Postulate is false, and hence that the category solution involves an objectionable loosening of the concept of necessity. My counterexample to the Imbedding Postulate will suggest the line along which a successful solution to the problem raised by truth-valuelessness in modal logic should be developed.

What I want to show is that a possible world in respect to which, by the category solution, a sentence is not evaluated, may nonetheless be a world which is so "out of line" with the import of the sentence that because of this world the sentence cannot be judged necessary. Thus to determine necessity, one cannot leave out of account such a world.

Consider two languages, SL and AL, which have, among others, the following features. SL contains the temporal and causal predicates 'earlier than' and '(a cause of)$_S$'. They are called temporal and causal since 'earlier than' is interpreted simpliciter as signifying a temporal precedence relation, and '(a cause of)$_S$' is interpreted simpliciter as signifying a causal relation. The precedence relation is such as to allow that time closes on itself. The causal relation is to be transitive but is not asymmetrical. The causal relation is not reducible by definition to the temporal one, but the language is also characterized by criteria for the application of the causal predicate, and these criteria mention the temporal relation. The notion of a criterion is still a vague one in philosophy, but I think this much is clear about it, that a statement of a criterion is not aptly described as empirical, analytic, or necessary. Since it is not analytic or necessary, it is both possible for a property to be present when a criterion for its predicate is not satisfied and, conversely, possible for the criterion to be satisfied in the absence of the property.

AL contains 'earlier than' interpreted as in SL, but in place of the causal predicate of SL, AL contains '(a cause of)$_A$', which is transitive but asymmetrical. Thus : ·

(s4)   Being (a cause of)$_A$ is asymmetrical

is analytic in AL. The criterion for 'x is (a cause of)$_A$ y' is that some relation C holds along the shortest temporal path from x to y but not along the same path from y to x. The criterion for 'x is (a cause of)$_S$ y' is that C holds along the shortest path from x to y. Thus, whenever the criterion for the former is satisfied so is that for the latter. Being empirically decidable, the criteria for '(a cause of)$_A$' are not concerned with the long path around a possible closed time sequence.

Let SW be a world which can be described using SL. Specifically, SW is a world of events occurring one at a time. The events are temporally extended but not divisible into shorter events. Further, SW is temporally closed. So it is a single string of events closing on itself. The criteria for the causal relation of AL, and hence of SL, are satisfied between neighboring events and the causal relation of SL, but not of AL, does indeed hold between them, so as to form a causal chain.

On the other hand, AW, though it is like SW in every other

respect, has in addition the causal relation signified by '(a cause of)$_A$' between all neighboring events. So events in AW are related both by (causality)$_S$ and by (causality)$_A$. So in AW, as distinct from SW, not only are the criteria for '(a cause of)$_A$' satisfied between neighboring events but also (causality)$_A$ holds between them.

One could reasonably assume that SW is a possible world. But it is clear that AW is impossible. The closure of time in AW and the transitivity of (causality)$_A$ imply that for any two events, x and y, x will (be a cause of)$_A$ y and y will (be a cause of)$_A$ x. Nonetheless, (s4) asserts that this is not the case. Hence a contradiction within AW.

If the predicate '(a cause of)$_A$' is interpreted in respect to SW on SW, it must be given the null extension. For if any two neighboring events are related by (causality)$_A$, then, since the criteria are satisfied between all neighboring events, all neighboring events would be related by (causality)$_A$. SW would then be the impossible world AW. But even if it is the null extension an absurdity results. For then (s4) would be true in respect to SW. This is clear since (s4) has the logical form:

(s4') $(x)(y)(x$ is (a cause of)$_A$ $y \supset \sim(y$ is (a cause of)$_A$ $x))$,

and, by the choice of the null extension, the antecedent is always false. We would then be committed to saying that the causality relation signified by the causal predicate of AL is indeed asymmetrical in respect to a world in which events are not related by an asymmetrical causal relation. This is certainly not a contradiction, but it is so clearly an undesirable consequence that we are bound to turn to another premiss. The other premiss is precisely that '(a cause of)$_A$' is, in respect to SW on SW, given the value U, rather than the null extension. This choice is reasonable in itself since it is reasonable to maintain that the events of SW are events of a type which belong to a world in which causality is not asymmetrical.

They could not appropriately have asymmetrical causal predicates ascribed to them.

On the category solution, SW is not to be considered in determining whether (s4') is necessary. For since $\phi($'(a cause of$)_A$', SW$)_{SW}$ = U, (s4') is, on the category solution, assigned no value in respect to SW. The Imbedding Postulate says there is a possible world in which SW is imbedded and in respect to which '(a cause of$)_A$' has an interpretation on it. Which world might this be? It is not obtained from SW merely by adding everywhere (causality)$_A$; for that gives AW. Nor is it a world obtained by adding to SW pairs of events for which (causality)$_A$ is an appropriate relation. For, once (causality)$_A$ is allowed as an appropriate relation between the added events, it would be arbitrary to exclude (causality)$_A$ from between the neighboring events taken over from SW, since they satisfy the criteria for (causality)$_A$. But again because of time closure and causal transitivity, such a world is impossible. In effect, when new events are added, the type of the original events has here changed. They are no longer events of a type which belong to a world in which causality is not asymmetrical. The assumption that they do not change is inadmissible since in one and the same world, one pair of events, though it satisfies the criterion for a certain relation, could not fail to be appropriate for that relation while another pair is appropriate for it. Extending these considerations to other candidates, one is readily convinced that SW cannot be imbedded in any possible world H such that $\phi($'(a cause of$)_A$', $H)_H \neq$ U.

What are the consequences for modality? It can no longer be plausibly maintained that just because a sentence is analytic it is necessary.[14] (s4') is analytic in AL, but it is not necessary

14. A similar conclusion comes from the argument, quite different from this one, that, in some sense of 'same' a sentence may say the same thing before and after a change in meaning of one of its terms and hence, while saying the same thing, change from being analytically true to being synthetically true or

in respect to SW, nor is it necessary in respect to any world relative to which SW is a possible world. The reason is not that it is false in respect to SW, for it has no truth-value in respect to SW. Rather, the reason is that it is "too strong" for SW, in a sense I shall try to explain. Roughly, a sentence is too strong for a world if in order to give it a truth-value in respect to that world, without violating type restrictions, that world must be so changed as to become an impossible world. I regard it as natural to hold that a sentence is not necessary in respect to a world if it is too strong for some world possible relative to that world.

In our example, AW differed from SW only in that '(a cause of)$_A$' was uninterpreted in respect to SW on SW and, hence, in that the type of events of AW made them eligible to stand in both kinds of causal relation. The lack of interpretation in SW was artificial at least in that the criteria for '(a cause of)$_A$' were satisfied in SW. So:

(D3)   The lack of interpretation of a predicate P is *artificial in respect to criteria* in respect to a world W on W iff the criteria for applying P are satisfied at one or more places in W, even though P is uninterpreted in respect to W on W.

(D4)   (a) If A is an atomic sentence, A is *too strong* for a possible world H iff
           (i) the predicate P of A is uninterpreted in respect to H on H, and thus $\phi(A,H) = U$, (ii) there is an impossible world H' such that H' differs from

---

false. Cf. L. Jonathan Cohen, *The Diversity of Meaning* (New York, Herder and Herder, 1965), p. 160. In the present paper, the contingency of some analytic sentences is argued for without assuming such a sameness through a change of meaning. This represents an abandonment of an argument used in the author's "Analyticity and Conceptual Revision," *Journal of Philosophy*, 63 (1966), 627–37.

H only in that P and predicates analytically related to it in the language in question are interpreted in respect to H' on H', and (iii) the lack of interpretation of P in respect to H on H is artificial in respect to criteria;

(b) If A is $\sim B$, then A is *too strong* for H iff (i) A is not a valid sentence of nonmodal logic and (ii) B is too strong for H;

(c) If A is $B \supset C$, then A is *too strong* for H iff (i) A is not a valid sentence of nonmodal logic and (ii) A is assigned S (too strong) by the following table, in which the values of B and C are in respect to H:

B	C	A
T	S	S
S	T	U
F	S	U
S	F	S
S	S	S

(d) If A is $(x)B$, then A is *too strong* for H iff for any t, Bt/x is too strong for H.

The (i)-clauses of (b) and (c) prevent the classification of logical truths as contingent. Thus, since we want A's being too strong to make $\Box A$ false, without (i) of (c), $\Box(A \supset A)$ would be false when A is too strong. However, since the notion of strength will appear only in the semantics of modal sentences [cf. (IV′), below], no circularity results from relying on the concept of nonmodal validity here. Since $\Box A$ is to be F when A is S, $\Box A \supset A$ is U, not S, when A is S, by the third row of the table. So $\Box(\Box A \supset A)$ is not falsified by such a case. Further, since $\sim A \supset (B \cdot \sim B)$ is equivalent to A, when A is S, $\sim A \supset (B \cdot \sim B)$ should also be S, as it is by the fourth or fifth row of the table.

The category solution, by not considering truth-valueless sentences, overlooks cases in which a sentence is too strong for a possible world. Thus the category solution admits as necessary sentences which cannot reasonably be regarded as such. (s4′), which is analytic in AL, is thus not false in any possible world, but it is contingent precisely because it is too strong for SW, which is a possible world.

For a less contrived example than SW, consider a world describable by Einstein's Special Relativity Theory. The following sentence, which is analytic in the language of Newtonian Mechanics,[15] is too strong for the relativistic world:

(s5)   If x is (prior)$_N$ to y in frame S, then there is no frame in which x is (simultaneous)$_N$ with y,

where the subscript 'N' indicates that the temporal relations are Newtonian. The observational criteria for applying the temporal terms of both languages are, if the old Newtonian criteria are properly improved, the same. By reasoning similar to that in connection with causation, it can be seen that '(prior)$_N$' and '(simultaneous)$_N$' are uninterpreted in respect to and on the relativistic world. In respect to criteria, this lack of interpretation is artificial, in the sense of (D3). There will be an impossible world, E′W, in which the relativistic one, EW, is imbedded and which differs from EW only in that the Newtonian temporal expressions of (s5) are interpreted in E′W on E′W, and hence in that the type of events in E′W is not such that only relativistic temporal relations can appropriately stand between them. The world E′W will be impossible since in it there is and there is not a frame in which some x and y are (simultaneous)$_N$. (s5) is then too strong for EW, and,

15. Cf. Hans Reichenbach, *The Philosophy of Space and Time*, Eng. trans. M. Reichenbach and J. Freund (New York, Dover, 1958), pp. 146–47.

though analytic, is not necessary in respect to EW or in respect to any world relative to which EW is possible.

THE SEMANTICS OF STRENGTH

So the category solution is unsatisfactory since it allows a sentence to be necessary in respect to a world even though it is too strong for some world possible relative to that world. It is easy to see that this objection can be turned against both the classical solution and the free modal logic solution. On the classical solution, '(a cause of)$_A$' would doubtless have the null extension in respect to SW. Thus (s4') would be true in respect to SW, and SW would then present no obstacle to the necessity of (s4'). On the free modal logic solution, (s4') is neither true nor false in respect to SW, and hence, by (IV), SW poses no obstacle to the necessity of (s4'). But there is an even more obvious objection which applies to the free modal logic solution, based as it is on the precritical interpretation. If '3 is anguished' is a category mistake in respect to any possible world, then it turns out to be necessary in respect to every possible world, since there is no such world in respect to which it is false!

A new semantics is called for to avoid this accumulation of objections. The one I shall propose preserves the laws (3), (4), and (8) of Lewis' system S1. I call it the "semantics of strength" because it gives explicit consideration to whether a sentence is too strong for some possible world in determining whether it is necessary in respect to a given world. There are other features of this semantics which resolve other difficulties. It recognizes, as did the precritical interpretation, that a sentence may be necessary in respect to H though truth-valueless in respect to some world possible relative to H. Yet to be necessary a sentence must be true in some possible world. Though '3 is anguished' is never false, it is not necessary since it is never true.

So, only if there is an H' such that HRH' and $\phi(A,H') = $ T, can it be the case that $\phi(\square A,H) = $ T. Still it is allowed that $\square A$ may be true or false in respect to some H, even though A itself is neither true nor false in respect to that H.

Thus the semantics of strength differs from the precritical interpretation through the replacement of (IV) with:

(IV')   (a) $\phi(\square A,H) = $ T iff (i) there is an H' such that HRH' and $\phi(A,H') = $ T, (ii) for any H' if HRH' then $\phi(A,H') \neq $ F, and (iii) there is no H' such that HRH' and A is too strong for H',

        (b) $\phi(\square A,H) = $ F iff either (i) there is an H' such that HRH' and $\phi(A,H') = $ F or (ii) there is an H' such that HRH' and A is too strong for H', and there is also an H' such that HRH' and $\phi(A,H') = $ T or F,

        (c) $\phi(\square A,H) = $ U otherwise, that is, iff for any H' if HRH' then $\phi(A,H') = $ U.

Taken together, (i) of (b) and the right hand side of (c) exhaust the alternatives implied by the negation of (i) of (a). It is then easy to see that as stated the rule exhausts all cases.

The objection to MInst, raised in connection with (s3), can no longer be raised. In view of (IV'c), '$\square$(3 is anguished)' is U in respect to any H; so the occurrence of '3 is anguished' in the antecedent of (s3) is now a U-occurrence. When the occurrence of '3 is anguished' in the consequent is assigned F by an F-function, its counterpart in the antecedent is also assigned F. One fault of the precritical interpretation was, then, its assumption that, since $\phi(A,H') = $ U is compatible with $\phi(\square A,H) = $ T for *some* H' such that HRH', $\phi(A,H) = $ U is compatible with $\phi(\square A,H) = $ T for *every* H' such that HRH'.

Obviously, it is clause (iii) of (IV'a) which takes account of the objection to the category solution made in the previous section. In view of this clause we can avoid having to say that the causal relation of AL is necessarily asymmetrical in respect to SW, a world in which events are not related by asymmetrical causality.

It remains only to state the semantics of possibility as derived from (6) and (IV'):

(VI') (a) $\phi(\diamondsuit A, H) = \mathrm{T}$ iff either (i) there is an H' such that HRH' and $\phi(A, H') = \mathrm{T}$ or (ii) there is an H' such that HRH' and $\sim A$ is too strong for H' and there is also an H' such that HRH' and $\phi(A, H') = \mathrm{T}$ or F,

      (b) $\phi(\diamondsuit A, H) = \mathrm{F}$ iff (i) there is an H' such that HRH' and $\phi(A, H') = \mathrm{F}$, (ii) .for any H' if HRH' then $\phi(A, H') \neq \mathrm{T}$, and (iii) there is no H' such that HRH' and $\sim A$ is too strong for H',

      (c) $\phi(\diamondsuit A, H) = \mathrm{U}$ otherwise, that is, iff for any H' if HRH' then $\phi(A, H') = \mathrm{U}$.

There is then no longer any objection to MGen, for now the antecedent and consequent of '3 is anguished $\supset$ $\diamondsuit$ (3 is anguished)' will both be U in respect to any H. Both occurrences of '3 is anguished' are U-occurrences; so an F-function that assigns the one T assigns the other T. It is also clear that MPartic is valid on the semantics of strength, in view chiefly of (i) of (IV'a).

There are some apparently odd properties of possibility as understood here. Since clause (ii) of (VI'a) gives a sufficient condition for possibility, a sentence can be possible in respect to a given world and still not be true in that world or any world possible relative to it. But this fits very nicely the case of the denial of one of our analytic contingencies. It is possible that Newtonian simultaneity is not absolute in precisely the sense that there is a world, EW, which the absolute Newtonian simultaneity simply does not fit. Of course, in (ii) of (VI'a) and where A is not a valid nonmodal sentence, the requirement that $\sim A$ be too strong for some H is not different from the requirement that A itself be too strong for some H', as is clear from (D4). It is also noteworthy that, by (VI'b), a sentence which is impossible in respect to a given world need not be false in all worlds possible relative to it. But this cannot be surprising once it is agreed that a necessary proposition need not be true in all possible worlds.

I started with the observation that in modal logic there is an anomaly parallel to the anomaly which in quantificational logic led to free logic. In quantificational logic the anomaly concerns in part what is to count as a nameable individual. If individuals outside the domain in question are nameable, then the difficulty arises that $(\exists x)A$ cannot be inferred from At/x. In modal logic the anomaly concerns what is to count as a possible world. If possible worlds are admitted in respect to which and on which certain predicates are uninterpreted— that is, if semantically incomplete possible worlds are admitted—then a necessary sentence, one which is not false in any possible world, need not be true.

The notion that nonexistent individuals are nameable and that semantically incomplete worlds are possible was embodied in the so-called precritical interpretation of quantificational and modal logic. It became clear that acceptance of the precritical interpretation demanded a rejection of both classical quantificational logic and classical modal logic and an acceptance of a free logic in both areas.

In modal logic, the desire to retain the classical modal laws, (3), (4), and (8), of Lewis' S1 leads most easily to the demand that all sentences have a truth-value. Under this demand, either all predicates are fully interpreted and all sentences that would otherwise not have a truth-value are assigned a truth-value, or uninterpreted predicates are left uninterpreted but all sentences without truth-values are simply dropped from account. The former procedure was called the classical solution and the latter the category solution. The classical solution countenances no possible worlds in respect to which predicates are uninterpreted. The category solution does countenance such semantically incomplete worlds, but it does not regard them as relevant to the necessity of sentences with the uninterpreted predicates.

The classical solution requires that category mistakes be put alongside other sentences as bearers of truth-values. The category solution avoids this, but is itself subject to the objection of treating as necessary sentences which are, though not false, too strong for some possible world. In effect, a sentence is too strong for a possible world if the possible world is turned into an impossible one in the attempt to interpret the predicates of that sentence on it. The same objection holds for the pre-critical interpretation, under which free modal logic is valid.

I introduced the semantics of strength, then, in an effort to realize three aims, which seemed to be nearly incompatible. The aims of the semantics of strength are: first, to deny necessity to any sentence which is too strong for some possible world; second, to avoid making category mistakes in the extensional interpretation of predicates; and third, to preserve the classical modal laws, MInst, MGen, and MPartic. The first goal is realizable only if certain analytic sentences are judged contingent; the second requires that truth-valueless sentences be allowed in modal logic, and that worlds in respect to which and on which some predicates are uninterpreted be allowed as possible worlds; if the third has been realized, and an examination of (IV') and (VI') makes it clear that it has, then the classical modal laws MInst, MGen, and MPartic do not presuppose that all sentences have a truth-value, though an advocate of free modal logic would claim that they do.

8. On the Logic of the Ontological Argument: Some Elementary Remarks

Jaakko Hintikka

It is much harder than one might first suspect to see what is wrong—if anything—with the ontological argument, in some of its variants at least. By way of criticism, it is often said that the argument fails because "existence is not a predicate." However, there are senses—and what is more, senses other than the purely grammatical one—in which existence clearly *is* a predicate. It is sometimes said that existence is not the kind of property that can be included in the essence of anything; but the reasons for saying so are far from clear, and the notion of essence is a notorious mess in the best of circumstances. One might suspect that something goes wrong with the logic of definite descriptions in the modal contexts involved in the argument; but I shall try to reconstruct some of the most important aspects of the ontological argument in terms having little to do with ordinary modalities and nothing whatsoever with definite descriptions. In fact, the independence of the essential features of the ontological argument from the theory of definite descriptions ought to be clear enough without much detailed argument. If what we are trying to do is to establish that there exists a unique being "than which nothing greater can be conceived"—in short, a unique supremely perfect

Being—surely the great difficulty is to show that there exists *at least one* such being, whereas we can face the problem of uniqueness with relative calm.

Furthermore, it has been complained that the notion, "being greater than anything else that can be conceived of," and the notion of supreme perfection are unclear. More than that, it is sometimes suggested that they are systematically ambiguous— that they make no sense until it has been specified in what respect greatness or perfection is to be measured. Certainly greater evil or more perfect vice cannot be what is meant—but even if there be no such things as these, what precisely *is* meant?

Yet a straightforward answer to this question is forthcoming. What is at stake is surely greatness or perfection with respect to existence. It does not take a neo-Platonist to agree that the greatest or most supreme being intended in the argument is certainly one whose powers of existing are maximal or whose mode of being is, as existence qua existence goes, supremely perfect.

Can we express in some reasonable way that some x is such a being—at least one such being? There are very natural-looking candidates for this task. One thing we can do is to say that x is an existentially perfect being, in short $Pr(x)$, if and only if it exists, provided that anything at all exists:

(1) $Pr(x) \equiv (\exists z)(z = z) \supset (\exists z)(z = x).$

Here I have rendered 'x exists' by '$(\exists z)(z = x)$.' The reasons why one has to do so are given in an earlier paper of mine.[1]

It is to be noticed that the role of x in (1) is that of a placeholder for singular terms, not one of a bindable variable.[2]

1. Jaakko Hintikka, "On the Logic of Existence and Necessity. I Existence," *The Monist*, 50 (1966), 55–76.

2. This remark is necessitated by the difference in logical behavior between free singular terms and bound (or bindable) variables which they evince as soon as we give up the "existential presuppositions" to the effect that each free singular term refers to some individual. For details, see the paper referred to above.

Prima facie at least, $Pr(x)$ as defined by (1) seems to express accurately and fully the idea that x is existentially the most perfect being (or one such being): nothing at all can exist without this x also existing—or, if the expression is allowed, all the other beings are existentially dependent on x.

It is easily seen that, provided the world is not completely empty, such a perfect being must exist:

(2) $(\exists z)(z = z) \supset (\exists x)Pr(x)$

is *logically true*. Hence a version of the ontological argument seems to possess perfectly good logical validity after all. Moreover, it can be shown that the logical truth of (2) does not depend on any hidden existential presuppositions.[3]

I strongly suspect that the logical truth of (2) (together with a number of related truths) is an important part of the tacit and half-understood reasons why the ontological argument is so perennially tempting.

Though logically true, this "ontological argument" is useless for the purposes which it was calculated to serve, as one can see simply by rewriting (2) or

$$(\exists z)(z = z) \supset (\exists x)((\exists z)(z = z) \supset (\exists z)(z = x))$$

by means of an elementary transformation into

(3) $(\exists x)(x = x) \supset ((\exists z)(z = z) \supset (\exists x)(\exists z)(z = x)).$

It is patent that (3) is completely vacuous. In fact, (3) shows at once that *any* existing individual will serve as the desired kind of x whose existence is asserted in the consequent of (2). [Notice that if a value of z exists which makes $(\exists z)(z = z)$ true, then *this same* individual serves as the value of both x and z

---

3. This is easily seen by means of the technique employed in the paper cited above.

which makes $(\exists x)(\exists z)(z = x)$ true.] Hence the existence of no particular entity is established by the logical truth of (2).[4]

This may be thrown into sharper focus by observing that (2) is to all practical purposes an instance of the schema

(4) $(\exists z)(z = z) \supset (\exists x)((\exists z)A(z) \supset A(x))$.

The logical truth of (4) may seem impressive to an uninitiated; it e.g. seems to imply that, given any problem whatsoever, there is a man who is able to solve it if anybody is (provided the universe is not empty). Yet the trick involved is exposed in many elementary logic texts. If at least one man can solve a problem, *any* such man serves as an instance of the kind of x claimed to exist in the consequent of (4).

The failure of (2) to give us a characterization of the kind of existentially perfect being we are looking for is not accidental: no other attempted characterization would have fared any better. Any condition on x that you may care to formulate in the sole terms of bindable variables, quantifiers, connectives, identity, and a predicate of existence, will be logically equivalent either to a vacuous predicate which applies to all existing individuals, or to a contradictory one, or to a simple numerical condition on one's domain of individuals (e.g. to the condition that x is the only individual, or that there are at least two other individuals, or to some such thing). This can be proved in the treatment of presupposition-free logic which I outlined in my 1966 *Monist* paper (referred to in the first footnote of the present paper). I argued there that $(\exists z)(z = b)$ will always do the duty for the expression "b exists"; hence the reference to a special predicate of existence can be omitted. The rest can be proved formally by a simple argument.

4. The basic difficulty about the ontological argument is thus not so much that it is invalid, but that it only appears to establish what it seems to prove, and that the argument is not readily seen to be the tautology it is. Its critics have for this reason levelled their objections at a wrong aspect of the argument. The same will be found to apply to certain modal versions of the argument.

Likewise, one can argue that any characterization of a kind of individual x in terms of given predicates, bindable variables, quantifiers, connectives, identity, and a predicate of existence can always be replaced by a straightforward description without any special predicate of existence and with the identity-relation occurring only in the following contexts: $(\exists y)(y \neq z_1$ & $y \neq z_2$ & ... & $y \neq z_k$ & $F(y, z_1, z_2, \ldots, z_k))$; and $(y)(y = z_1)$ $\vee y = z_2 \vee \ldots \vee y = z_k \vee F(y, z_1, z_2, \ldots, z_k))$. In other words, if an exclusive interpretation of quantifiers is used, no identity signs are needed.[5]

This simple result shows clearly what is true in the misformulated cliche that "existence is not a predicate." Existence *is* a predicate. There is no grammatical or logical harm whatsoever in treating it like one, and in using it for the purpose of characterizing different kinds of individuals. What is peculiar about it is that it is redundant for all descriptive purposes. If this is what is meant by statements of the well-known Kantian kind, to the effect that "by whatever and by however many predicates we may think a thing—even if we completely determine it—we do not make the least addition to the thing when we further declare that this thing is," then such statements are completely correct. Let us notice, moreover, that this correctness does not in any way depend on the problematic concept of essence.

Does the ontological argument fare any better if we introduce modal operators? Let us examine the situation. In order to be as clear as possible of the different assumptions involved, let me couch my discussion in terms of the epistemic operator "it is known that", in short, K. The dual operator P will have the force of saying "for all that is known, it is possible that." I prefer working with these because of their intuitive meaning,

5. For the idea of an exclusive reading of quantifiers, see Jaakko Hintikka, "Identity, Variables, and Impredicative Definitions," *Journal of Symbolic Logic, 21* (1956), 225–45.

and as a consequence many of their semantical properties, are much clearer than e.g. those of logical modalities "it is logically necessary that" and "it is logically possible that."[6] However, I expect that essentially the same points as I shall proceed to make in terms of the epistemic modalities K and P can be made in terms of logical modalities, in so far as they are viable at all.

In terms of K and P it seems to be easy to formulate a characterization of an existentially perfect being, say x. Of any such being (if any) it is surely known that if anything exists, it will do so too:

(5) $K((\exists z)(z = z) \supset (\exists z)(z = x))$.

Let us abbreviate this with $Pr'(x)$. Can we then prove that such beings exist, i.e. can we prove the following:

(6) $(\exists x)Pr'(x)$?

Proving (6) would mean showing that its negation cannot be a member of any "model set," i.e. of any consistent description μ of a possible world.[7] Let us assume that it is, and see whether anything impossible results:

(7) $(x)P((\exists z)(z = z) \ \& \ (z)(z \neq x)) \in \mu$.

Nothing follows from (7) unless we have some term b at hand of which it is known whom it refers to:[8]

(8) $(\exists z)K(z = b) \in \mu$.

---

6. I have tried to spell out the logic of the epistemic operators "K" and "P" in my book, *Knowledge and Belief* (Ithaca, Cornell University Press, 1962). I shall rely on what is said there in the present paper. For some problems which one encounters in this area and for their resolution, see also the symposium on epistemic logic in the first issue of *Nous*, *1* (1967).

7. This is the typical mode of argument employed in *Knowledge and Belief*.

8. Cf. *Knowledge and Belief*, section 6.8, and my paper, "Individuals, Possible Worlds, and Epistemic Logic," *Nous*, *1* (1967), 33–62, especially 35–38.

By well-known principles, (7) and (8) imply

(9) $P((\exists z)(z = z) \mathbin{\&} (z)(z \neq b)) \in \mu$

hence[9]

(10) $(\exists z)(z = z) \in \mu^*$

and

(11) $(z)(z \neq b) \in \mu^*$

for some alternative state of affairs μ^*. Furthermore, we must have[10]

$$a = a \in \mu^*$$
$$(\exists z)(z = a) \in \mu^*$$

for some a. Nothing further follows, however, unless we assume that (8) implies

(12) $(\exists z)(z = b) \in \mu^*$.

However, if this is assumed, (12) will contradict (11).

If the two assumptions that were mentioned in the course of the argument are made, our new "ontological proof" thus succeeds. What does this result show?

The validity of the second assumption which enabled us to carry out the proof is easily seen to be tantamount to the validity of the implication

(13) $(\exists x)K(x = a) \supset K(\exists x)(x = a)$.

In plain English, the assumption says that we can know *who* someone is only if we know *that* he exists.[11] This assumption

9. Cf. the conditions (C.P*) and (C.&), of *Knowledge and Belief*.

10. In virtue of (10), keeping in mind that the name of some *existing* individual must be able to replace z in (10).

11. For a defense of this reading, see *Knowledge and Belief*, especially pp. 131–32, and "Individuals, Possible Worlds, and Epistemic Logic," pp. 50–53.

has a great deal of initial plausibility; so much so that I assumed it in *Knowledge and Belief* as a valid principle.[12] However, for several concurrent reasons I have come to consider it as invalid. Now we can see that the question of its validity is of a considerable interest to the evaluation of the ontological argument. If the validity of (13) is assumed, a version of the ontological argument can be carried out.

What are my reasons for rejecting the validity of (13)? An illustration of them is obtained by pointing out that if it is assumed, we could not formulate in all the natural ways we might want to use such perfectly natural statements as "there is someone who is not known by *a* to exist." One possible formalization of this statement is

$$(14)\ (\exists x) \sim K_a(\exists y)(x = y)$$

the negation of which is easily seen to be implied by (13) (or which can be shown to be contradictory by means of the assumption that enabled us to vindicate a version of the ontological argument). Analogous remarks pertain to such statements as

$$(\exists x)B_a \sim (\exists y)(y = x)$$

and

$$(\exists x) \sim B_a(\exists y)(y = x).$$

(This does not quite settle the matter, however, as I shall try to explain in a supplementary note appended to the present paper.)

Hence there seem to be good reasons for denying the validity of (13), and hence our version of the ontological argument goes by the board.

It is important to realize, however, that my rejection of the validity of (13) is not due to a desire to make the ontological

12. *Knowledge and Belief,* p. 160.

argument invalid, although the rejection results in the overthrow of a version of the argument. By considering the argument given above, it can be seen that it does not establish the desired result in any case, independently of whether or not the validity of (13) is assumed.

This is seen by recalling that an additional premise of the form $(\exists x)K(x = b)$ (i.e. "it is known who b is") was needed in any case, for some free singular term b. This term was needed as a substitution-value of x in (7). In other words, this term was brought in in order to provide a counter-argument to the assumption that a perfect being (in the sense of a being satisfying $Pr'(x)$) does not exist. (In fact, the consideration of all the other singular terms is seen to be beside the point in our argument.) To all intents and purposes, we thus had to assume that it is known who the perfect being is before we could prove the He exists. But we could prove His existence only by assuming the validity of the principle that knowing who b is presupposes knowing that b exists. Hence, if this principle is assumed, it is strictly circular to assume that the additional premise (8). Hence our reconstrued "epistemic" version of the ontological argument must be said to fail already on account of this circularity.

Moreover, if the validity of (13) were assumed, the characterization of God as the most perfect being (in the sense of a being satisfying $Pr'(x)$) would be quite unnecessary, for it is seen from the above argument that no use is made in it of the antecedent of the implication for which $Pr(x)$ is a shorthand. (This point is similar to the point made earlier—that the validity of (2) does not go to show the existence of any particular being.) The whole force of the argument would reduce to saying that since it is known who God is, He is known to exist. And merely saying this without further explanation is scarcely taken by anyone to amount to an argument for God's existence, although it is perhaps not too far from the traditional idea that our having an adequate idea of God is sufficient to prove His existence.

Our argument was couched in terms of one particular attempt to define God as the existentially most perfect being—"a being than which a greater (existentially greater!) cannot be conceived." It can be shown, however, that no other characterization along similar lines can succeed any better. By reviewing all the different characterizations that one may try to give of an existentially perfect being—or of any being, for that matter—in the sole terms of the predicates of identity and existence, the concept of knowledge, quantifiers, and propositional connectives, one can see that no one of them makes an essential difference to our attempts to prove the existence of a being so characterized. I shall not try to prove this result here, nor state it more explicitly. Suffice it to say that it is a straightforward consequence of the adequacy of any reasonable system of epistemic logic that I know of. It extends to epistemic logic the result which (I suggested earlier) is the gist in the idea that existence is not the kind of attribute which can constitute the essence of any one thing.

How close does our attempted reconstrual of the ontological argument come to the real thing? The argument was formulated by Anselm in terms of "existence in the mind" vs. "existence in reality." This distinction is often explicated in terms of possible existence vs. actual existence. In this note, I have in effect replaced this explication by another one, to wit, by a distinction between something's (say b's) existing in the mind (say in the mind of a) in the sense of a's *knowing who* b is, and b's existing actually.

This way of going about it seems to me preferable for several reasons. First, it appears to come much closer to Anselm's language of *understanding* or *being able to conceive of* "a being than which a greater cannot be conceived" than any talk of what is possible. Second, the notions of (conceptual) possibility and (conceptual) necessity are notoriously obscure; their characteristics have been debated back and forth. In comparison, the idea of knowledge, including the idea of *knowing who* someone is are commonplace, however difficult their full analysis is likely to be. Hence we are apt to be much more knowledgeable about these concepts than about the somewhat artificial philosophers' notions of conceptual necessity and conceptual possibility. In particular, we have a much better grasp of the idea of *knowing who* someone is than we have of the philosophical concepts of essence and conceptual possibility. It may in fact be said that the concept of essence was in our sample argument replaced by the concept of knowing who someone is.

Perhaps this does not make much difference, however, for it seems to me that in so far as one can build a satisfactory theory of (conceptual) necessity, it will be in the relevant respects sufficiently similar to the logic of knowledge to enable us to say essentially the same things about our chances of reconstructing the ontological argument in terms of ordinary modal logic as we already said about these chances in epistemic logic (the logic of knowledge). Gaunilo, Aquinas, and Kant thus appear to have been shrewder—or perhaps merely sounder—logicians than St. Anselm and Descartes.

Supplementary Note

As was mentioned in the text, I have come to give up the conditions (C.EK =) and (C.EK =)* of *Knowledge and Belief.* I announced this initially as a response to some critic's remarks. Although I still think that the two conditions have to be given up, I have meanwhile realized that most of these criticisms fall much short of establishing this. For instance, Hector-Neri Castañeda has claimed that the following consistent statement of ordinary language cannot be consistently expressed in my symbolism:[13]

(15) "there is a person such that Jones does not know that the person in question exists,"

and the formulation

(16) $(\exists x) \sim K_{\text{Jones}}(\exists y)(x = y)$,

which appears to be the most straightforward rendering of (15) in my symbolism, is indeed inconsistent unless (C.EK =) and (C.EK =)* are given up.

However, this is not the whole story. I have indicated repeatedly how a distinction can be made between what is said of the reference of a singular term, "whoever he is or may be," and between what is said of the definite individual to which a singular term in fact happens to refer.[14] If the person whose existence is asserted in (15) is Smith, then the natural formulation of

(17) Jones does not know that Smith exists

will surely construe it as a statement about the individual in question (i.e. about Smith, the flesh-and-blood person). In other words, (17) is really of the form

(18) $(\exists x)(x = \text{Smith} \ \& \sim K_{\text{Jones}}(\exists y)(y = x))$

or

(18)* $(x)(x = \text{Smith} \supset \sim K_{\text{Jones}}(\exists y)(y = x))$

But if this is so, the natural translation of (15) surely is not (16) but rather

(19) $(\exists z)(\exists x)(x = z \ \& \sim K_{\text{Jones}}(\exists y)(y = x))$

or

(19)* $(\exists z)(x)(x = z \supset \sim K_{\text{Jones}}(\exists y)(y = x))$.

13. Castañeda has repeated this claim quite a few times. For a sample, see "On the Logic of Self-Knowledge," *Nous*, *1* (1967), 9–21, especially p. 9.

14. See e.g. "Individuals, Possible Worlds, and Epistemic Logic," pp. 46–48.

Of these (19)* is not inconsistent even if the two critical conditions are presupposed. Although (19) is inconsistent if (C.EK =) or (C.EK =)* is assumed, its (conditional) inconsistency is not altogether surprising. It merely reflects the plausible (but misleading) basis of Castañeda's criticism : If Smith's existence is not known to Jones, Smith cannot be identical with one of the individuals whose identity is known to Jones. But this does not make (19)* any worse a translation of (15), and Castañeda's objection is therefore rebutted even if the critical conditions are assumed to be satisfied.

9. Some Puzzles About Agency[1]

Roderick M. Chisholm

I shall first present a number of philosophical puzzles about the nature of agency. Then I shall formulate a "philosophical theory" in the endeavor to throw light upon some of the concepts that are exemplified in human action. And finally I shall attempt to show how the theory enables us to solve the puzzles.

> *Puzzle (1)* Human beings are responsible agents. But this fact appears to conflict with a deterministic view of human action—the view that every event that occurs is preceded or accompanied by a set of events constituting a sufficient causal condition for that event. And the same fact also appears to conflict with an indeterministic view of human action—the view that the things we do have no causes at all. For if the things we do have no causes at all, then our actions are entirely capricious.

1. Presented in part as the third of three Carus Lectures, entitled "Some Metaphysical Questions about the Self," at the meeting of the Pacific Division of the American Philosophical Association, Berkeley, California, December 29, 1967. I have selected this essay for the present volume, because it is an attempt to extend the important work that was begun in Henry Leonard's "Authorship and Purpose," *Philosophy of Science*, 26 (1959) 277–94, and because I would like to think it represents that view of philosophy and its relation to science and to language which is expressed in Part I of his Presidential Address and exhibited throughout his writings.

How can it be, then, that human beings are responsible agents?

Puzzle (2) 'At eight o'clock this morning I could have arranged things in such a way that I would be in San Francisco now, but I did not.' What does this mean? (i) Not simply that my being in San Francisco now is logically possible; for my being on Jupiter now is logically possible, but I couldn't have arranged *that*. (ii) Nor does it mean that my being in San Francisco now was epistemically possible at eight o'clock this morning— that it is consistent with everything that was known at that time this morning. For I knew at that time that I would *not* be in San Francisco now. Yet I *could* have arranged things in such a way that I *would* be in San Francisco now. (iii) Nor does it mean that there are states of affairs of the following sort: *If* this morning I had brought it about that those states of affairs occurred, or if I had undertaken (chosen, endeavored, willed, tried, set out) to bring it about that those states of affairs occurred, then I *would* be in San Francisco now. For suppose, first, that there are such states of affairs, that the if-then statement we have just made is true; suppose secondly, that I would be in San Francisco now only if I *had* brought about, or undertaken to bring about, those states of affairs; and suppose, thirdly, that I *couldn't* have brought them about, or couldn't have undertaken to bring them about. Then, surely, despite the truth of the if–then statement, I could *not* have arranged things in such a way this morning that I would be in San Francisco now. (iv) Is it to say, then, that there is no sufficient causal condition for my not being in San Francisco now? It cannot be this. After all, for some time now, there has *been* a sufficient causal condition for my not being in San Francisco now (consider the distance between here and there, the fact that I have been here for at least the past fifteen minutes, and the means of transportation that have been available to me). Yet this morning I *could* have arranged things in such a way that I would be there by now. (v) Does it mean, then, that at eight o'clock this morning there was no sufficient causal condition for my not being in San Francisco now? The 'could' that we are looking for must tell us more than this. Consider a subatomic particle such that there is now no sufficient causal condition for its not remaining here and no sufficient causal condition for its not moving from here to there. Shall we say of it that it *could* now arrange things in such a way that it would move from here to there? Or consider a man whose hand twitches from time to time without sufficient causal condition and also remains still from time to time without sufficient causal condition. These facts would hardly imply that the man *can* now arrange things in such a way that his hand remains still or that his hand will twitch. What, then, is there left for us to mean when we say "At eight o'clock this morning I could have arranged things in such a way that I would be in San Francisco now, but I did not"?

Puzzle (3) Physiology tells us that when a man raises his arm there is a set of physiological events, including the motion of muscles, which constitutes a sufficient causal condition for his arm going up. (a) What justification can there be, then, for saying that sometimes when he raises his arm, he could have kept it down instead? (b) If he has learned what the muscle motions are that cause his arm to go up and if he wishes to produce those motions, he can do so by raising his arm. But how can this be if they are what causes his arm to go up?

Puzzle (*4*) If there are any states of affairs that the man himself causes to happen, then there must be certain states of affairs *q* such that he causes *q* to happen without first causing still other states of affairs *p* such that *p* causes *q* to happen. If there are such "basic actions," then raising the arm must be among them, since (if our agent is like most of the rest of us) there is nothing else he needs to *do* in order to raise his arm. But if the motion of his arm is caused by physiological events, then there are no "basic actions." And therefore there is nothing that the agent himself causes to happen.

Before setting forth my own way of dealing with these puzzles, I shall comment briefly upon an alternative treatment which many contemporary philosophers find attractive.

These philosophers will point out (i) that very often, when we say of a man that he has done something, we are making a kind of performative utterance. For example, we may be pronouncing a verdict. Or we may be serving notice that we hold the man responsible for a certain state of affairs, thus conveying to our hearers that we intend to treat him accordingly. Or we may be adjuring others to hold him responsible and to submit him to similar treatment. Or we may be speaking of ourselves and confessing, admitting, or apologizing. Since the making of such performative utterances is quite different from the description of matters of fact, the philosophers in question will then go on to deduce (ii) that the "language game" we play when we talk about human action is quite different in its "rules" from the "language game" we play when we talk about natural events. Or, appealing to a different metaphor, they may say that the language we use ·when we talk about human action "does not mesh with" the language we use when we talk about natural events. If they were right in saying this, then they might plausibly go on to say, as they do, (iii) that if we attempt to play both games at once, or to use the two languages as though they were one, we are very likely to end up in confusion. The hypothesis will then suggest itself (iv) that such puzzles as those we have set forth, involving the relations among human actions and certain natural events, are simply the results of such linguistic confusion. And from this hypothesis, our philosophers conclude (v) that once the various confusions are brought to light, the puzzlement will vanish.

It is not difficult to understand the appeal of this way of looking at our puzzles. I think it is fair to say, however, that there has been no positive confirmation, as yet, of (v). And what is to be said in defense of (ii)? If our talk about human action were simply a matter of making the type of performative utterance referred to in (i)—if it were simply a matter of pronouncing verdicts, serving notices, confessing, or apologizing—then we would be justified in saying, as in (ii), that the "language game" we play when we make such utterances is quite different from the one we play when we talk about natural events. But obviously our talk about human action is not simply a matter of making such performative utterances. There are, after all, certain facts to which we appeal in order to *justify* these utterances—certain facts which justify us in pronouncing verdicts, in serving notices, and in adjuring others. And these are facts involving human action, facts that may be set forth in purely descriptive language. It is clear, then, that the truth of (i) above does not warrant the affirmation of (ii). But (i), so far as I know, is the only positive reason that has been offered in defense of (ii).

I shall assume, therefore, that our puzzles cannot be dealt with merely by affirming (ii). What they require is, in Russell's phrase, a certain amount of honest toil.

I shall now attempt to describe a language in which we may

lay bare the descriptive element in the concept of an action, stripping from it all implications of moral and legal responsibility. In this language, our action talk must be, to a certain extent, recast. But if we have such a language, then I think we may be able to throw some light upon the relations that hold among actions and other types of event. In confirmation of this way of looking at human action, I shall try to show how such a language will enable us to solve our puzzles.

Let us assume that we already have at our disposal a language capable of describing the causal relation as it obtains among states of affairs. We now add just one undefined locution to this language. The locution is:

"He makes it happen that ——— in the endeavor to make it happen that ...",

where the blanks may be filled by sentences. It may be expanded in obvious ways (e.g. by substituting a description or proper name for the subject term, and by introducing tenses and time and place designations).

The following sentences are instances of our undefined locution: (i) "He makes it happen that his arm goes up in the endeavor to make it happen that the chairman sees him"; and (ii) "He makes it happen that a shadow of his arm appears unseen on the back wall in the endeavor to make it happen that the chairman sees him." (To prevent possible ambiguity, we might allow ourselves the following alternative reading of the second sentence: "In the endeavor to make it happen that the chairman sees him, he makes it happen that a shadow of his arm appears unseen on the back wall.") There is an important difference between these two examples, if we think of them as being asserted in ordinary situations. For if we say, as in (i), that the man makes it happen that his arm goes up in the endeavor to make it happen that the chairman sees him, then, in all probability, the situation is one in which the man knows that he makes it happen that his arm goes up and in which he does it intentionally. But if, in the same circumstances, we say, as in (ii) that he makes it happen that a shadow of his arm appears unseen on the back wall, then, in all probability, the man does not know that he makes such a shadow of his arm appear, and he can hardly be said to do so intentionally. Both situations, however, are describable by means of our undefined locution. By introducing further definitions, we can make out the difference between them.

Let us introduce "M————, ..." as an abbreviation for our locution, "He makes it happen that ———— in the endeavor to make it happen that ...". Using this abbreviation, we may now formulate three assumptions about the interpretation of our locution.

(A1)   Any instance of 'M————, ...' implies '$(\exists p)(\exists q)(Mp,q)$'

where the variables 'p' and 'q' may be thought of as referring to states of affairs.[2] Hence if our agent made it happen that his

2. This use of propositional or state-of-affairs variables does not preclude the use of individual variables. Consider a man who makes it happen that his house is red in the endeavor to make it happen that his house looks new. Then we may say: there is a p such that he makes it happen that p in the endeavor to make it happen that his house looks new; there is a q such that he makes it happen that his house is red in the endeavor to make it happen that q; there is an x such that he makes it happen that x is red in the endeavor to make it happen that x looks new; there is an x and a p such that he makes it happen that x looks red in the endeavor to make it happen that q; and so on. (If a man believes his house to be red and also believes some of the same things his brother believes, we might say that there is an x and a p such that he believes x to be red and he believes p in common with his brother.) Among the variants of our primitive locution, therefore, would be sentences of the following forms:

$(\exists x)(\exists y)[M(Fx),Gy]$
$(\exists y)[M(\exists x)(Fx),Gy]$
$(\exists x)M(Fx), (\exists y)(Gy)$
$M(\exists x)(Fx), (\exists y)(Gy)$

arm went up in the endeavor to make it happen that the chairman sees him, then there is a state of affairs p and a state of affairs q, such that he made it happen that p in the endeavor to make it happen that q.

(A2)   Any instance of 'M———,...' implies the corresponding instance of '———.'

Thus "He makes it happen that his arm goes up in the endeavor to make it happen that he attracts the chairman's attention" implies "His arm goes up."

(A3)   Any instance of 'M———,...' implies the corresponding instance of 'M(M———,...),...'.

If he makes it happen that his arm goes up in the endeavor to make it happen that he attracts the chairman's attention, then this whole state of affairs—his making his arm go up in the endeavor to attract the chairman's attention—is itself something he makes happen in the endeavor to attract the chairman's attention. This third assumption may be suggested by an observation that Suarez makes in this context: "If we understand the term 'effect' so that it includes not only the thing produced, but also everything that flows from the power of the agent, then we may say that the action itself is in a certain sense the effect of the agent."[3]

Thus any instance of our locution will refer to the agent as a cause, and it will imply that he makes something happen.

Still other possibilities are obtained by quantifying over property variables. (If he makes it happen that his house is red in the endeavor to make it happen that his house looks new, is there a property F and a property G such that he makes it happen that his house has F in the endeavor to make it happen that his house has G?) A complete "logic of action" would concern itself with the logical relations obtaining among these various forms.

3. F. Suarez, *Disputationes Metaphysicae*, Disp. XVIII, Sec. 10, Para. 6.

It will also imply that he makes it *happen* that he makes that something happen. But although any instance of "M————, ..." implies the corresponding instance of "————," it is not true that any instance of "M————, ..." implies the corresponding instance of "....". He may make it happen that his arm goes up in the endeavor to make it happen that he attracts the chairman's attention, and yet not make it happen that he attracts the chairman's attention.

An adequate logic of intentional action would also include the following assumptions in addition to the three above: that an agent makes p and r happen in the endeavor to make q happen, if and only if, he makes p happen in the endeavor to make q happen and he makes r happen in the endeavor to make q happen; that if he makes p happen on the endeavor to make q happen and if p's happening contributes causally to r's happening, then he, the agent, contributes causally to r's happening; and if, at a given time, he makes p happen in the endeavor to make q happen and makes r happen in the endeavor to make s happen, then, at that time, he makes r happen in the endeavor to make q happen. (It may be noted that our second, third, and fourth assumptions are analogues of familiar modal principles.)

We may now set forth a series of definitions.

(D1)   He *undertakes* (*endeavors*) to make it happen that ...
         $= $ df $(\exists p)(Mp, \ldots)$

("He undertakes at t to make it happen that ..." might be defined as: "There is a p such that he makes it happen that p in the endeavor at t to make it happen that ...".) This definition allows us to say, "He undertakes to make it happen that his arm goes up" if we can say, "There is a p such that he makes it happen that p in the endeavor to make it happen that his arm goes up." The expressions to undertake, or to endeavor, as here understood, do not mean to try, if to try connotes making or exerting an effort. Nor does it imply the exercise of "an act of will." But many philosophers, I believe, have used the expressions to try and to will merely to describe those situations for which I have introduced the technical term to undertake, or to endeavor.

(D2)   He *makes it happen* that ———— $= \mathrm{df}\,(\exists p)(M$————$, p)$

(D3)   He *intentionally makes it happen* that ———— $= \mathrm{df}$
        $(M$————$,$ ————$).$

It should be noted that (D3) yields a somewhat broad sense of "He intentionally makes it happen that ————". A more narrow sense is introduced in (D6) below.

Among the consequences of our definitions and assumptions are those that we may abbreviate as follows: Making p happen implies p, but it does not imply undertaking p. Undertaking p does not imply p and therefore it does not imply making p happen. But intentionally making p happen implies undertaking p as well as making p happen. Undertaking p implies making undertaking p happen, but it does not imply undertaking undertaking p.

We may say, in short, that to act is to endeavor to make happen.[4] But from this it does not follow that when a man acts,

4. Sometimes we may say of a man that he does something, or that he makes a certain thing happen, without implying that he has performed an act and without implying, as we would be if we affirmed what is intended by the definiendum of (D2), that he himself is a cause. Thus if a man faints and tips over the table, we may say later: "Look at what you did. You broke the table and made the lights go out." If he had known, or should have known, that he was likely to faint, then we might say that he was negligent in failing to take precautions and we might hold him responsible for breaking the table and making the lights go out. But if there was no reason at all for him to suspect that he was going to faint, then in saying that there was something that he did and something that he made happen, we would not be implying that he performed an act. And although we would seem to be saying that he, the *agent*, caused the breaking of table, what we would be saying in fact is that that *event*, which was the agent's falling, caused the breaking of the table.

he endeavors to act—much less, that he endeavors to endeavor to act. What the liar endeavors to do, for example, is not to *lie*, but to make it happen that his hearers are deceived.

Our undefined locution enables us to say, not only that the agent is a cause, but also that his causation is purposive or teleological. But although the statement, "He makes it happen that a shadow of his arm appears on the back wall in the endeavor to make it happen that the chairman sees him," describes something that is teleological, it does not tell us that the agent made the shadows move *for the purpose of* making it happen that the chairman sees him. Yet this ordinary concept of purposive activity is readily explicated in terms of our primitive locution. "He makes it happen that *p for the purpose of* making it happen that *q*," unlike "He makes it happen that *p in the endeavor to* make it happen that *q*," implies that he intentionally makes it happen that *p* (see (D3)). I propose this definition:

(D4)   He makes it happen that —— *for the purpose of* making it happen that . . . = df. He makes it happen that —— in the endeavor to make it happen that (i) —— and (ii) . . . and (iii) his undertaking to make it happen that —— causes it to happen that . . .

It should be noted that the expression "He undertakes to make it happen that his undertaking of *p* causes *q*" does not imply "He undertakes to make it happen that *p* causes *q*." A man may make it happen that an orange tree grows next year and he may do so for the purpose of making it happen that he gets his pay next week. In such a case, he is endeavoring to make it happen that *his endeavor* to make it happen that an orange tree grows next year will cause him to be paid next week. He is not endeavoring to make it happen that the growth of an orange tree next year will cause him to be paid next week.

The definition of "undertaking to make it happen that
——— for the purpose of making it happen that . . ." would be
analogous to that just given:

(D5)   He undertakes to make it happen that ——— for the
purpose of making it happen that . . . = df. There is a
p such that he makes it happen that p in the endeavor
to make it happen that (i) ——— and (ii) . . . and (iii)
his undertaking to make it happen that ——— causes
it to happen that . . .

With the concept just defined, we may now refine upon the
concept of intentional action that was defined in (D3):

(D6)   He makes it happen that . . . and does so just in the
way in which at t he intends = df. (a) He intentionally
makes it happen that . . . , and (b) for all p, such that
he undertakes at t to make it happen that p for the
purpose of making it happen that . . . , he makes p
happen.

When the definiendum of (D6) applies, then we may say of the
undertaking in question that it was a complete success.

Now we are in a position to define "basic actions," those
things which, as one might say, we do without having to do
other things to get them done. For most of us, raising our arms
and blinking our eyes are thus basic. Unlike the man who
cannot do such things "at will," we don't have to do anything
for the purpose of getting them done.[5] The following definition,

5. The term "basic action" was introduced by Arthur Danto, in "What
We Can Do," *Journal of Philosophy*, *60* (1963), 435–45. The following quotation from St. Augustine suggests that what Danto calls the "repertoire of basic
actions" may vary considerably from one person to another:

      We know, too, that some men are differently constituted from others,
and have some rare and remarkable faculty of doing with their body
what other men can do by no effort do, and, indeed, scarcely believe
when they hear of others doing. There are persons who can move their

I believe, is adequate to this concept of basic action:

(D7)   At *t* he makes it happen that ———— and his doing so
        is a *basic act* = df. At *t* he intentionally makes it
        happen that ————, and there is no *p* such that at *t*
        he undertakes to make it happen that *p* for the
        purpose of making it happen that ————

Finally, let us consider the concept of power or ability. I shall
assume that whenever it is within the agent's power to perform
a certain action, then there is no sufficient causal condition for
his not undertaking to perform that action. Thus if there is a
man in the back of the room who now has it within his power
to get himself to this platform, then there is not at this time,
nor has there been prior to this time, any set of states of affairs
constituting a sufficient causal condition for his *not* now undertaking to make it happen that he gets himself to this platform.
Let us say, then:

(D8)   It is *within his power at t to undertake* to make it
        happen that ———— = df. There is no sufficient causal
        at *t*, or prior to *t*, for his not undertaking at *t* to make
        it happen that ————

---

ears, either one at a time, or both together. There are some who,
without moving the head, can bring the hair down upon the forehead,
and move the whole scalp backwards and forwards at pleasure.
Some, by lightly pressing their stomach, bring up an incredible quantity
and variety of things they have swallowed, and produce whatever they
please, quite whole, as if out of a bag. Some so accurately mimic the
voices of birds and beasts and other men, that, unless they are seen,
the difference cannot be told. Some have such command of their bowels,
that they can break wind continuously at pleasure, so as to produce
the effect of singing. I myself have known a man who was accustomed
to sweat whenever he wished. It is well known that some weep when
they please, and shed a flood of tears...
The City of God, Book XIV, Chapter 24; translated by M. Dods.

(To say "There is no sufficient causal condition for his not undertaking to make it happen that ———" will be to say "There is no sufficient causal condition for it not being the case that there is a *p* such that he makes *p* happen in the endeavor to make it happen that ———".)

We may now define two technical concepts—"directly in his power" and "indirectly in his power"—and then, in terms of these, the desired concept of "within his power."

(D9)   It is *directly within his power* at *t* to make it happen
       that ——— = df. There is a *p* such that (i) it is within
       his power at *t* to undertake to make it happen that *p*,
       and (ii) if he were to undertake at *t* to make it happen
       that *p*, he would make it happen that ——— in the
       endeavor at *t* to make it happen that *p*.

The man in the back of the room may now have it directly within his power to make it happen that he gets himself three feet closer to this platform. For, let us assume, it is within his power to undertake to get himself to the platform and if he were to undertake that then he would get himself three feet closer to the platform in the endeavor to get himself to the platform.

We have noted that undertaking *p* implies making it happen that one undertakes *p*. Hence if undertaking *p* is within the agent's power, in the sense of (D8), then it is also directly within the agent's power, in the sense of (D9).

The man in the back of the room may not have it *directly* within his power to get himself to the platform, in the sense of the technical expression we have just defined in (D9). For it may be that, if he undertakes to get himself here, he will change his mind **en route**, in which case the second clause of our definiens will not be satisfied. Yet there is a sense in which we may be able to say that it is *indirectly* within his power to get here. He has it directly within his power to get himself three feet closer. And he may be such that, if he does thus get himself three feet closer, then he will have it directly within his power to get himself three feet closer still; then, if he does that, he will have it directly within his power to get himself another three feet closer still; and, if he were to keep on in that way, then he would finally have it directly within his power to get himself to this platform.

I believe that the following definition of "indirectly within his power" captures the essentials of this situation:

(D10)   It is *indirectly within his power* at t to make it happen that ——— = df. There is a p such that it is directly within his power at t to make it happen that p; and there is a series of successive states of affairs, beginning with his undertaking at t to make it happen that p, and ending with its happening that ———, which is such that, for each state of affairs in the series prior to its happening that ———, his making that state of affairs happen would cause it to be directly within his power to make the successor of that state of affairs happen.[6]

The following, I believe, gives us the desired sense of "within his power":

(D11)   It is *within his power* at t to make it happen that ——— = df. Either it is directly within his power at

6. An alternative procedure would be the following. We would first define "to directly enable" (e.g. "His making p happen would directly enable him to make q happen provided only: if he makes p happen, then his making q happen will be directly within his power"), and we would then use this concept to formulate a definition of "indirectly within his power" in the manner of Frege's definition of the ancestral. Thus we might say: "It is indirectly within his power at t to make it happen at t' that ———, provided only: (a) there is a state of affairs p such that his making p happen is directly within his power at t; and (b) its happening at t', that ———, is a member of every class of states of affairs C such that (i) p is a member of C and (ii) whatever any member of C directly enables him to make happen is also a member of C."

t to make it happen that ———, or it is indirectly within his power at t to make it happen that ———.

Now we may return to our puzzles.

Puzzle (*1*) Human beings are responsible agents. But this fact appears to conflict with a deterministic view of human action—the view that every event that occurs is preceded or accompanied by a set of events constituting a sufficient causal condition for that event. And the same fact also appears to conflict with an indeterministic view of human action—the view that the things we do have no causes at all. For if the things we do have no causes at all, then our actions are entirely capricious. How can it be, then, that human beings are responsible agents?

In every responsible act, at least one of the states of affairs involved—the agent's undertaking of that act—is not preceded or accompanied by any set of events constituting a sufficient causal condition for it. Hence 'determinism,' as defined, is false. But it is not true that that state of affairs has no cause at all, for it is caused by the man. Moreover, the man causing that state of affairs is also a state of affairs that is caused by the man. And his causing of these things need not have been capricious. For there is a state of affairs such that he caused these things to happen in the endeavor to make that state of affairs happen. Making that state of affairs happen, therefore, was one of his reasons for acting as he did. And he may have had other reasons; perhaps he desired that that state of affairs happen, or perhaps he thought he ought to make it happen.

Puzzle (*2*) What, then, is there left for us to mean when we say "At eight o'clock this morning I could have arranged things in such a way that I would be in San Francisco now, but I did not"?

We mean that, although at eight o'clock this morning I did not make it happen that I arranged things in such a way that I would be in San Francisco now (D2), nevertheless it was then within my power to make it happen that I so arranged things (D11). The "could," therefore, is "constitutionally iffy" (D9) and (D10). And the proposed explication is consistent with saying that for some time there has been a sufficient causal condition for my not being in San Francisco now. But the freedom of the so-called "*actus voluntatis elicitus*" is preserved. For we may say that there was no sufficient causal condition this morning for my not undertaking to arrange that I would be in San Francisco now; and from this it would follow that such an undertaking was then within my power (D8). The undetermined particle does not have this type of freedom. In its case, the absence of equipment for undertaking or endeavoring constitutes a sufficient causal condition for its *not* undertaking or endeavoring. Since undertaking *p* implies making undertaking-*p* happen, therefore, if it was within my power this morning to undertake to make it happen that I am in San Francisco now, it was directly within my power this morning to make it happen that I undertake to make it happen that I am in San Francisco now (D9). But undertaking does not imply undertaking to undertake (endeavoring does not imply endeavoring to endeavor). If we understand "to will" as "to undertake," or "to endeavor," then we may say with Hobbes: "I acknowledge this liberty, that I can do if I will: but to say, I can will if I will, I take to be an absurd speech."[7] But we may go beyond Hobbes and also acknowledge the liberty of "I can will" along with that of "I can do if I will."

7. Thomas Hobbes, *The Questions concerning Liberty, Necessity, and Chance*, the quotation may be found in the excerpt in Sidney Morgenbesser and James Walsh, eds., *Free Will* (Englewood Cliffs, N.J.; Prentice-Hall, 1962), p. 42.

> *Puzzle* (*3a*) Physiology tells us that when a man raises his arm there is a set of physiological events, including the motion of muscles, which constitutes a sufficient causal condition for his arm going up. What justification can there be, then, for saying that sometimes when he raises his arm, he could have kept it down instead?

Suppose it was within the agent's power to make it happen that his arm go up (D8); and suppose that if he had undertaken to make it happen that his arm go up, then he would have made it happen (i) that the various physiological states, including the muscle motions, occur, and (ii) that his arm go up. Then the occurrence of the physiological states as well as the motion of the arm was directly within his power (D9). It is a mistake to suppose that "He makes *p* happen" and "*p*'s happening causes *q* to happen" together imply "He does not make *q* happen." It is also a mistake to suppose that "He makes *p* happen in the endeavor to make *q* happen" (e.g. "He made it happen that his muscles moved in the endeavor to make it happen that his arm go up") implies "He makes *p* happen for the purpose of making *q* happen."

> *Puzzle* (*3b*) If he has learned what the muscle motions are that cause his arm to go up and if he wishes to produce those motions, he can do so by raising his arm. But how can this be if they are what cause his arm to go up?

The man who moves his muscles by raising his arm makes it happen that his arm goes up for the purpose of making it happen that his muscles move. This means that he undertakes to make it happen that his *endeavor* to make the arm go up will make it happen that the muscles move (D4). It does not mean that he undertook to make it happen that *his arm going up* make it happen that his muscles move. We may recall the man who makes it happen that an orange tree grows next year for the purpose of making it happen that he gets his pay next week.

> *Puzzle* (*4*) If there are any states of affairs that the man himself causes to happen, then there must be certain states of affairs *q* such that he causes *q* to happen without first causing still other states of affairs *p* such that *p* causes *q* to happen. If there are such "basic actions," then raising the arm must be among them, since (if our agent is like most of the rest of us) there is nothing else he needs to *do* in order to raise his arm. But if the motion of his arm is caused by physiological events, then there are no "basic actions." And therefore there is nothing that the agent himself causes to happen.

The third premise ("If the motion of his arm is caused by physiological events, then there are no 'basic actions'") is false. "At *t* he makes *q* happen, and his doing so is a basic act" implies "There is no *p* such that at *t* he makes *p* happen for the purpose of making *q* happen." But it does not imply "There is no *p* such that at *t* he makes *p* happen and *p* causes *q* to happen" (D7).

I would suggest to the reader that, in evaluating the present way of dealing with these questions, he do so in part by comparing it with the available alternatives.

10. Metaphysics and the Concept of a Person

Wilfrid Sellars

In the first edition "Paralogisms of Pure Reason" Kant suggests that "the substance which in relation to outer sense possesses extension" might be "in itself the possessor of thoughts and that these thoughts can by means of its own inner sense be consciously represented." On this hypothesis, which is a purely speculative one, "the thesis that only souls (as particular kinds of substances) think would have to be given up, and we should have to fall back on the common expression that *men* think, that is, that the very same being which, as outer appearance is extended is, in itself, internally a subject and is not composite, but is simple and thinks." (A359–60)

Kant, of course, does not commit himself to this hypothesis. Indeed it is a part of his methodology to advance alternative hypotheses concerning things as they are in themselves, which hypotheses can be neither refuted nor established by speculative reason, as a means of keeping what he calls dogmatic metaphysics in check. Thus, another such speculative hypotheses would be a dualistic one to the effect that as things in themselves, persons consist of a real mind and a real body, the latter appearing in perception as a complex material thing. In the course of his critique of traditional metaphysical theories of mind and body, he suggests still other hypotheses that are of even greater interest, a theme to which I shall return.

To set the stage for an appreciation of Kant's insights, both critical and constructive, let us take as our point of departure his reference to the "common expression" that *men* think, that is, "that the very same being which is . . . extended is . . . a subject . . . and thinks." This "common expression" is, of course, characteristic of the Aristotelian tradition, extending from antiquity to the Oxford Aristotelianism being reborn before our very eyes. According to this tradition it is the same thing, a *man* or, as we now say (since the equality of the sexes has moved into the higher levels of ideological superstructure), a *person*, which both thinks and runs.

Even a Cartesian dualist, of course, can acknowledge that it is one and the same thing, a person, which runs and thinks, for sameness is ubiquitous. Thus it is one and the same thing, a family, which gets and spends. But perhaps the family gets by the husband getting and spends by the wife spending. The Aristotelian counterpart would be the bachelor who does both the getting and the spending. The dualist thinks of the person as a family or team, a mind that thinks and a body that runs. The Aristotelian, on the other hand, construes reference to minds as reference to persons qua having those states and capacities which are distinctive of rational animals, and references to human bodies as references to persons qua having those states and capacities by virtue of which they belong to the larger family of corporeal substances. The Aristotelian can grant, then, that there are minds and bodies without being in any more interesting sense a dualist. References to minds and bodies are *façons de parler*. They have a derivative existence or "mode of being."

It is worth pausing to note that since one must, as Aristotle himself emphasizes, be careful to distinguish between priority in the order of knowing or conception, and priority in the order of being, a dualist could grant that our primary concept of a person is Aristotelian, and yet insist that when we explore the behavior of the things to which we apply this concept, we discover facts that force us to postulate a dualism of minds and bodies. A useful parallel is provided by the development of microphysical theory. It is clear that in the order of knowing concepts pertaining to perceptual objects are primary. Yet, from the standpoint of Scientific Realism, perceptual objects are derivative and secondary—however these terms are to be construed—in the order of being.

Considerations of many different types have been advanced to support dualism—ranging from the interpretation of dreams and religious experience to abstruse metaphysical arguments. In the modern period, the mechanistic revolution in physical science provided the chief motive power for mind–body dualism. If the body is a cloud of particles, must not the unitary thinking, feeling subject be a distinct existent—perhaps, as some have thought, like a captain in his ship; perhaps, as others thought, like a dog tied to a chariot.

My aim here is to do some hard-core metaphysics. I shall therefore begin by taking the Aristotelian framework seriously and assume that persons are, in the toughest of senses, single logical subjects: that persons are in no sense systems of logical subjects. If it is objected that according to well-confirmed scientific theory persons are, at least in part, made up of molecules, and as such are systems of individual things, I shall take temporary refuge in the familiar line that such scientific objects are "conceptual fictions"—useful symbolic devices.

As for such perceptible "parts" as arms, legs etc., your true Aristotelian construes them as merely potential parts, much as the two sides of a uniformly colored expanse are potential parts—a line could be drawn dividing it in two. And just as statements can be made about the two sides of the expanse without presupposing that it is actually divided in two, so, on strict Aristotelian principles, statements can be made about the arms or legs of a person without presupposing that they are distinct individual things in their own right. Of course, the arms or legs can be made really distinct from the person, by cutting them off; but then, as Aristotle points out, they would no longer be arms or legs in the primary sense—any more than a corpse is a man.

A person, then, according to the Aristotelian analysis, is a single individual which does not have subordinate individuals as its parts. Its unity is not that of a system. A person is a complex individual, of course, but his complexity is a matter of the many predicates applying to that one individual who is the person.

Identity or sameness is one of the least informative of concepts. As Bishop Butler pointed out long ago, "everything is what it is and not another thing." Thus, even if a person were a system he would be self-identical, for anything—even a system—is self-identical. Consider identity through time. Philosophers often attempt to distinguish between a "loose" and a "strict" sense of identity. The language is misguided, although the contrast they have in mind is sound. As far as I can see, to insist that a person is literally identical through time—as the Aristotelians do—is simply to insist that a person is not a system of successive "person-stages." On the other hand, even if a person were a series of person-stages, he would still be self-identical through time, for he would be the same series with respect to each moment of his existence.

It has sometimes been argued that anything which endures through time must be a series. If this is presented not as revisionary metaphysics, but as an analysis of the conceptual framework we learned at our mother's knee, it is sheer confusion. One such argument, recently elaborated by Gustav Bergmann,[1] is interesting as an example of how mistaken a metaphysical argument can be even when buttressed by all the

1. "Some Reflections on Time," in *Meaning and Existence* (Madison, University of Wisconsin Press, 1960).

technical resources of the new logic. It has the form of a *reductio ad absurdum* and goes as follows:

(1) Suppose (contrary to fact) a Substance S—a logical subject of which the identity through time is *not* that of a series—and suppose that S becomes successively red and green.

(2) Then redness and greenness would both be true of S.

(3) But redness and greenness are incompatible.

(4) To be coherent, then, we must say that redness is true of S at one moment or period of time t_1 and that greenness is true of S at another moment or period of time t_2.

(5) Thus, to describe S coherently we must mention moments or periods of time.

(6) But [argues Bergmann] moments or periods of time are conceptual constructions and must not be mentioned in a list of ontological ultimates.

(7) Hence basic statements about the world must not mention moments or periods of time.

(8) But, according to the substance theory, this is exactly what basic statements about substances must do.

(9) Hence the theory of substance commits one to a false ontology and must be rejected.

Roughly, a substance ontology is committed to a "container" or "absolute" theory of time.

The flaw in this argument is that, in its attempt to formulate a substance ontology within the tidy language of *Principia Mathematica*, it overlooks the role of tenses and temporal connectives in actual usage. Thus, to take account of the incompatibility of redness and greenness, a substance theorist is not forced to move directly to propositions of the form

S is red at t_1
S is green at t_2

let alone to such supposititious PMese counterparts as

Red(S,t_1)
Green(S,t_2).

The latter, indeed, are counter-intuitive, for they present colors as relations between substances and times, rather than as qualitative characteristics. If a substance theorist were forced to make this move, he would indeed be in trouble.

If, on the other hand, we introduce the relational predicates 'red at' and 'green at', and write:

Red at (S,t_1)
Green at (S,t_2)

we see intuitively that these locutions presuppose the propriety of the nonrelational forms

Red(S)
Green(S).

But is this not to admit that the substance theorist cannot solve the incompatibility problem without countenancing times as ontological ultimates and doing violence to the intrinsic grammar of color predicates?

The answer is "no," for he needs only point to the availability of such forms as

S is red
S will be green

which preserve the nonrelational character of color predicates.

It might be objected to this that sentences containing the tensed verbs 'is,' 'was,' and 'will be' are covertly relational. Thus one might be tempted to construe

S is red

as

S be red *now*

where 'be' is a "tenseless" (or "pure") copula; and the latter, in turn, as

Red(S, *now*)

and as unfolding into

Red(S, t_1) and Simul(t_1, context of utterance).

Similarly, one might construe

S will be green

as

S be green after *now*

and as unfolding into

(Et) Green (S, t) and After(t, context of utterance).

But once one sees that the job done by sentences involving tokens of 'now' requires *not* that they *mention* a relation to the context of utterance, but rather that they *stand in* a relation to the situation they describe, it becomes clear that the same is true of the tensed verbs 'is,' 'was,' and 'will be.' The concept of a pure tenseless copula is a myth—at least as far as our ordinary conceptual framework is concerned.[2]

Again, the substance theorist can point to the related forms

S was red before it was green
S is red and will be green
S will be green after it is red.

---

2. That there might be a use for such a copula in a contrived conceptual framework is argued in "Time and the World Order," In *Minnesota Studies in the Philosophy of Science* (Minneapolis, University of Minnesota Press, 1963), 577–93. For a discussion of the copula 'is' as a pseudotenseless copula equivalent to the 'be' introduced by the equivalence 'S be P ≡ S was P or S is P or S will be P,' see p. 533.

It is surely a mistake to assume that 'before,' 'while,' 'after,' and other temporal connectives[3] are to be analysed in terms of a reference to moments or periods of time, as we saw it to be a mistake to assume that 'is,' 'was,' and 'will be' are to be analysed in terms of a tenseless copula and a reference to a relation.

Thus it is open to the Aristotelian to agree with Bergmann that moments and periods of time are conceptual constructions, but to claim that they are constructible within the framework of a substance ontology in terms of such concepts as before, after, while—rather than in terms of relations between events, where "event" is taken to be the basic ontological category.

Even more transparent is a closely related argument for the thesis that the identity of a person is the identity of a series. It involves a confusion between a person and his history. The history of a person is the sequence of events in which he is relevantly involved. There clearly are such things as events; and the events in which a person participates *do* constitute a series. But if we look at one such event, say,

> the event of Caesar crossing the Rubicon

it becomes apparent that what can be said by referring to the event in which Caesar participated can also be put without such reference. Thus, instead of saying,

> The event of Caesar crossing the Rubicon took place

we can simply say,

> Caesar crossed the Rubicon.

---

3. I speak of them as connectives, for unlike relation words they are not contexts calling for abstract singular terms (e.g. that-clauses). A broad theory of temporal and other nonlogical connectives is urgently needed. See pp. 550–51 of the essay cited above.

Indeed, it is clear that in ordinary discourse event-talk is in some sense derivative from substance-talk. If one did not understand the simple subject-predicate sentence

Socrates ran

one could not understand the more complex locution

(The event of) Socrates running took place.

The latter presupposes the former in a very straightforward sense. Indeed, it contains it, with a slight grammatical modification.

To appreciate the sense in which the latter statement contains the former, as well as to understand how the two statements can be strongly equivalent without having the same sense, an analogy will help. Consider the pair of statements

Snow is white
It is true that snow is white.

These statements are strongly equivalent, but not identical in meaning. Furthermore, the second statement in some sense contains the former. (In a literal sense it contains the sign design of the former.)

I have argued in a number of places[4] that '-ity,' '-hood,' '-ness,' and 'that' (as used to form propositional clauses) are to be regarded as quoting devices which (a) form sortal predicates which apply to expression tokens in any language or conceptual scheme which are doing in that language or conceptual scheme that which is done in our language by the design with which they are conjoined; (b) turn these sortal predicates into distributive singular terms. Thus "andness" is to be construed as 'the ·and·' where '·and·' is the sortal predicate formed from the design *and*. On this analysis the singular term

that snow is white

4. Most recently in *Science and Metaphysics* (London, 1968), Chapter 3.

becomes

> the ·snow is white·

and

> That snow is white is true

becomes

> The ·snow is white· is true.

Since statements which have distributive singular terms as subjects

> The lion is tawny

can be "reduced" to statements which have the sortal predicate from which the singular term is constructed as their grammatical subjects,

> Lions are tawny

the above analysis enables the reduction of

> That snow is white is true

to

> ·snow is white·s are true

which tells us that in a relevant mode of correctness

> ·snow is white·s are correctly assertible

i.e. authorizes one, so to speak, to step down from ones metalinguistic stilts and *use* a ·snow is white·, which is, in our language, to use a 'snow is white.' My generic term for such assertibility is "semantic assertibility" (abbreviated to "S-assertibility").[5]

5. For an elaboration of this account of truth see *Science and Metaphysics*, Chapter 4.

To focus these considerations on our original topic of events, notice first that there are a number of locutions which, used in appropriate contexts, are equivalent to the predicate 'true.' Thus:

That snow is white is the case.

Of particular interest are examples in which it seems appropriate to take seriously the prima facie tensed character of the copula in 'is the case.' Consider, for example, the statements

That Socrates runs is the case (right now).
That Socrates runs was the case (yesterday at 2 PM).
That Socrates runs will be the case (tomorrow at 3 PM).

The suggestion I wish to make is that 'is taking place,' 'took place,' and 'will take place' are to be construed as specialized truth-predicates that are used in connection with statements in which the predicate is a verb standing for a kind of change, activity, or process. The most interesting case, as we shall see, is that of statements in which the predicate stands for a kind of action.

To return to our example of event talk, the statement

(The event of) Socrates running took place

has, in the first place, the form

That Socrates runs was true

and, more penetratingly considered, the form

The ·Socrates runs· was true.

A further step in the analysis (though by no means the final one) takes us to

The ·Socrates runs· was S-assertible

and

·Socrates runs·s were S-assertible.

To develop this analysis into a full-fledged theory of event-talk would take us into problems pertaining to quantifying into statements containing abstract singular terms. My present purpose has been to sketch a strategy for explaining the sense in which event-talk is dependent on substance-talk, and the sense in which statements about events taking place can be strongly equivalent to statements about substances changing, without being synonymous with the latter. It may be possible, as I have indicated above, to construct a conceptual framework and a use of 'event' in which events are more basic than their counterparts in the substance framework of ordinary discourse. But to construct such a framework would not be to analyse the concept of event which we actually employ.[6]

Having taken the metaphysical bit into our teeth, let us turn to issues more directly related to the topic of persons. Consider, for example, the endless perplexities which have arisen about the ownership-relation between persons and their "experiences." The fundamental point to be made is of a piece with the considerations advanced above: Philosophers should be wary of verbal nouns. Failure to do so has generated about as much bad metaphysics as has been sponsored by 'is' and 'not.' Words like 'sensation,' 'feeling,' 'thought,' and 'impression' in such contexts as

Jones has a sensation (feeling, etc.)

have mesmerized philosophers into wondering what Jones' mind is, as contrasted with his sensations, feelings, etc. If

6. In the essay referred to in n. 2, however, I failed to appreciate the kinship of event-expressions with abstract singular terms. With this exception, the argument of the essay and the distinctions it draws still seem to me to stand up reasonably well.

Jones qua mind is a haver of "experiences," then, since to be a haver is to have a relational property, must not the mind be a *mere* haver—in other words a "bare particular"? Are we not confronted by a choice between accepting bare particulars[7] with ontological piety, and avoiding them at the price of committing ourselves to a "bundle theory" of the self?

Since the above dialectic is a special case of a more general dialectic pertaining to subject-predicate statements, we find philosophers pressing their brows in anguish over the dilemma of choosing between "things are havers (bare particulars)" and "things are bundles of what they are said to have." The fundamental mistake, of course, is that of construing subject-predicate statements as relational. It is that of construing, for example,

Tom is tall

as expressing a relation between two objects, Tom and tallness. The issues involved are complex, and I cannot do justice to them here.[8] I shall simply point out that if we consider the contexts listed at the beginning of this section, it is surely implausible to take such statements as

Tom has a feeling

7. The term 'bare particular' has come to be ambiguous. Traditionally it was used in connection with the view that ordinary things (e.g. horses) are composites of a *this* factor and a *such* factor, where the *this* factor was conceived to be a pure substratum in the sense that it has no empirical character, but only the metaphysical character of standing in the *having* relation (or *nexus*) to a *such* factor. Neither the *this* nor the *such* factor would be the horse.

Recently, however, the term has come to be used in connection with the view that particularly is an irreducible category, i.e. that particulars are not "complexes of universals." To accept bare particulars in the first sense is to accept them in the second, but not vice versa.

8. I have examined it in some detail in Chapter 7 of *Science, Perception and Reality* (London, 1963). See also *Philosophical Perspectives* (Springfield, Ill., 1967), Chapter 6.

to be anything but a derivative (but legitimate) way of saying what is said adequately and nonrelationally by such statements as

Tom feels . . .

Thus, in general,

Tom has a V-tion,

where 'V-tion' is a verbal noun for a kind of "experience," would be a derivative (but legitimate) way of saying what is said adequately and nonrelationally by

Tom Vs.

Clearly there is a strong equivalence between

Tom feels

and

Tom has a feeling

and, in general, between

Tom Vs (e.g. Tom senses)

and

Tom has a V-tion (e.g. Tom has a sensation),

but this is no more a sign of synonymy than is the strong equivalence between

Snow is white

and

It is true that snow is white.

Clearly, 'Snow is white' is, in a straightforward sense, more basic than 'It is true that snow is white.' The strategy employed above with respect to events suggests that the sense in which 'Tom Vs' is more basic than 'Tom has a V-tion' is essentially the same. According to such an analysis,

> Tom has a sensation

would be reconstructed as

> That he senses is true of Tom.

We have already construed *events* as a special kind of proposition, and *taking place* as a special form of truth. It is but a small step along this path to construe an object's *participating in* an event as a special case of an attribute being true of the object.

Now it might be objected that what I have been advancing is interesting and possibly even true—but irrelevant. It might be conceded that the relational locution

> Tom has a V-tion

can, in many cases, be "reduced" to the "more basic"

> Tom Vs

but urged that the latter statement is itself—when made explicit—relational. In other words it might be urged that the basic thesis of the relational theory of "experiencing" concerns *not* the metaphysical relation of *having*, but the *empirical* relations of feeling, sensing, thinking, etc. For even if we turn our attention from

> Tom has a V-tion(sensation)

to

> Tom Vs(senses)

we see, on reflection, that the latter is equivalent to

> Tom senses *something*

which, prima facie, has the form

(Ex) Senses(Tom,x).

Here is where the so-called "adverbial" theory of the objects of sensation becomes relevant. For, joining in the move from

Tom has a sensation of a red triangle

to

Tom senses a red triangle

the adverbial theory denies that the latter has the form

(Ex) x is a red triangle and Tom senses x.

To take a more intuitive example, the adverbial theory denies that

Tom feels pain

has the form

Feels(Tom,pain)

but interprets it rather as

Tom feels-pain

and, thus, ascribes to it the form

Tom Vs.

The example is more intuitive because we are struck by the rough equivalence of 'Tom feels pain' to 'Tom hurts.'

To make this move is to construe 'pain,' in the above context, as a special kind of adverb; one which modified 'feels' to form a verbal expression which stands to the latter as "determinate" to "determinable": roughly, as species to genus.

If the verb in

Tom feels pain

is 'feels-pain' thus construed, then in the context

> Tom has a feeling of pain

the 'of pain' must be construed as the corresponding adjective which makes a specific verbal noun out of the verbal noun root 'feeling.'

The adverbial theory views such verbs as 'feels,' 'experiences,' 'senses'—and, as we shall see, 'thinks'—as generic verbs, and the expressions formed from them by "adding a reference to the objects felt, experienced, etc." as specific verbs. It follows from this that in a perspicuous language, we would not use the generic verb in forming its species, but, instead, say

> Tom pains

rather than

> Tom feels pain

just as we say

> The book is rectangular

rather than

> The book is rectangularly shaped.

In this perspicuous language we would not say,

> Tom senses a red triangle

but

> Tom a-red-triangles

where the verb 'a-red-triangle' stands for that kind of sensing which is brought about in standard conditions, and in standard perceivers, by the presence of a literally red and triangular object.

In the case of conceptual activity, on the assumption that

thinking is to be construed as "inner speech,"[9] parallel considerations lead to parallel results. In the first place,

> S has the thought that snow is white

or

> The thought that snow is white occurs to S

would be the higher-order equivalence of

> S thinks (i.e. is thinking) that snow is white.

And, in the second place, the latter statement would not have the form

> Thinks(S, that snow is white)

but rather

> S Vs.

For 'thinks that snow is white' would stand to 'thinks' as specific verb to generic verb. Here, again, we are to construe the expression following the verb as a special kind of adverb. And, as before, in a perspicuous language the verb root 'thinks' would drop out of the specific verbs. What would the perspicuous specific verb be? The answer lies in our previous account of abstract singular terms as classifying expressions. There we abstracted from the fact that the primary mode of being of language was nonparroting verbal activity by one who knows the language, and construed

> That snow is white

as

> The ·snow is white·

9. For a discussion of the concept of thinking as a quasi-theoretical concept modeled on the concept of meaningful verbal behavior, see Chapter 5 of *Science, Perception and Reality*; also Chapter 6 of *Science and Metaphysics*.

where '·snow is white·' applies to any expression in any language which does the job done in ours by the design *snow is white*. But, as we must now realize, the primary mode of being of "expressions" is people speaking (writing, etc.). Thus what we are really classifying are linguistic activities. To take this into account, instead of saying

'Schnee ist weiss's (in German) are ·snow is white·s

we should say

'Schnee ist weiss'ings (in G) are ·snow is white·ings

and once we have these verbal nouns we are led to form the corresponding verbs. Thus when all the proper moves have been made,

Jones said that snow is white

becomes

Jones ·snow is white·ed.

Parallel considerations lead to parallel results in the case of thinking as inner speech. Thus,

The thought that snow is white occurred to Jones

which is doubly relational in appearance, turns out to have as its foundation the nonrelational state of affairs expressed by

Jones ·snow is white·ed[10].

The above considerations will play a crucial role in the argument to follow. As a preliminary means of grasping their significance, consider the following objection often raised

10. The dot-quoted expressions in the context of inner speech are analogical counterparts of dot-quoted expressions in the context of speech proper. For an elaboration of this point see Chapter 6 of *Science and Metaphysics*.

against Descartes. It is argued that instead of claiming that

> I think (*cogito*)

formulates a piece of primary knowledge, Descartes should have given this role to something like

> This thought exists.

To get to the existence of the "I," then, we would have to make the inferential move

> This thought exists
> So, a thinker (i.e. the thinker of this thought) exists.

"I" would then be identified as the thinker who "has" the thought. To start down this path is obviously to raise the question: what would justify this inference?

From the perspective we have reached we can see that this objection overlooks the fact that reference to thoughts is derivative from references to thinkers thinking. Thus the fundamental form of the mental is not

> There are thoughts (or, more generally, representations)

but rather as Kant saw,

> x thinks (represents),

of which a special case is

> I think (represent).

Before I turn my attention to Kant's treatment of the "I" and the relevance of this treatment to the views I have been developing, I must enlarge my canvass to take into account other features of the Aristotelian metaphysics of the person. The theme I have particularly in mind is that of causation.

Off hand, one would be inclined to say that Richard Taylor

belongs in the mainstream of the perennial tradition, and, indeed, his recent study of *Action and Purpose* contains much to warm the hearts of those who seek to defend classical insights against the dogmas of reductionist empiricism and naturalism. Yet in spite of the many positive virtues of his analysis, the total effect must be counted a failure, largely because of the inadequate account of causation on which it rests. Actually, this comment is a bit unfair, since Taylor has many interesting and perceptive things to say about causation. The trouble is that he overlooks the ambiguity of the term, the fact that it stands for a whole family of concepts. Once he commits himself to a paradigm it becomes the paradigm of all causality and blurs key distinctions.

One familiar sense of "cause" is embodied in locutions of the form

X caused Y to Z by doing A

e.g.

Jones caused the match to light by striking it.

This concept of causation can be called "interventionist." In its primary form, as the illustration suggests, the cause *is* a person and a person causes something to happen by *doing* something. This concept, by a metaphorical extension, is applied to inanimate objects, thus

The stone caused the glass to shatter by striking it.

The extended use, as a frozen metaphor, is invaluable, but philosophers have often sensed in it the original life. This accounts for the traditional conviction that, strictly speaking, only persons can be causes.

Now I take it as obvious that persons are or can be causes in this sense of "cause." Let us, therefore, explore it by means of examples, thus

Jones caused the pawn to move by pushing it.

This is an excellent example of personal causation, of a piece with many Taylor gives. But at a critical stage in his argument, we find him arguing that, on occasion at least, persons cause their actions. Thus, as he sees it, when Jones moves his finger, we can appropriately say

Jones caused his finger to move.

Now if we were to ask

By doing what?

which our original paradigm requires, the answer must surely be "nothing." For if we were to say, for example,

Jones caused his finger to move by pushing it

Taylor would, correctly, object that in this event the motion of the finger would not be an action, but the result of an action—the pushing. This indicates that something is wrong. Our previous concept of a person as a cause is out of place in this context. The point must, however, be made carefully, for when we leave the context of "minimal actions," this concept of persons as causes *is* relevant. Thus the assertion that

Jones killed Smith

can be met with the question

By doing what?

that is

What did Jones do which caused Smith to die?

to which the answer,

Jones caused Smith to die *by firing the gun at him*

is appropriate and falls under our canonical form. A minimal action is exactly one to which the question

By doing what?

is inappropriate. And for this reason the concept of persons as causes with which we have been working is inapplicable.

Notice that to admit that in the context of nonminimal actions a person caused something to happen is not to admit that what the person caused is an action. Minimal actions are not the causes of nonminimal actions, they are rather the initial stages of nonminimal actions. (Of course, not every "initial stage" of an action is itself an action; consider nerve impulses or, more to the point, volitions.) Thus granting, for the moment, that crooking one's trigger finger is a minimal action, whereas the action of firing a gun is not, the relation of the former to the latter is not that of cause to effect, but that of an action to a larger action of which it is a part. To be sure, the crooking of the finger causes the firing of the gun in the sense of the gun's going off. But in *this* sense the firing of the gun is not an action, but a purely physical event. The relation of minimal actions to nonminimal actions should not be pictured *thusly*,

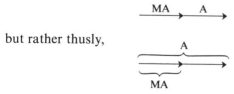

but rather thusly,

Now it might be said that by using the paradigm

X caused *Y* to *Z* by *A*-ing

to explore Taylor's idea that persons cause their actions, I am being seriously unfair. After all, it could be pointed out, Taylor explicitly contrasts "personal" causation with "natural" causation, whereas my comments amount to the idea that he fails to draw this distinction. There is some truth to this charge. I do claim that Taylor fails to draw this distinction; but as I see it this is because his concept of personal causation is vacuous. For, in effect, I have been arguing that the sense in which, according to Taylor, persons cause their actions amounts to no more than that they do them; indeed, in the last analysis, to no more than that persons act. Thus, as used by Taylor,

> Jones caused action A

is a misleading way of saying

> Jones did action A

which amounts to

> Jones did an A-ing

and is, as I put it, the higher order equivalent of

> Jones Ad.

Nobody would think of dancing a waltz as causing a waltz. Taylor may have been misled by the fact that we do speak, for example, of "making" a gesture, and "making" in some contexts is certainly "causing." But, surely,

> Jones made a gesture

stands to

> Jones gesticulated

as "Jones performed a waltz" stands to "Jones waltzed," and the appearance of causation is an illusion.

I conclude that persons do not cause their actions, though, except in the case of minimal actions, by doing one thing they can cause something else to happen, and can, therefore, be said to have done a correspondingly more complex action. Thus, by firing a gun and causing a death, one kills.

If persons do not cause their actions, does anything else cause them? On occasion, yes. I can be caused to do something by someone else, as when I am caused by someone in authority to make amends. By a metaphorical extension of this usage, inanimate objects can also cause one to do something. Two points must, however, be made in this connection. In the first place, it is obvious that not every action is in *this* sense caused. And in the second, one must be careful to distinguish between those causes in which an action is caused, and those in which one is not, properly speaking, an agent at all, but rather a patient, as when one is overpowered by superior force.

If, now, we turn to other senses of 'cause,' and take Aristotle as our guide, we find it quite sensible to say that actions have causes indeed, in Aristotle's sense, *efficient* causes. For not all efficient causation is to be construed on the above model.

Taylor's account of the teleological explanation of purposive behavior consists of two theses:

(1) A negative thesis to the effect that purposive behavior is not caused by anything other than the agent, i.e. he is not caused to do it;

(2) A positive thesis to the effect that purposive behavior is to be explained in terms of such locutions as 'X did Y in order to bring about Z.'

Unfortunately, he leaves the latter thesis unexplicated except in tautologous ways, thus 'X did Y with the aim of bringing about Z.'

Taylor does consider the possibility that actions are caused by volitions. But his account of volitions and causation by volition is a caricature. The following points need to be made:

(1) Taylor assumes that volitions are actions in the practical sense, pieces of conduct (in this case mental

conduct)—the sort of thing which, *if there were any*, could themselves be caused by volition. Thus he argues that according to the theory of volitions, in order to do one action (*A*) one must first do another (willing to do *A*). This, he points out, if taken seriously, would generate a vicious regress.

To this the answer is simple and straightforward. Volitions are not to be construed as pieces of conduct. They are "actions" only in that broadest sense in which anything expressed by a verb in the active voice (e.g. sleeping) is an action. They are actualities, indeed episodes, but not actions in any more interesting sense.[11]

    (2) Taylor assumes that because playing a phrase on the piano consists of striking successive notes, the willing that causes the playing of the phrase must consist of a volition for each note.

To this, the obvious answer is that learning to play a piece of music, and, in general, learning to play the piano, involves the building of behavioral elements into patterns which can be intended as wholes. It is only the beginner who has to think out each step as he goes along. The point is familiar to anyone who has learned to ride a bicycle or to swim.

    (3) Taylor agrees (with Melden) that since (with the necessary qualifications) there is no logical connection between cause and effect, and since there *is* a logical connection between the volition to raise one's arm and the raising of the arm, the volition cannot be the cause of the action.

To this the proper reply is that the so-called "logical" connection between the volition and the action is the "aboutness"

11. For a more complete account of this and other methods pertaining to volition, see *Science and Metaphysics*, Chapter 7.

relation between a thought and the state of affairs it represents, and not a putative relation of entailment between events. If Taylor's argument were correct, it would follow that a red book couldn't be the cause of the perceptual belief that one is confronted by a red book. Taylor, indeed, overlooks the point that volitions are to be construed as thoughts and have intensionality. It is obvious that when we act purposively we must be thinking of the state of affairs to be realized. This thinking can't be merely matter-of-factual thinking about the future. What generates action is not descriptive thinking to which has been added a nonconceptual impetus or push. It is practical thinking.

>   (4) Taylor ridicules volitions by arguing that all that can be said of the volition which causes ones finger to go up is that it is a "finger-raising volition."

This claim overlooks the complex logical and conceptual relations that can be traced between volitions and other modes of practical thinking.[12] For our present purposes, it is sufficient to note that Taylor's objection could also be raised against the concept of perceptual taking or belief. What is the perceptual taking (normally) caused by a red book in front of one? It is a red-book-in-front-of-one taking. Why not?

>   (5) Taylor argues that if volitions are the causes of our actions, they must cause us to do them.

This argument is a simple consequence of his assimilation of all senses of 'cause' to his paradigm. His conclusion that if volitions are the cause of actions then we are not free, but are caused or compelled to do what we do, is sheer confusion.

12. I have discussed these relations in some detail in "Thought and Action," in Keith Lehrer, ed., *Freedom and Determinism* (New York, Random House, 1966).

Finally, it should be noted that just as motions are things moving, so volitions are persons willing. To suppose that in "personal" causation (or "agency") one is confronted by a mode of causation which can be schematized as

Person causes event

and contrasted with "natural" causation, the latter being schematized as

Event causes event

is to make a radical mistake. Even in the case of purely physical causation it is permissible to say, for example

The bomb caused the disaster

which has the form

Thing caused event.

Here, however, we recognize that although this form of statement is legitimate, the truth of such statements requires that of statements of the form

Event caused event

thus,

The explosion of the bomb caused the disaster.

It is, therefore, essential to see that exactly the same situation obtains in the case of personal causation. The truth of statements of the form

Jones brought about E

requires that of statements of the form

(In the circumstances) Jones' willing to bring about E' caused E

which also has the form

Event caused event.

That the causing event is a volition, i.e., a conceptual event of the kind which is central to practical thinking is what distinguishes 'actions' from 'mere events.' To construe the difference in terms of the contrast between 'person causes event' and 'event causes event' is sheer error.

I shall now return to the Kantian idea that "I think" or "I represent" is the basic and irreducible form of self-awareness with respect to distinctively human states of one's person. Traditional metaphysicians had argued that the subject of representations (the represener) is a simple, noncomposite substance which is "strictly" or, as it is sometimes put, "literally" identical through time—i.e. does not have the identity of a series. Kant argues, *per contra*, that for all we know the subject or represener might be:

(a) an attribute of something more basic
(b) a system (composite)
(c) a series.

Of these possibilities, the first (although it has other overtones) amounts to the idea that from God's point of view a person's mind might be an Aristotelian unitary person qua having mental states and capacities, as contrasted with those states and capacities which are the real counterparts of bodily states and capacities. Kant defends this possibility by showing that a traditional argument to the contrary is a fallacy. His reconstruction of this fallacy or "paralogism" can be paraphrased as follows:

(1) The concept of the "I" (represener) is the concept of a subject of representations.

(2) The concept of the "I" is not the concept of derivative or dependent logical subject.

(3) Therefore the concept of the "I" is the concept of a
    nonderivative subject.[13]

Kant concedes that the argument would not be a fallacy if we
could add the premise that our concept of the "I" is the concept
of a determinate kind of object, as the concept of a species of
material thing is the concept of a determinate kind of object.
For this premise would entail that the concept of the "I" is
the concept of a specific type of logical subject; and from this,
together with the premise that it is not the concept of a logical
subject of specific type T, one could establish that it is the
concept of a logical subject of specific type T, if these were the
only relevant alternatives.

But the concept of the "I" is the concept of that which thinks
(thus, as Kant uses the term 'I,' it is equivalent to 'mind'), and
concepts pertaining to mental acts are "functional" in a way
which leaves open the question as to the "qualitative" or, as I
prefer to say, contentual character of the items that function
in such a way as to be the kind of mental act they are. To use a
well-worn analogy, one may distinguish between the contentual and the functional aspects of the activities involved in a
game of chess. The contentual aspects concern the material
out of which the pieces and the board are made, and the specific
kinds of changes which are to count as the various moves.
We can conceive of widely different contentual embodiments of
chess, i.e. we can conceive of the functionings in ways which
abstract from specific embodiments, though they lay down
abstract requirements which any specific embodiments must
satisfy. Notice that these abstractly conceived functionings
could be embodied in different types of logical subject. Thus

13. To get an initial insight into the surface structure of the argument,
consider the following:

We conceive of x as colored
We do not conceive of x as red
Therefore we conceive of x as nonred.

there could be a game of chess in which the pieces were simple substances, or composite substances, or persons qua bodies, or, in the case of mental chess, conceptual entities. This can be put by saying that these abstractly conceived functionings are "transcategorial" with respect to the type of logical subjects in which they might be embodied (e.g. simple, complex, person qua moveable).

Now the peculiar feature of concepts pertaining to conceptual activity is that they are purely functional. To get purely functional concepts pertaining to chess, we start with concepts involving specific content and proceed by abstraction. Our concepts pertaining to conceptual activity, on the other hand, are purely functional *ab initio*. This lack of a specific contentual aspect is what lies behind the temptation to think of mental acts as "diaphanous." And Kant's point can be put by saying that conceptual acts are transcategorial with respect to the type of logical subject which might engage in them (e.g. simple, complex, person qua capable of conceptual activity).

Thus, to represent the mind as a substance (as contrasted with a person qua capable of conceptual acts) is not to know that the mind is such a substance. For to know that latter we would have to have an adequate contentual concept of mental activity (i.e. we would have to know the mind "as a determinate object"), and this we do not have. Thus, from the standpoint of knowledge "representing the mind as a substance" amounts to no more than "not representing it as a contentually specific dependent subject". Indeed, by parity of reasoning, "representing the mind as a dependent subject" would amount to no more than "not representing it as a contentually specific substance".

To sum up, if we conceive of the "I" (or mind) determinately as a determinate object of knowledge, without conceiving of it as a dependent logical subject, we must be conceiving of it as an independent or nonderivative object of knowledge. Thus

Kant traces the fallacy to a failure to note that the term 'I' (or 'mind') does not express the concept of a determinate kind of object. It is because of this that, even granted that we do not conceive of the "I" as a derivative subject, it does not follow that we are conceiving of it as a nonderivative subject, or substance.

Kant finds a similar fallacy in the argument "rational psychologists" had used to prove the simplicity of the "I"—to prove that its identity is not that of a system or composite. His reconstruction of the argument can be paraphrased as follows:

(1) The concept of the "I" (representer) is the concept of one subject.
(2) The concept of the "I" is not the concept of a composite.

Therefore

(3) The concept of the "I" is the concept of a non-composite entity. Its unity is not that of a system.

As before, Kant concedes that if our concept of the "I," as a *one* subject, were the contentually determinate concept of a determinate object, then the conclusion would be established. If we are not conceiving of it as a system or composite, we must be conceiving of it as a determinate noncomposite or simple object of knowledge. But, again, our knowledge of the mind is the knowledge of that which acts in ways which we conceive of in purely functional terms. And since these functions could, in principle, be activities of either (a) a simple substance, (b) a composite substance, or (c) a substance (simple or composite) qua capable of conceptual activity, our knowledge does not determine to which of these types of logical subject the "I" belongs.

In connection with this second Paralogism, Kant makes two points that show the subtlety of his thought. It is, he argues, indeed true that the subject of thoughts cannot be a *many* in the sense of *many subjects of thought*. To make the point in terms of a familiar type of example, if one thinker thinks 'Tom,' another thinks 'is,' and yet another thinks 'tall,' this does not entail that there is an "I" which thinks 'Tom is tall.' But, Kant points out, it does not follow that the "I" which thinks cannot be a plurality or system.

> The subject of thoughts, the "I," is a plurality is not the same as
>
> The subject of thoughts is a plurality of "I"s.

The third Paralogism concerns the claim that the identity of the "I" through its successive states is not the identity of a series. It has a similar form, and Kant's treatment of it is equally sound and illuminating. Here, too, it should be noted that the idea that the "I" is a series must not be confused with the idea that it is a series of "I"s.

I have often characterized my metaphysical views as strongly Kantian in structure. Thus I have argued that the common-sense world, the world of the "manifest image" is, in the Kantian sense, phenomenal; the way in which things as they really are appear to minds endowed with a certain conceptual framework. The fact that this framework is a subtle one, particularly in those respects which concern action and practice, by no means guarantees that its ontology is an adequate representation of the way things are.

In the manifest image, our concept of a person is not the concept of something of which the behavior can be assimilated to the triggering off of causal properties in the interaction of material things. Persons acquire second natures—in the literal sense, dispositions. But their *first* nature is not that of a system of causal properties—dispositions in the metaphorical sense—but rather that of a system of capacities pertaining to the various modes of thinking.

In the Paralogisms Kant has kept the way clear for the view that in reality the "I" is a system, and, in particular for the view that it is a system of scientific objects, the true counterparts of Kant's things-in-themselves. Again he has kept the way clear for the view the thoughts and other representations are in reality complex states of a system and, in particular, of a neurophysiological system. Here again one must beware of assimilating scientific intelligibility to Taylor's paradigm of causation. Kant also kept the way clear for the view that in reality the identity of the "I" through its successive acts of representation is the identity of a series.

Kant's fundamental error was to construe the phenomenal world in Cartesian terms. The Aristotelian–Strawsonian reconstruction is along sounder lines. But, as I see it, this (unavoidable) error was but one more symptom of his pre-evolutionary commitments. Correctly rejecting standard empiricism, he was forced into the platonic alternative of innate ideas. This led him to tie together in one bundle the diversity of concepts in terms of which we explain the course of nature. Different levels of spatial and temporal concepts were identified and construed in terms of the Space and Time of Newtonian mechanics. The framework of emerging microphysics was assumed to be already in the mind awaiting its Socrates, as did geometry in the soul of Meno's slave.

Today we are in a better position to distinguish between the conceptual framework of which nature was the cause, and the freely elaborate conceptual frameworks with which we now challenge nature. It is the greater explanatory power of the latter which stands behind the claim that things as they are in themselves are things as ideal science would find them to be. But the details of this neo-Peircean conception of truth and reality must be left to another occasion.[14]

14. For an initial attempt see Chapters 3–5 of my *Science and Metaphysics*.

Part III

Intensions, Combinators, and Sheffer Functions

11. On Leonardian Intensions of Class-Terms

R. M. Martin

Sets of characteristics common and jointly peculiar to the extensions of terms are called by Leonard the *intensions* of those terms.[1] Roughly speaking, a *characteristic* is a property or attribute, and an attribute "purports ... to *apply* to things" rather than to refer to or name them. A characteristic is *common* to a group of objects if and only if every object in that group has that characteristic. And a characteristic is *peculiar* to an object if and only if "nothing except this object has that characteristic." A set of characteristics is *jointly peculiar* to an object if and only if that object has all the characteristics in that set. And finally, a set of characteristics is jointly peculiar to a *set* of objects if and only if every member of that set has every characteristic in that set of characteristics. There are many sets of characteristics common and jointly peculiar to the extension of a term, and hence many intensions of a term. The two most important Leonard calls the *total contingent intension* and the *total strict intension* of the term.

Characteristics are presumably taken by Leonard "in intension," as the traditional phrase has it. Thus two characteristics P and Q are *not* to be identified just because every

1. H. S. Leonard, *Principles of Right Reason* (New York, Holt, 1957), pp. 234 ff.

object which has P has Q and conversely. Classes *are* so identified, however. A pellucid condition under which two characteristics are identical remains to be given. No clear identity—no clear characteristic, to paraphrase Quine.

Elsewhere it has been suggested that attributes can perhaps be construed somewhat as follows.[2] Let α^2 be a class of individuals and let a be any expression which *designates* it. Consider now the ordered couple

$$(1) \qquad\qquad \langle \alpha^2, a \rangle,$$

of α^2 with a, where a designates α^2. This ordered couple is a new entity, as it were, namely, the given class *with respect to its being designated by a.* We may regard it as the class α^2 *taken in intension,* more particularly, taken *in the intension specified by a.* It is also akin to Frege's notion of an *object-taken-in-a-given-mode-of-presentation (Art des Gegebenseins).*[3]

Let us construe characteristics or properties hereafter as ordered couples of the kind (1). To say that an individual α^1 *has* a characteristic or property $\langle \alpha^2, a \rangle$ is then merely to say that α^1 is a *member* of the class α^2 and that a designates α^2. We cannot say in an object-language, however, that α^1 has such and such a characteristic. This can be said only in the appropriate semantical metalanguage. The notion of a characteristic, or of having a characteristic, thus becomes a semantical notion, as clear-cut and precise as such notions ever are.

When, now, are two characteristics to be identified? Strictly there are *many* relations here to be distinguished. Consider $\langle \alpha^2, a \rangle$ and $\langle \beta^2, b \rangle$. Suppose a is *equivalent* to b, in the sense that they designate the same class. The two characteristics

2. See the author's "On Abstract Entities in Semantic Analysis," *Nous,* forthcoming.

3. See G. Frege, "On Sense and Reference," in P. Geach and M. Black, eds., *Philosophical Papers of Gottlob Frege* (Oxford, Blackwell, 1952), p. 57.

may then be said to be equivalent. Suppose a and b are *L-equivalent* in an appropriate sense : the two characteristics may then be said to be L-equivalent. Suppose a and b *mutually entail* each other in some quite strict sense : the two characteristics then also. There are many relations of entailment here to be distinguished, depending upon the inner structure of a and b. The inner structure need not be explored here ; the only point to be noted is that there is a multiplicity of semantical relations here to be distinguished, some of which may give reasonable notions of identity.

If we construe characteristics in this sense we can give an exact formulation to what seems to be a theory of intensions very close to Leonard's. The fit is not perhaps quite perfect, but it rarely is anyhow. It will be close enough surely to see that Leonard was working with important ideas that can be given a full explication only in modern semantics.

As object-language let us take a system T^k based upon the simplified theory of types, but containing variables of the first k types only ($k \geq 1$). The lowest type is that of individuals. Let 'α^n' be a variable of type n. 'α^{n+1}' is then a variable for classes of type $n + 1$, and 'α^1', for individuals. Relations we may assume to be handled familiarly as classes of ordered couples, triples, etc. In the semantical metalanguage of T^k, variables of a few types higher than k are also admitted. Let 'Des', for designation, be the semantical primitive significant in contexts of the form 'a Des α^n', which reads 'the expression a designates the class α^n'. As additional variables we have 'β^n', 'γ^n', etc., and as variables over *expressions* of T^k we have 'a', 'b', etc.

The atomic formulas of T^k are of the form '$\alpha^{n+1} \alpha^n$', which reads 'α^n is a member of α^{n+1}', or just 'α^n is an α^{n+1}'. In addition to the variables, suitable nonlogical individual- and class-constants are admitted as primitives. Also expressions of the form '$\hat{\alpha}^n(-\alpha^n-)$', called *abstracts* (or defined class-constants), are admitted primitively. '$\hat{\alpha}^n(\!\!-\!\!\alpha^n\!\!-\!\!)$', where '$(\!\!-\!\!\alpha^n\!\!-\!\!)$' is a sentential function of T^k containing 'α^n' as its only free variable, designates the class of all α^n's such that $(\!\!-\!\!\alpha^n\!\!-\!\!)$. Suitable axioms governing membership as construed in type-theory are presupposed, as well as axioms of identity and of concretion and abstraction.

The structure of the semantical metalanguage is somewhat more complicated, but need not be described more fully for present purposes. In addition to suitable axioms for syntax, we have the following familiar Rules of Designation.

DES R1 $\vdash \mathbf{a} \operatorname{Des} \alpha^1$, where in place of '$\alpha^1$' we put in a primitive individual-constant and in place of '$\mathbf{a}$' its structural-descriptive name.

DES R2 $\vdash \mathbf{a} \operatorname{Des} \alpha^{n+1}$, where in place of '$\alpha^{n+1}$' we put in a primitive class-constant of type $n+1$ and in place of '$\mathbf{a}$' its structural-descriptive name.

DES R3 $\vdash \mathbf{a} \operatorname{Des} \hat{\alpha}^n(\!\!-\!\!\alpha^n\!\!-\!\!)$, where in place of '$\mathbf{a}$' we put in the structural-descriptive name of the abstract '$\hat{\alpha}^n(\!\!-\!\!\alpha^n\!\!-\!\!)$'.

DES R4 $\vdash (a)(\alpha^1)(a \operatorname{Des} \alpha^1 \supset \operatorname{InCon} a)$, where '$\operatorname{InCon} a$' expresses that a is a primitive individual-constant.

DES R5 $\vdash (a)(\alpha^{n+1})(a \operatorname{Des} \alpha^{n+1} \supset \operatorname{ClsCon}^{n+1} a)$, where '$\operatorname{ClsCon}^{n+1} a$' expresses that a is a class-constant of type $n+1$.

DES R6 $\vdash (a)(\alpha^n)(\beta^n)((a \operatorname{Des} \alpha^n \cdot a \operatorname{Des} \beta^n) \supset \alpha^n = \beta^n)$.

Let the expressional variables 'a', etc., be regarded as of lowest type in the semantical metalanguage. The ordered couple $\langle \alpha^1, a \rangle$ is then the class

$$\{\{\alpha^1\},\{\alpha^1,a\}\},$$

of type 3. $\langle \alpha^2, a \rangle$ may be regarded as the class

$$\{\{\alpha^2\}, \{\alpha^2, \{a\}\}\},$$

of type 4. And so on. Hence in general $\langle \alpha^{n+1}, a \rangle$ will be a class of type $n + 3$. Characteristics being construed as such classes, they are then of type $n + 3$ where the objects to which they apply are of type n.

Let us give now a few definitions leading up to the notion of a Leonardian intension in general.

As we know from the foregoing, a characteristic is to be a class of type $n + 3$ consisting of a class α^{n+1}-in-a-given-mode-of-presentation-a. Hence

(D1)   'Char α^{n+3}' may abbreviate '$(E\alpha^{n+1})(Ea)(\alpha^{n+3} = \langle \alpha^{n+1}, a \rangle \cdot a \text{ Des } \alpha^{n+1})$'.

The definiendum here reads 'α^{n+3} is a characteristic'.

What is it now to *have* a characteristic? Clearly we may let

(D2)   'α^n Has α^{n+3}' abbreviate '$(E\alpha^{n+1})(Ea)(\alpha^{n+3} = \langle \alpha^{n+1}, a \rangle \cdot a \text{ Des } \alpha^{n+1} \cdot \alpha^{n+1} \alpha^n)$'.

The relation of *having* relates an entity to an entity of three types higher, in view of the ordered couple involved. To have the characteristic $\langle \alpha^{n+1}, a \rangle$ is merely to be a member of α^{n+1}. But the mode of presentation must be specified, for otherwise we would be speaking of membership in a class rather than of having a characteristic.

Let us consider now Leonard's notion of a characteristic's being *common* to a class of entities when every entity which is a member of that class has that characteristic. For this we may let

(D3)   'α^{n+3} Com α^{n+1}' abbreviate '$(\text{Char } \alpha^{n+3} \cdot (\alpha^n)(\alpha^{n+1}\alpha^n \supset \alpha^n \text{ Has } \alpha^{n+3}))$'.

The definiendum reads 'the characteristic α^{n+3} is common to the members of the class α^{n+1}'.

A class of characteristics is *jointly peculiar* to a class of entities, we recall, provided every member of that class of entities has every characteristic in that class of characteristics. Thus

(D4)   'α^{n+4} JPclr α^{n+1}' abbreviates '$(\alpha^{n+3})(\alpha^{n+4}\alpha^{n+3} \supset$ (Char $\alpha^{n+3} \cdot (\alpha^n)(\alpha^{n+1}\alpha^n \supset \alpha^n$ Has $\alpha^{n+3})))$'.

The definiendum here reads 'α^{n+4} is a class of characteristics jointly peculiar to the members of the class α^{n+1}'.

We recall now that a Leonardian intension of a term is any class of characteristic common and jointly peculiar to the extension of that term. The extension of a term, in the present kind of a semantics, is merely the entity which that term designates. Hence, without more ado, we may say that α^{n+4} is a Leonardian intension of an expression a as follows.

(D5)   'α^{n+4} LndInt a' abbreviates '$(E\alpha^{n+1})(a$ Des α^{n+1} $\cdot (\alpha^{n+3})(\alpha^{n+4}\alpha^{n+3} \supset \alpha^{n+3}$ Com $\alpha^{n+1})$ $\cdot \alpha^{n+4}$ JPclr $\alpha^{n+1})$'.

The *total contingent intension* of a class-term a is, in Leonard's words, "the set of all characteristics common to the extension of that term." In the system here, we may thus let

(D6)   'α^{n+4} TotContInt a' abbreviate '$(E\alpha^{n+1})(a$ Des α^{n+1} $\cdot \alpha^{n+4} = \hat{\alpha}^{n+3}(\alpha^{n+3}$ Com $\alpha^{n+1}))$'.

The *total strict intension* of a term is "that intension of the term in question which consists of all and only the necessary members of the total contingent intension." It seems best not to attempt to define this notion in just this way, but a little differently. 'Necessary' here is to be construed in the sense of 'analytically true'. And we shall not speak of a "necessary member" but instead will require that a certain sentence concerning membership be analytic in T^k.

Let 'Anlytc c' express that the sentence c is *analytically* or *logically true* in T^k, i.e. that a is a truth wholly in virtue of its truth-functional, quantificational, or identity-theoretic structure. And let 'a AnlytcInc^{n+1}b' express that the class-constant a of type $n+1$ is analytically included in the class-constant b of the same type. To say this is merely to say that the sentence which consists of the universal quantifier '(α^n)' followed by '(' followed by a followed by 'α^n' as argument followed by '$\supset$' followed by b followed by 'α^n' as argument followed by ')', is an analytic sentence. Thus, to speak roughly, where a Des α^{n+1} and b Des β^{n+1}, a AnlytcInc^{n+1}b if and only if '$(\alpha^n)(\alpha^{n+1}\alpha^n \supset \beta^{n+1}\alpha^n)$' is analytic, where in place of 'α^{n+1}' and 'β^{n+1}' we put in appropriate constants.

The total strict intension may then be introduced as follows.

(D7)   'α^{n+4} TotStrInt a' abbreviates '(ClsCon$^{n+1}a \cdot \alpha^{n+4} = \hat{\alpha}^{n+3}(E\alpha^{n+1})(Eb)(b$ Des $\alpha^{n+1} \cdot \alpha^{n+3} = \langle \alpha^{n+1},b \rangle \cdot a$ AnlytcInc$^{n+1}b))$'.

Clearly we have the following theorems.

> *T1* $\vdash \alpha^{n+4}$ TotContInt $a \supset \alpha^{n+4}$ LndInt a.
>
> *T2* $\vdash \alpha^{n+4}$ TotStrInt $a \supset \alpha^{n+4}$ LndInt a.
>
> *T3* $\vdash (\alpha^{n+4}$ TotStrInt $a \cdot \beta^{n+4}$ TotContInt $a) \supset \alpha^{n+4} \subset \beta^{n+4}$.

Elsewhere the notion of being an *objective analytic intension* of a class-constant has been introduced.[4] But this is precisely the same as Leonard's total strict intension as construed by (D7). There are other semantical notions which likewise give rise to intensions, the notion of being *true*, the notion of being *factually true*, and the notion of being a *theorem*. Hence we may introduce the following notions also.

4. In "On Abstract Entities in Semantic Analysis." For an alternative theory, along somewhat more Aristotelian lines, as it were, see the author's *Belief, Existence, and Meaning* (New York, New University Press and London, University of London Press, forthcoming).

Let 'a VerInc^{n+1} b' express that the class-constant a of type $n + 1$ is *veridically* included in the class-constant b of the same type. This is defined, similar to the way in which 'a Anlytc-Inc^{n+1} b' is, but by requiring that the given sentence consisting of such and such expressions (precisely as above) be *true* rather than analytic. And similarly let 'a FctlInc^{n+1} b' express that a is *factually* included in b. For this it is required that the given sentence be factually true, i.e. true but not analytically so. And finally, let 'a ThmInc^{n+1} b' express that a is *theoremically* included in b. Here the requirement is that the given universal conditional be a *theorem*. All four of these notions, of being analytic, of being true, of being factual, and of being a theorem, are useful in semantics generally. It is interesting to note that each gives rise to a kind of intension of Leonardian type.

The notion of being an *objective veridical intension* of a class-constant is now definable. Let

(D8)   'α^{n+4} ObjVerInt a' abbreviate '(ClsCon$^{n+1}a \cdot \alpha^{n+4} =$
$\hat{\alpha}^{n+3}(E\alpha^{n+1})(Eb)(b$ Des $\alpha^{n+1} \cdot \alpha^{n+3} = \langle \alpha^{n+1},b \rangle$
$\cdot a$ VerInc$^{n+1}b))$'.

And similarly let 'α^{n+4} ObjFctlInt a' and 'α^{n+4} ObjThmInt a' express respectively that α^{n+4} is the objective *factual* intension of a or the objective *theoremic* intension of a.

It is not difficult to see that (D8) introduces essentially the same notion as (D6). In fact

T4 $\vdash \alpha^{n+4}$ TotContInt $a \equiv \alpha^{n+1}$ ObjVerInt a.

The proof utilizes the fundamental semantical law concerning truth, that a sentence **a** is true if and only if (————), where '(————)' is a sentence of T^k and '**a**' is taken as its structural-descriptive name.

Each intension of the kinds introduced is a Leonardian intension, as has already been remarked. Thus in addition to

$T1$ and $T2$ we have the following.

$T5$ $\vdash \alpha^{n+4}$ ObjFctlInt $a \supset \alpha^{n+4}$ LndInt a.

$T6$ $\vdash \alpha^{n+4}$ ObjThmInt $a \supset \alpha^{n+4}$ LndInt a.

For the proof of $T5$ we note that every factual sentence is true, and for that of $T6$, that every sentence which is a theorem is true.

Finally, we should note that the four kinds of Leonardian intensions are all distinct from one another under reasonable assumptions concerning T^k. Clearly

$T7$ $\vdash (\alpha^{n+4}$ ObjAnlytcInt $a \cdot \beta^{n+4}$ ObjVerInt $a \cdot \gamma^{n+4}$ ObjFctlInt $a \cdot \delta^{n+4}$ ObjThmInt $a) \supset (\alpha^{n+4} \neq \beta^{n+4} \cdot \alpha^{n+4} \neq \gamma^{n+4} \cdot \alpha^{n+4} \neq \delta^{n+4} \cdot \beta^{n+4} \neq \gamma^{n+4} \cdot \beta^{n+4} \neq \delta^{n+4} \cdot \gamma^{n+4} \neq \delta^{n+4})$.

The proof presupposes that we can prove that, for T^k, not every true sentence is analytic, no analytic sentence is factual, not every theorem which is a sentence is analytic, not all truths are factual, not all truths are theorems, and not all theorems are factual.

We have been concerned in this paper only with the semantical core of Leonard's theory; the flesh and blood, so to speak, are given in his book. Although the semantics is not explicitly characterized there, the pages concerned with the flesh and blood of the theory of intensions are surely among the finest in the history of the subject.

12. Combinatory Logic and Negative Numbers

Frederic B. Fitch

1. Introduction[1]

1.1. Most systems of combinatory logic contain operators 'I', 'K', 'W', 'C', and 'B' such that:

$$
\begin{aligned}
\mathrm{I}a &= a,\\
\mathrm{K}ab &= a,\\
\mathrm{W}ab &= abb,\\
\mathrm{C}abc &= acb,\\
\mathrm{B}abc &= a(bc).
\end{aligned}
$$

In such systems it is possible to obtain the effect of abstraction without introducing an operator analogous to Church's lambda operator. It is also possible to define numerical operators '0', '1', '2', '3', and so on, corresponding to the non-negative integers and having the properties,

$$
\begin{aligned}
0ab &= b,\\
1ab &= ab,\\
2ab &= a(ab),\\
3ab &= a(a(ab)), \text{ and so on.}
\end{aligned}
$$

1. This research was supported by NSF-GP-3899.

These latter equations can also be written thus:

$$a^0b = b,$$
$$a^1b = ab,$$
$$a^2b = a(ab),$$
$$a^3b = a(a(ab)), \text{ and so on.}$$

(Grouping not indicated by parentheses is assumed to be to the left as much as possible.)

1.2. The corresponding equations for negative integers, however, are lacking in all previously published systems of combinatory logic, so far as the writer knows. This lack will be remedied in the system **S** by the presence of a minus operator '$-$' and of numerical operators '-0', '-1', '-2', and so on, satisfying the following equations:

$$-0ab = b,$$
$$-1a(ab) = b,$$
$$-2a(a(ab)) = b,$$
$$-3a(a(a(ab))) = b, \quad \text{and so on.}$$

These equations can also be written as follows:

$$a^{-0}b = b,$$
$$a^{-1}(ab) = b,$$
$$a^{-2}(a(ab)) = b,$$
$$a^{-3}(a(a(ab))) = b, \quad \text{and so on.}$$

The presence of the minus operator in **S** entails that the formation rules for forming well-formed formulas in **S** be somewhat more restrictive than would otherwise need be the case.

1.3. In the system **S**, and indeed in all systems possessing the operators described in 1.1 above, there exist operators for addition, multiplication, and exponentiation which are appropriate to use in connection with the numerical operators of 1.1 and 1.2. If these operators for addition, multiplication, and exponentiation are respectively denoted by '+', '*', and '$\in$' (where '*' may be viewed as the same as 'B' of 1.1), the following equations express their basic properties in combinatory logic:

$$+abcd = ac(bcd),$$
$$*abc = a(bc),$$
$$\in ab = ba.$$

If '+', '*', and '$\in$' are written as infix operators, the above equations become:

$$[a + b]cd = ac(bcd),$$
$$[a * b]c = a(bc),$$
$$[a \in b] = ba.$$

The last equation could also be written in either of the following two ways, since whenever one operator operates on another, the former may be written as a superscript (or exponent) of the latter:

$$[a \in b] = a^b,$$
$$\in ab = a^b.$$

To illustrate the use of '+', '*', and '$\in$' in connection with the numerical operators of 1.1, the following three equations will be informally derived:

$$[2 + 3]cd = 5cd,$$
$$[2 * 3]cd = 6cd,$$
$$[2 \in 3]cd = 8cd.$$

In these derivations recall that grouping not indicated by parentheses is assumed to be to the left as much as possible:

$$\begin{aligned}
[2 + 3]cd &= 2c(3cd)\\
&= c(c(3cd))\\
&= c(c(c(c(cd))))\\
&= 5cd.
\end{aligned}$$

$$[2 * 3]cd = 2(3c)d$$
$$= 3c(3cd)$$
$$= c(c(c(3cd)))$$
$$= c(c(c(c(c(cd)))))$$
$$= 6cd.$$
$$[2 \in 3]cd = 2^3cd$$
$$= 2(2(2c))d$$
$$= 2(2c)(2(2c)d)$$
$$= 2c(2c(2(2c)d))$$
$$= 2c(2c(2c(2cd)))$$
$$= c(c(2c(2c(2cd))))$$
$$= c(c(c(c(c(c(c(cd)))))))$$
$$= 8cd.$$

1.4. The operators for addition, multiplication, and exponentiation may also be applied in connection with negative integers in the system **S**, although the process is somewhat more complicated. A simple example, however, is as follows:

$$[-2 + 3]cd = -2c(3cd)$$
$$= -2c(c(c(cd)))$$
$$= cd$$
$$= 1cd.$$

1.5. Operators of the form, '$[a * b^{-1}]$', where 'a' and 'b' stand for integers, may themselves be viewed as standing for fractions or rational numbers. Other operators of appropriate form may be viewed as standing for various real numbers and complex numbers. The theory of real and complex numbers thus obtained in the system **S** is somewhat weaker than the classical theory, but it is still fairly adequate. There is no need in the system **S** to redefine addition, multiplication, and exponentiation whenever a new sort of number (e.g. negative, rational, imaginary, etc.) is defined. The same definitions of these operations work for all the number systems. These mathematical details, however, will not be included in the present paper.

1.6. The system **S** contains a descriptive operator, '$\imath$' (inverted Greek small iota), that operates on an expression denoting a unit class to give the only member of that unit class. This descriptive operator is used in defining the minus operator, ' $-$ '. It can also be used to define operators corresponding to a wide variety of other functions that cannot be defined in the usual systems of combinatory logic.

1.7. There is an over-all enumerating operator 'v' in **S** that associates each well-formed formula in **S** with exactly one positive integer.

1.8. It seems likely that the system **S** can be proved free from contradiction. An attempt to carry out this proof will not be included in the present paper.

1.9. The operators 'I', 'K', 'W', and 'C', and the operators for the positive integers are treated as defined operators in **S**, and they are defined as follows: 'I' for '00', 'C' for '$\in$**$\in$**$\in$**' (that is, for '**$\in$(**$\in$)(**$\in$)'), 'K' for C0, '1' for 'I', '2' for '1 + 1', '3' for '1 + 2', and so on, and 'W' for 'C(*2$\in$)'. As already noted, 'B' is the same as '*'.

2. The Class of Wffs and the Class of Theorems

2.1. The class of wffs (well-formed formulas) of **S** and the class of theorems of **S** will be simultaneously defined by means of a double induction (2.4–2.32 below). It seems impossible to define the class of wffs independently of the class of theorems because, for example, in order to determine whether or not '$\imath a$' is to be considered a wff, the most suitable criterion appears to be one that makes reference to theorems. The class of theorems is, of course, a subclass of the class of wffs. Neither of these two classes is decidable or even recursively enumerable, but this does not appear to the writer to be much of a disadvantage as long as consistency can be established, as seems likely. Furthermore, it is even an advantage, because thereby a serious kind of incompleteness is avoided, the kind that Gödel showed to be present in every constructively defined system.

2.2. Italic lower-case letters are used within single quotes, either singly or as parts of longer expressions within single quotes, to stand for arbitrary wffs. Hence, when single quotes are used to enclose an expression containing italic lower-case letters, reference is not being made to the actual expression between the single quotes, but rather to various expressions got from that expression by replacing the italic lower-case letters in it by wffs.

2.3. The following abbreviations will be used:

'*ab*' for '(*ab*)',
'*abc*' for '((*ab*)*c*)',
'*abcd*' for '(((*ab*)*c*)*d*)',

and so on. Also:

'[*a b c*]' for '*bac*' and hence for '((*ba*)*c*)',
'[*ab c d*]' for '*c*(*ab*)*d*',
'[*a b cd*]' for '*ba*(*cd*)',
'[*ab c de*]' for '*c*(*ab*)(*de*)',

and so on. (Notice importance of spaces on each side of the central expression within square brackets.) Outermost square brackets can be omitted if ambiguity does not result. Thus, e.g. when '[*a* = *b*]' is not part of a larger wff, it may be abbreviated as '*a* = *b*', retaining the spaces on each side of ' = '.

2.4. The primitive wffs are ' = ', '0', ' + ', '*', '∈', '∼', 'ᴠ', '∃', '*ω*', 'ι', and '*v*'. The meanings of most of these have already been indicated. ' ∼ ', 'ᴠ', '∃', and '*ω*' respectively stand for (propositional) negation, (propositional) disjunction, non-emptiness (of classes or properties), and the property of being a natural number. It is assumed that every primitive wff is a wff.

2.5. '$=a$' and '$=ab$' ('$[a = b]$', '$a = b$') are wffs (for all wffs 'a' and 'b').

2.6. '$a = a$' is a theorem (for every wff 'a').

2.7. If '$a = b$' is a theorem, then the result of replacing 'a' by 'b' or 'b' by 'a' anywhere in a wff is a wff, and the result of such a replacement in a theorem is a theorem.

2.8. '$0a$' and '$0ab$' are wffs.

2.9. '$0ab = b$' is a theorem (cp. 1.1).

2.10. '$+a$', '$+ab$' ('$[a + b]$'), and '$+abc$' ('$[a + b]c$') are wffs.

2.11. A necessary and sufficient condition for '$+abcd$' ('$[a + b]cd$') to be a wff and for '$+abcd = ac(bcd)$' to be a theorem is that '$ac(bcd)$' should be a wff.

2.12. '$*a$' and '$*ab$' ('$[a * b]$') are wffs.

2.13. A necessary and sufficient condition for '$*abc$' ('$[a * b]c$') to be a wff and for '$*abc = a(bc)$' to be a theorem is that '$a(bc)$' should be a wff.

2.14. '$\in a$' is a wff.

2.15. A necessary and sufficient condition for '$\in ab$' ('$[a \in b]$') to be a wff and for '$\in ab = ba$' to be a theorem is that 'ba' should be a wff.

2.16. '$\sim a$' is a wff.

2.17. '$\sim(\sim a)$' is a theorem iff (if and only if) 'a' is a theorem.

2.18. At least one of the wffs, 'a' and '$\sim a$', is not a theorem.

2.19. At least one of the wffs, '$a = b$' and '$\sim[a = b]$', is a theorem.

2.20. 'va' and 'vab' ('$[a \vee b]$') are wffs.

2.21. '$a \vee b$' is a theorem iff 'a' or 'b' is a theorem.

2.22. '$\sim[a \vee b]$' is a theorem iff '$\sim a$' and '$\sim b$' are theorems.

2.23. '$\exists a$' is a wff.

2.24. '$\exists a$' is a theorem iff there is a wff 'b' such that 'ab' is a wff and is also a theorem. (The requirement that 'ab' should be a wff is really superfluous since all theorems are wffs.)

2.25. '$\sim(\exists a)$' is a theorem iff, for every wff 'b' such that 'ab' is a wff, '$\sim(ab)$' is a theorem.

2.26. 'ωa' is a wff.

2.27. 'ωa' is a theorem iff there is a wff 'b' such that '$a = b$' is a theorem and 'b' is one of the wffs '0', '00 + 0', '00 + [00 + 0]', '00 + [00 + 0', and so on. The latter wffs may be said to denote respectively the natural numbers 0, 1, 2, 3, and so on.

2.28. At least one of the wffs, 'ωa' and '$\sim(\omega a)$', is a theorem.

2.29. A necessary and sufficient condition for '$\imath a$' to be a wff, and for '$b = \imath a$' to be a theorem, is that 'ab' should be a theorem and '$\sim(ac) \vee [b = c]$' should be a theorem for every wff 'c' such that 'ac' is a wff.

2.30. 'va' is a wff.

2.31. If '$va = vb$' is a theorem, so is '$a = b$'.

2.32. At least one of the following wffs is a theorem: '$va = 0$', '$va = [00 + 0]$', '$va = [00 + [00 + 0]]$', and so on.

3. ABSTRACTION

3.1. The equations given in 1.1 for 'I', 'K', 'W', 'C', and 'B' are easily shown to be theorems of **S** (for all cases where these equations are wffs), if the first four of the above operators are defined as in 1.9, and if 'B' is defined as '*'. It is also convenient to define an operator 'S' as '$C * \in^{C+}$'. Then '$Sabc = ac(bc)$' can be shown to be a theorem of **S**, provided that it is a wff, by the following steps:

$$
\begin{aligned}
Sabc &= [C * \in^{C+}]abc, \\
&= *C(C + \in)abc, \\
&= C(C + \in a)bc, \\
&= C + \in acb, \\
&= + a \in cb, \\
&= ac(\in cb), \\
&= ac(bc).
\end{aligned}
$$

3.2. If 'x' is any wff different from 'I', 'K' and 'S', and not containing an occurrence of 'I', 'K' or 'S', then the 'x'-*abstract of a wff* 'b' is defined as follows by induction:

(1) If 'x' and 'b' are the same wff, then 'I' is the 'x'-abstract of 'b'. In other words, 'I' is the 'x'-abstract of 'x'.

(2) If 'x' and 'b' are not the same wff, and if 'x' does not occur in 'b', then 'Kb' is the 'x'-abstract of 'b'.

(3) If 'x' and 'b' are not the same wff, if 'x' does occur in 'b', and if 'b' is 'cd' where 'e' is the 'x'-abstract of 'c' and 'f' is the 'x'-abstract of 'd', then 'Sef' is the 'x'-abstract of 'cd', that is, the 'x'-abstract of 'b'.

3.3 It is easy to show by induction (but will not be done here) that if 'a' is the 'x'-abstract of 'b', and if 'c' is the result of replacing 'x' by 'y' throughout 'b', then the equations '$ay = c$' and '$[y \in a] = c$' are theorems. (Also, for the special case where 'x' and 'y' are the same wff, the equations '$ax = b$' and '$[x \in a] = b$' are theorems.) If we write '$(\ldots x \ldots)$' for 'b' and '$(\ldots y \ldots)$' for 'c', and write '$\hat{x}(\ldots x \ldots)$' for the 'x'-abstract of '$(\ldots x \ldots)$' (that is, for 'a', the 'x'-abstract of 'b'), then the theorems '$ay = c$' and '$[y \in a] = c$' can be written respectively as '$\hat{x}(\ldots x \ldots)y = (\ldots y \ldots)$' and as '$[y \in \hat{x}(\ldots x \ldots)] = (\ldots y \ldots)$'. These two latter equations, especially when written in this way, will be called *abstraction equations*. For example consider the abstraction equation, '$[2 \in \hat{x}[x = 2]] = [2 = 2]$'. (It is assumed that '$x$' appears in '$x = 2$' only where explicitly shown, so that 'x' is assumed to be a different wff from '$=$' and '2', and different from each part of '2,' and of course different from 'I', 'K', and 'S', and not containing any of the latter as occurrences.)Notice that '$\hat{x} =$' (the 'x'-abstract of '$=$') is 'K$=$', while '$\hat{x}x$' is 'I', so that '$\hat{x}(=x)$' is 'S(K$=$)I'. Furthermore, '$\hat{x}2$' is 'K2', so '$\hat{x}(=x2)$' (the same as '$\hat{x}[x = 2]$') is 'S(S(K$=$)I)(K2)'. Hence the abstraction equation '$[2 \in \hat{x}[x = 2]] = [2 = 2]$' may be proved in the following steps:

$$[2 \in \hat{x}[x = 2]] = \hat{x}[x = 2]2,$$
$$= S(S(K=)I)(K2)2,$$
$$= S(K=)I2(K22),$$
$$= S(K=)I22,$$
$$= K=2(I2)2,$$
$$= K=222,$$
$$= =22,$$
$$= [2 = 2].$$

Other abstraction equations are proved in a similar way.

3.4. '&' is defined as $(\hat{x}\hat{y}(\sim[\sim x \vee \sim y])$, that is, as the '$x$'-abstract of the '$y$'-abstract of '$\sim[\sim x \vee \sim y]$'. By a double use of abstraction equations it can be shown that '$[a \& b] = \sim[\sim a \vee \sim b]$' is a theorem.

3.5. '$(\exists x)(\ldots x \ldots)$' is defined as '$\exists \hat{x}(\ldots x \ldots)$' (that is, as '$(\exists \hat{x}(\ldots x \ldots))$'), while '$(x)(\ldots x \ldots)$' is defined as '$\sim(\exists x)(\sim(\ldots x \ldots))$'. Here triple dots are being used in essentially the same way as in 3.3. The results stated as 3.6–3.8 are derived rules dealing with '&', with the existence quantifier, and with the universal quantifier.

3.6. '$a \& b$' is a theorem iff 'a' and 'b' are both theorems.

3.7. '$(\exists x)(\ldots x \ldots)$' is a theorem iff there is a wff 'a' such that '$(\ldots a \ldots)$' is a theorem (and a wff).

3.8. '$(x)(\ldots x \ldots)$' is a theorem iff '$(\ldots a \ldots)$' is a theorem for every wff 'a' such that '$(\ldots a \ldots)$' is a wff.

4. THE MINUS OPERATOR

4.1. By use of 2.29, 3.6, 3.8 and the abstraction equations of 3.3, the following result can be established: A necessary and sufficient condition for '$\imath\hat{x}(\ldots x \ldots)$' to be a wff and for '$a = \imath\hat{x}(\ldots x \ldots)$' to be a theorem is that '$(\ldots a \ldots) \& (x)[\sim(\ldots x \ldots) \vee [a = x]]$' should be a theorem (or, equivalently, that '$(\ldots a \ldots)$' should be a theorem and that

'$\sim(\ldots x \ldots) \vee [a = x]$' should be a theorem for every wff 'x' such that '$(\ldots x \ldots)$' is a wff).

4.2. The minus operator, '$-$,' is defined as '$\hat{x}\hat{y}\hat{z}(\imath\hat{w}[xyw = z])$.' By use of the abstraction equations of 3.3 it can be shown that if '$\imath\hat{w}[caw = b]$' is a wff, then '$-cab$' is a wff and '$-cab = \imath\hat{w}[caw = b]$' is a theorem.

4.3. It can also be shown that a necessary and sufficient condition for '$-cab$' to be a wff and for '$d = -cab$' to be a theorem is that '$[cad = b]$ & $(x)[\sim[cax = b] \vee [d = x]]$' should be a theorem (or, equivalently, that '$cad = b$' should be a theorem and that '$\sim[cax = b] \vee [d = x]$' should be a theorem for every 'x' such that 'cax' is a wff).

4.4. In particular, a necessary and sufficient condition for '$-1a(ab)$' to be a wff and for '$b = -1a(ab)$' to be a theorem is that '$1ab = ab$' should be a theorem (which, indeed, it is if 'ab' is a wff) and that '$\sim[1ax = ab] \vee [b = x]$' should be a theorem for every 'x' such that '$1ax$' is a wff.

4.5. Since '$1ab = ab$' is a theorem iff 'ab' is a wff, it follows from 4.4 that a necessary and sufficient condition for '$-1a(ab)$' to be a wff and for '$-1a(ab) = b$' to be a theorem is that 'ab' should be a wff and that '$\sim[ax = ab] \vee [b = x]$' should be a theorem for every 'x' such that 'ax' is a wff.

4.6. It is seen from 4.5 that '$-1a(ab) = b$' is a theorem just in case that '$-1a(ab)$' is a wff. Similarly it can be shown that each of the equations of 1.2 is a theorem just in case the left side is a wff. This amounts to saying that each of the equations of 1.2 is a theorem if that equation is a wff, since, in general, an equation is a wff if both sides are wffs. The right sides of the equations of 1.2 are wffs because it is understood that lower-case italic letters stand for wffs.

4.7. Consider '$-1=(=b)$' for any wff 'b'. This can be shown to be a wff by 4.5 because '$=b$' must be a wff and because '$\sim[=x = =b] \vee [b = x]$' is a theorem for every wff 'x' such that '$=x$' is a wff, and indeed for every wff 'x,' since '$= x$' is a wff for every wff 'x'.

4.8. In order to see that '$\sim[=x = =b]\vee[b = x]$' is a theorem for every wff 'x', observe that, by 2.19, at least one of the wffs '$=x = =b$' and '$\sim[=x = =b]$' is a theorem. If '$=x = =b$' is a theorem, then since '$=xx$' (or '$x = x$') is a theorem by 2.6, '$=bx$' (or '$b = x$') is a theorem by 2.7, replacing '$=x$' by '$=b$' in '$=xx$', and so '$\sim[=x = =b]\vee[b = x]$' is a theorem by 2.21. On the other hand, if '$\sim[=x = =b]$' is a theorem, so is '$\sim[=x = =b]\vee[b = x]$' by 2.21.

4.9. Similarly it can be shown that '$-0 = b$', '$-2 = (=(=b))$', '$-3 = (=(=(=b)))$', and so on, are wffs for every wff 'b', and that the equations '$-0 = b = b$,' '$-1 = (=b) = b$,' '$-2 = (=(=b)) = b$,' '$-3 = (=(=(=b))) = b$,' and so on, are the theorems for every wff 'b'.

4.10. In conclusion some general remarks will be made about the enumerating operator 'v.' This operator not only provides an enumeration (and hence a well-ordering) of all entities dealt with in **S**, but it also makes provision for attaining a limited sort of extensionality in the system **S**. For example, 'v' makes possible a definition of an operator 'χ' which, relatively to each operator 'b', specifies the first-enumerated operator of all those operators 'a' such that '$axy = bxy$' is a theorem for all wff 'x' and 'y' for which 'axy' and 'bxy' are wffs. Thus '$\chi b = c$' is a theorem if 'c' is this first-enumerated operator, and 'χb' would, in a sense, be the extensional counterpart of the operator 'b', since, if '$\chi bxy = \chi dxy$' for all wffs 'x' and 'y' for which 'χbxy' and 'χdxy' are wffs, then '$\chi b = \chi d$' would be a theorem.

BIBLIOGRAPHY

A. Church, *The Calculi of Lambda-Conversion*, Princeton, Princeton University Press, 1941.

H. B. Curry and R. Feys, *Combinatory Logic, 1*, Amsterdam, North Holland, 1958.

F. B. Fitch, "Combinatory Logic and Whitehead's Theory of Prehensions," *Philosophy of Science, 24* (1957), 331–35.

———, "Representations of Sequential Circuits in Combinatory Logic," ibid., *25* (1958), 263–79.

———, "A System of Combinatory Logic," Technical Report, Office of Naval Research, Group Psychology Branch, Contract No. SAR/Nonr-609(16), November, 1960.

———, "The System CΔ of Combinatory Logic," *Journal of Symbolic Logic, 28* (1963), 87–97.

S. C. Kleene, A Theory of Positive Integers in Formal Logic, *American Journal of Mathematics, 57* (1935), 153–73, 219–44.

J. B. Rosser, *Deux esquisses de Logique*, Louvain, 1955.

13. On the Concepts of Sheffer Functions

Herbert E. Hendry and Gerald J. Massey

CUSTOMARY CONCEPT OF SHEFFER FUNCTIONS

The concept of a Sheffer function, bequeathed to us in works by Martin and Salomma,[1] may be explained as follows. Let E be a nonempty set of elements. Let Ω_i be the set of all i-ary functions[2] on E, and let $\Omega = \bigcup\limits_{i=1}^{\infty} \Omega_i$. Then a set Δ_1 of functions, $\Delta_1 \subseteq \Omega$, is called a *Sheffer set* with respect to a set Δ_2 of functions, $\Delta_2 \subseteq \Omega$, if every member of Δ_2 can be defined by a finite number of compositions from the members of Δ_1. If a Sheffer set Δ_1 happens to be a singleton, the member of Δ_1 is called a *Sheffer function for* Δ_2.

ALIEN vs. INDIGENOUS SHEFFER FUNCTIONS

Consider the set Λ of all truth functions definable in a particular Lukasiewicz–Tarski many-valued C–N logic. If we

1. Norman M. Martin, "Some Analogues of the Sheffer Stroke Function in n-Valued Logic," *Indagationes Mathematicae*, 12 (1950), 393–400. Arto Salomma, "Some Analogues of Sheffer Functions in Infinite-Valued Logics," *Acta Philosophica Fennica*, 16 (1963), 227–35. See also Atwell Turquette, Review of Arto Salomma's "On the Composition of Functions of Several Variables Ranging over a Finite Set," *Journal of Symbolic Logic*, 25 (1960), 291–93.

2. In the sense used by Alonzo Church, *Introduction to Mathematical Logic*, (Princeton, Princeton University Press, 1956), *1*, 15 ff.

take $0, 1, \ldots, m$ as the set of truth-values, the functions associated with N and C are given thus: For the value i of p, the value of Np is $m - i$; and for the values i,j of p,q, the value of Cpq is 0 if $i \geq j$, and otherwise the value is $j - i$.[3] By the customary concept of a Sheffer function, Webb's binary stroke is a Sheffer function for Λ, since it serves to define every truth function in a many-valued logic, as proved in Webb.[4] (Where W is Webb's stroke function, for the values i,j of p,q, the value of Wpq is minimum $(i,j) + 1$, unless $i = j = m$; in the latter event, the value is 0.) But one might feel uncomfortable about calling Webb's stroke a Sheffer function for Λ for the well-known reason that it is not definable in terms of members of Λ. On the other hand, McKinsey's connective E is not only a Sheffer function for Λ but is also definable in terms of members of Λ, namely:

$$Epq =_{df} CpC\{CNq\}qNCqN\{Cq\}Nq$$

where the braces indicate $m - 1$ occurrences of the term inside. McKinsey's definitions of N and C run thus:[5]

$$Cpq =_{df} EpEEEqqEEqqEqqq$$

$$Np =_{df} EpEEppEEppEpp$$

The foregoing considerations prompted Quine[6] to remark that McKinsey's result differs from Webb's in that McKinsey's

3. We use 'p,' 'q,' etc., with or without subscripts as metalinguistic variables for formulas. Where there is no danger of ambiguity we will use connectives as surrogates for both their names and the associated functions.

4. Donald Webb, "Definition of Post's Generalized Negative and Maximum in Terms of One Binary Operation," *American Journal of Mathematics, 58* (1936), 193–94.

5. For proof of the adequacy of the above definition, see J. C. C. McKinsey, "On the Generation of the Functions Cpq and Np of Lukasiewicz and Tarski by means of a Single Binary Operation," *Bulletin of the American Mathematical Society, 42* (1936), 849–51.

6. W. V. O. Quine, Review of McKinsey, ibid., in *Journal of Symbolic Logic, 2* (1937), 59.

E belongs to the C–N logic whereas Webb's stroke is "foreign" to it. Following Quine's lead, then, we propose to call a set Δ_1 an *indigenous* Sheffer set for a set Δ_2 if Δ_1 is a Sheffer set for Δ_2 and, in addition, every member of Δ_1 is definable by finite composition from Δ_2. A Sheffer set Δ_1 for a set Δ_2 will be called *alien* if it is not indigenous. Thus McKinsey's E and Webb's stroke are respectively indigenous and alien Sheffer functions for Λ.

We note in passing that there exist indigenous Sheffer functions much simpler than McKinsey's for any Lukasiewicz–Tarski logic with truth values 0, 1, ..., m in which m is not an integral multiple of 3, viz., the connective D defined below:

$$\mathrm{D}pq =_{\mathrm{df}} \mathrm{C}p\mathrm{N}q$$

Proof: Let '0' abbreviate a wff which always has the value 0. Now if we could write such a wff in terms of D alone, we could define N and C thus:

$$\mathrm{N}p =_{\mathrm{df}} \mathrm{D}p0$$
$$\mathrm{C}pq =_{\mathrm{df}} \mathrm{D}p\mathrm{N}q$$

So it remains for us to show how to write a wff 0 in terms of D. Let ϕ^1 be $\mathrm{D}pp$, and let ϕ^{k+1} be $\mathrm{D}\phi^k\phi^k$. We claim that the wff $\mathrm{D}\phi^m\phi^{m+1}$, which we shall call Z, is a wff which comes out with the value 0 for every value of p, and we sketch a proof by induction of this claim. For the value i of p, it is readily verified that the value of Z is 0 if $\frac{1}{2}m \leq i$. Given this, it is easy to see that the value of Z is 0 if $i \leq \frac{1}{4}m$. Given the two preceding results, it follows that the value of Z is 0 if $\frac{3}{8}m \leq i$. Again given the two preceding results, it is easily verified that the value is 0 if $i \leq \frac{5}{16}m$; etc. By induction, it follows that the value of Z is 0 for any value of i except $i = \frac{1}{3}m$. But unless m is an integral multiple of 3, there is no truth-value $i = \frac{1}{3}m$. Thus, for the C–N logics under discussion, Z is a wff with constant value 0. The connective D is therefore an indigenous Sheffer function for such logics. (For the record we remark that D is not a

Sheffer function for $\{C,N\}$ when m = 3i, since i will then be a fixed point of D.)

SHEFFER-SPECTRUM PROBLEM

Martin[7] would reserve the title "Sheffer function" for Sheffer functions (in the above sense) which are binary. The fact that often the problem of finding indigenous ternary Sheffer functions is trivial compared to the corresponding problem for binary ones shows that there is some merit to Martin's suggested terminology. For example, the ternary function $*$, where $*(p,q,r) \equiv_{df} [\Box(p \equiv q) \supset (q \downarrow r)] \& [\sim \Box(p \equiv q) \supset \Box r]$ is an indigenous Sheffer function for *any* of the Lewis modal calculi, but indigenous binary Sheffer functions have been found only for the system S5.[8]

Proof:

$$p \downarrow q =_{df} *(p,p,q)$$
$$\sim p =_{df} p \downarrow p$$
$$\Box p =_{df} *(\sim p,p,p)$$

(The precise sense in which a connective is a Sheffer function for a modal system is explained in the next section.) But it sometimes happens that there are indigenous Sheffer functions of degree n > 2 for a set Δ of functions but no smaller degree indigenous Sheffer functions for Δ. For example, there are no singulary or binary indigenous Sheffer functions for $\{\&,\supset\}$ but there are ternary ones, e.g., $*(p,q,r) =_{df} (p \supset q) \& (p \supset r)$.

Proof:

$$p \supset q =_{df} *(p,q,q)$$
$$t =_{df} p \supset p$$
$$p \& q =_{df} *(t,p,q)$$

7. Martin, "Some Analogues of the Sheffer Stroke Function."

8. See Gerald J. Massey "Binary Connectives Functionally Complete by Themselves in S5 Modal Logic," *Journal of Symbolic Logic, 32* (1967), 91–92.

Thus we prefer not to follow Martin but rather to apply the term "Sheffer function" to Sheffer functions of arbitrary degree. (We will later liberalize the concept of a Sheffer function even further to include functions of variable degree, viz. multigrade functions.)

Attention to the degree of a Sheffer function suggests the following problem which we call the *Sheffer-spectrum problem.* Let Δ be some set of functions. Does there exist, for each positive integer n, a subset Δ_n of Δ such that there are indigenous n-ary Sheffer functions for Δ_n but no indigenous Sheffer functions of smaller degree? The Sheffer-spectrum problem is rather simple for modal systems. For example, let Δ be the set of all connectives (functions) definable in S5, and let Δ_n be $\{\otimes\}$ where $\otimes(p_1, \ldots, p_n) =_{df} \sim (\Diamond C_1 \And \Diamond C_2 \And \ldots \And \Diamond C_2{}^n)$ and $C_1, C_2, \ldots, C_2{}^n$ are the 2^n terms of the full disjunctive normal form of the tautology $(p_1 \lor \sim p_1) \lor p_2 \lor p_3 \lor \ldots \lor p_n$. Obviously $\otimes$ is itself an indigenous n-ary Sheffer function for Δ_n. Where $*$ is any m-ary connective m $<$ n definable by composition from $\otimes$, it is easy to see that $*$ is truth-functional, viz., $*$ is the m-ary truth function with constant value truth. So obviously $\otimes$ cannot be defined in terms of $*$. Thus we have a positive solution to the Sheffer-spectrum problem for S5, and *a fortiori* for any *modal* system contained in S5.

The Sheffer-spectrum problem for the set of all truth functions is much more difficult, but we can derive a positive solution to it as a corollary of the central result of the monograph Post.[9] To explain this result, which we will call *Post's Sheffer-theorem,* we need additional terminology. Where Δ_1 is an indigenous Sheffer set for a set Δ_2 of truth functions, if Δ_1 is finite and independent (no function in it is definable in terms of the others), then Δ_1 is said to be a *generator-set* for

9. Emil L. Post, *The Two-Valued Iterative Systems of Mathematical Logic,* Annals of Mathematical Studies, 5 (Princeton, Princeton University Press, 1941).

Δ_2. A generator-set is said to be of *rank* n if it contains functions of degree n but of no higher degree. A set of truth functions is said to be of *order* n if there is a rank n generator-set for it but no generator-set of lower rank for it. Post's Sheffer-theorem[10] can be stated thus:

> Every nonempty set of truth functions is of finite order. Moreover, for every positive integer n, there is a set of truth functions of order n.

Let Δ_n be a set of truth functions of order n, let Γ be a generator-set for Δ_n of rank n, and let Γ_n be the set of all the n-ary functions in Γ. And let us call a k-ary function *collapsible* if there is at least óne j-ary function, where j is any integer less than k, such that it and the given k-ary function are interdefinable. Now clearly not every member of Γ_n is collapsible, for otherwise there would be a generator-set of rank $<$ n for Δ_n, contrary to the assumption that Δ_n is of order n. So let $*$ be any of the noncollapsible members of Γ_n. We claim that for the set $\{*\}$ there is an n-ary indigenous Sheffer function, viz. $*$ itself, but that there are no indigenous Sheffer functions for $\{*\}$ of lesser degree. The latter half of the claim is also obvious, since otherwise $*$ would be collapsible. From Post's Sheffer-theorem, therefore, we have derived a positive solution to the Sheffer-spectrum problem for the set of all truth functions. We note that a positive solution to the Sheffer-spectrum problem for the Lewis modal logics follows directly from the positive solution just given for truth-functional logic. We chose, however, to give an independent and much simpler solution of the former problem.

To complete this section, we observe that there are sets of truth functions for which there are no indigenous Sheffer functions of any degree. For example, the set which contains conjunction, disjunction, and all the constant functions is such

10. Ibid., p. 94.

a set. Perhaps a more interesting example is $\{\sim, \equiv\}$. To prove that there is no indigenous Sheffer function for $\{\sim, \equiv\}$ we assume that $*$ is such a function and derive a contradiction. Suppose that $*(p_1, p_2, \ldots, p_n) \equiv \phi$ is a tautology defining $*$ in terms of $\sim$ and $\equiv$. Note first that ϕ must have an odd number of occurrences of $\sim$. Otherwise we could eliminate them two at a time, and we would be left with a definition of $*$ exclusively in terms of $\equiv$. Since $\sim$ cannot be defined in terms of $\equiv$, this is impossible. So we can reduce the number of occurrences of $\sim$ in ϕ to 1. And we are left with a formula equivalent to $\sim(p_1 \equiv p_2 \equiv \ldots \equiv p_n)$. Notice now that n is odd. For if n were even there would be an odd number of occurrences of $\equiv$, and the formula could be written equivalently as $(p_1 \not\equiv p_2 \not\equiv \ldots \not\equiv p_n)$. (Simply add tildes two at a time and distribute.) Then we would have a definition of $*$ exclusively in terms of $\not\equiv$. But, since $\equiv$ is not definable in terms of $\not\equiv$, this is impossible. At this stage it is easily verified that any result of replacing the p_i's in $*(p_1, p_2, \ldots, p_n)$ by occurrences of p and q is equivalent to either $\sim p$ or $\sim q$. Similarly it can be verified that any result of replacing the p_i's by occurrences of p, q, $\sim p$, and $\sim q$ is equivalent to p, q, $\sim p$, or $\sim q$. It follows by induction that any formula written exclusively from p, q, $*$ and parentheses is equivalent to one of p, q, $\sim p$, and $\sim q$. Thus we cannot define $\equiv$ in terms of $*$. But this contradicts our initial assumption that $*$ was a Sheffer function for $\{\sim, \equiv\}$. (Since $\{\sim, \equiv\}$ and $\{\equiv, \not\equiv\}$ are interdefinable the proof also shows that there is no indigenous Sheffer function for $\{\equiv, \not\equiv\}$.)

SYNTACTICAL CONCEPTS OF SHEFFER FUNCTIONS

Like the customary concept of a Sheffer function, the notion of an indigenous Sheffer function is a semantical concept which does not apply to formal systems directly, but does so indirectly through semantical models of such systems. For example, we may speak of the connective $\downarrow$ as an indigenous Sheffer function for a formal system of classical propositional logic since under the principal interpretation of the system the associated function of $\downarrow$ is an indigenous Sheffer function for the set of truth functions associated with the primitive and defined connectives of the system. What then are we to say of the following binary connective which serves to define all the primitive connectives (say $\sim$, $\supset$, and $\Diamond$) of a logistic system S5 and is in turn definable in terms of them? We have

$$p * q =_{df} \sim \Diamond(p \cdot q) \vee \Diamond(p \cdot q) \cdot \Diamond(p \cdot \sim q) \cdot \sim(p \cdot \sim q) \vee$$
$$\Diamond(p \cdot q) \cdot \sim \Diamond(p \cdot \sim q) \cdot \sim(p \cdot q)$$
$$\sim p =_{df} p * p$$
$$p \supset q =_{df} p * (p * q)$$
$$\Diamond p =_{df} ((\sim p * p) * p) \supset p$$

We remark that neither this connective nor its dual is the same as Massey's ✿.[11] Indeed, this $*$ is much simpler than Massey's ✿ in the sense that for any definition of ✿ in terms of *familiar* truth-functional and modal connectives there is a much simpler definition of $*$ in terms of the same connectives. The semantics of $*$ may be given by a complete set of truth tables just like the complete set given for ✿ by Massey, with the 13th and 14th tables replaced by these two tables:

p	q	$p * q$
T	T	F
F	T	T
F	F	T

p	q	$p * q$
T	F	T
F	T	T
F	F	T

The correctness of the above definitions can be verified by means of complete sets of truth tables.[12] Surely there is an

11. Massey, "Binary Connectives."

12. See Gerald J. Massey, "The Theory of Truth Tabular Connectives, Both Truth Functional and Modal," *Journal of Symbolic Logic, 31* (1966), 593–608.

important sense in which ✫ and * are *Sheffer connectives* for the S5 system: each is definable in terms of the primitive connectives of S5 and those primitives are in turn definable in terms of either. Yet on Kripke's semantics for S5,[13] neither ✫ nor * would be Sheffer connectives in the semantical sense, since Kripke's semantics do not associate (extensional) functions with modal connectives. There are, of course, characteristic infinitely many valued (extensional) Lindenbaum-type models of S5, but in most of them ✫ and * do not have indigenous Sheffer functions associated with them. But in some of the Lindenbaum models, those which are *natural* in a certain sense, the associated functions of ✫ and * are indeed indigenous Sheffer functions for the set of functions associated with the S5 primitives. For example, let $\Gamma_1, \Gamma_2, \Gamma_3, \ldots$ be a complete enumeration of the distinct equivalence classes of the wffs of the S5 system, where Γ_1 is the set of theorems, and let A_i be a particular member of Γ_i. Our truth-values will be the positive integers with 1 as the designated value. For the value i of p, the value of $\sim p$ is to be j, where $\sim A_i \in \Gamma_j$. Similarly, for the value i of p, the value of $\diamond p$ is to be j, where $\diamond A_i \in \Gamma_j$. And for the values i and j of p and q, the value of $p \supset q$ is to be k, where $(A_i \supset A_j) \in \Gamma_k$. It is apparent that under this *natural* Lindenbaum many valued characteristic interpretation, indigenous Sheffer functions are associated with ✫ and *.

The foregoing shows that one could extend the semantical concepts of a Sheffer function to modal and other non-extensional systems through the mediation of natural Lindenbaum-type models or through some analogous device. Such a move would, of course, require a precise account of naturalness. But the same end can be achieved more easily by a syntactical definition of a Sheffer connective like the following: a connective $\otimes$ will be called an (*indigenous*) *Sheffer connective*

13. S. Kripke, "A Completeness Theorem in Modal Logic," *Journal of Symbolic Logic, 24* (1959), 1–14.

for a system L if $\otimes$ can be defined in terms of the primitive connectives of L and each primitive connective of L can be defined in terms of $\otimes$.

But even such a syntactical concept of a Sheffer function is applicable only to systems which have an equivalence connective corresponding to the $\equiv$, since the usual rules of definition[14] are framed with reference to such a connective. So let us conceive of a definition of a connective in terms of a set Δ of connectives as an effective rule R for rewriting an arbitrary atomic formula B in which the connective occurs so as to get a formula R(B) in which only connectives in Δ occur. And consider a system L with primitive connectives Δ, together with a definition of each member of Δ in terms of $\otimes$ and a definition of $\otimes$ in terms of the members of Δ. Then we might say that the connective $\otimes$ is an *indigenous Sheffer function for* the system L if

(a) for every theorem A of L, R(ϕ(A)) is a theorem of L, and

(b) for every nontheorem A of L, R(ϕ(A)) is a nontheorem of L,

where R represents the definition of $\otimes$ in terms of the members of Δ and where ϕ(A) represents the result of rewriting A, by means of the definitions of the members of Δ, so as to yield a formula which contains no connectives except $\otimes$. This syntactical concept, however, is only as definite as is the notion of a connective.

MULTIGRADE CONNECTIVES

A given connective of a formal system is customarily permitted to attach only to a fixed number n of argument-expressions to form a wff; we will call such connectives *unigrade*

14. See Patrick Suppes, *Introduction to Logic* (Princeton, Van Nostrand Co., 1962).

connectives. We wish now to consider connectives which attach to any finite number of argument-expressions to form a wff; such connectives will be called *multigrade* connectives. (It is evident that there is a parallel distinction for operators of other sorts.)[15] Because of the prejudice mentioned in the first sentence of this section, the bulk of familiar examples of multigrade operators are to be found in informal mathematics and ordinary language. Perhaps the simplest examples are the set-forming operator '{...}' and the ordered n-tuple-forming operator '⟨...⟩,' for the following expressions are all clearly grammatical:

$\{1,3,5\}, \{1,2\}, \{4,10,5,2\}, \langle 1,1 \rangle, \langle 1,2,1 \rangle, \langle 3,3,3,4 \rangle.$

The English connectives 'and' and 'or' are also multigrade. Consider:

The Orioles will take first, the Tigers second, and (or) the Yankees last.

But the multigrade connectives pop up occasionally even in formal languages; e.g. the → of Gentzen-type systems is multigrade (but restricted in certain ways).

We shall confine our somewhat cursory and informal discussion of multigrade operators to unrestricted multigrade connectives in formal systems. For these connectives we need a grammatical rule of the following sort: If ⊗ is a multigrade connective, then for every positive integer k, if $A_1, \ldots, A_k$ are wffs, the expression $\otimes(A_1 \ldots A_k)$ is a wff.[16] (Note that multi-

15. We borrow the term 'multigrade' from Leonard and Goodman, "The Calculus of Individuals," *Journal of Symbolic Logic*, 5 (1940), 45–55. But in that essay it is used to refer not to connectives but to relations and predicates. There the authors were concerned with the calculus of individuals as a device to handle special problems involved in the introduction of such predicates into constructional systems.

16. One might choose to let k be 0. In this event, ⊗ would behave as a constant in its 0-ary use. Also one might allow connectives whose behavior is more erratic, e.g. connectives that take at most n arguments or connectives that take only an odd number of arguments.

grade connectives cannot be accommodated unambiguously in parenthesis-free notation.) For example, consider a propositional logic P with the multigrade conjunction connective &. The following are all wffs of P:

$$(\&(pqr) \equiv \&(\&(pq)\&(pr)\&(p)))$$
$$(\&(pqr) \equiv ((p \cdot q) \cdot r))$$
$$\&(pq)$$
$$\&(\&(p)\&(q)).$$

Let us call a denumerable set Σ of unigrade (truth-functional) connectives a (*truth-functional*) *semantic set* if, for each positive integer k, there is exactly one k-ary connective in Σ. We will say that a semantic set Σ *expresses* a multigrade connective $\otimes$ if, for every positive integer k, $\otimes(p_1 \ldots p_k)$ is equivalent to $*_k(p_1 \ldots p_k)$, where $*_k$ is the k-ary unigrade connective in Σ. We will call a multigrade connective *truth-functional* if a truth-functional semantic set expresses it. For example, the multigrade & is truth-functional since it is expressed by the semantic set consisting of the singulary assertion connective together with, for each j > 1, the j-ary unigrade conjunction connective. If we "identify" multigrade connectives expressed by the same semantic set, it is readily seen that there is a continuum of multigrade truth-functional connectives.

Let us assign positive integers as Gödel-numbers to the unigrade truth functional connectives, thus enabling us to regard semantic sets as (infinite) sets of positive integers. A truth-functional connective will be said to be (*recursively*) *definable* if it is a unigrade connective or if it is a multigrade connective for which there is a recursive semantic set which expresses it. Obviously the number of definable truth-functional connectives is denumerable. Now if we understand definition in the liberalized sense of the last paragraph of the previous section, it follows that $\downarrow$ is an indigenous Sheffer function for the set of definable truth-functional connectives.

To see this, let $\otimes$ be a definable multigrade connective. Using a recursive semantic set for $\otimes$, one can readily formulate an effective rule which instructs one how to eliminate $\otimes$ in favor of $\downarrow$ in each of the denumerably many atomic contexts of $\otimes$ which differ among themselves in respect to the number of argument-expressions. Hence each (recursively) definable truth-functional connective, unigrade or multigrade, is definable in terms of $\downarrow$. Wittgenstein's multigrade N is also a Sheffer function for the set of definable truth-functional connectives.[17] (The value of $N(p_1 \ldots p_k)$ is truth if falsehood is assigned to each p_i, and is falsehood otherwise. For we have $p \downarrow q =_{df} N(pq)$.)

Although *any* particular definable truth-functional connective could be introduced by definition into a logistic system of propositional logic with $\downarrow$ as sole primitive connective, it is not the case that *all* could be so introduced. For suppose that there is a logistic system L in which all the definable truth-functional connectives have been defined in terms of $\downarrow$. Let S be $\otimes_1, \otimes_2, \ldots$ where $\otimes_1, \otimes_2, \ldots$ is in order of their introduction into L a complete enumeration of the definable multigrade truth-functional connectives. Clearly S is effectively enumerable; otherwise the definitional rules of L would lack the requisite effectiveness. Let $*$ be the multigrade connective such that, for each positive integer k, $*(p_1 \ldots p_k)$ is equivalent to $\&(p_1 \ldots p_k)$ unless $\otimes_k(p_1 \ldots p_k)$ is also equivalent to $\&(p_1 \ldots p_k)$; in this latter event $*(p_1 \ldots p_k)$ has the constant value falsehood. Clearly $*$ is a truth-functional multigrade connective which is not in S. And since there is obviously a recursive semantic set which expresses $*$, it follows that $*$ is (recursively) definable, and hence that S does not contain all definable truth-functional multigrade connectives, which

17. See L. Wittgenstein, *Tractatus Logico-Philosophicus*, Eng. trans. D. Pears and B. McGuinness (London, Routledge, 1961), propositions 5.501–5.51.

contradicts our initial assumption. (We have, of course, appealed to Church's thesis in this informal treatment.)

Multigrade modal connectives can be given a treatment exactly parallel to the one just given multigrade truth-functional connectives. That is, corresponding notions of a semantic set and of (recursive) definability could be formulated, and corresponding results could be established. For example, for any of the common Lewis modal calculi it could be shown that there is a continuum of multigrade connectives, and that $\{\downarrow, \diamondsuit\}$ is an indigenous Sheffer set for the definable connectives of the system, etc. For each of these systems, there will be many multigrade Sheffer connectives for the set of definable connectives of the system. For example, the multigrade connective $*$ is such a Sheffer connective, where $*(p)$ is equivalent to $\diamondsuit p$ and where, for any $k > 1$, $*(p_1 \ldots p_k)$ is equivalent to $N(p_1 \ldots p_k)$.

Proof:

$$\diamondsuit p =_{df} *(p)$$
$$p \downarrow q =_{df} *(pq)$$

BIBLIOGRAPHY

Church, Alonzo, *Introduction to Mathematical Logic, 1* (Princeton, Princeton University Press, 1956).

Kripke, S., "A Completeness Theorem in Modal Logic," *Journal of Symbolic Logic, 24* (1959), 1–14.

Leonard, Henry S., and Nelson Goodman, "The Calculus of Individuals," *Journal of Symbolic Logic, 5* (1940), 45–55.

Martin, Norman M., "Some Analogues of the Sheffer Stroke Function in n-Valued Logic," *Indagationes Mathematicae, 12* (1950), 393–400.

Massey, Gerald J., "The Theory of Truth Tabular Connectives, Both Truth Functional and Modal," *Journal of Symbolic Logic, 31* (1966), 593–608.

————, "Binary Connectives Functionally Complete by Themselves in S5 Modal Logic," *Journal of Symbolic Logic*, *32* (1967), 91–92.

McKinsey, J. C. C., "On the Generation of the Functions Cpq and Np of Lukasiewicz and Tarski by means of a Single Binary Operation," *Bulletin of the American Mathematical Society*, *42* (1936), 849–51.

Post, Emil L., *The Two-Valued Iterative Systems of Mathematical Logic*, Annals of Mathematical Studies, 5 (Princeton, Princeton University Press, 1941).

Quine, W. V. O., review of McKinsey, "On the Generation . . . Binary Operations," *Journal of Symbolic Logic*, *2* (1937), 59.

Salomma, Arto, "Some Analogues of Sheffer Functions in Infinite-Valued Logics," *Acta Philosophica Fennica*, *16* (1963), 227–35.

Suppes, Patrick, *Introduction to Logic* (Princeton, Van Nostrand, 1962).

Turquette, Atwell, review of Arto Salomma's "On the Composition of Functions of Several Variables Ranging over a Finite Set," in *Journal of Symbolic Logic*, *25* (1960), 291–93.

Webb, Donald, "Definition of Post's Generalized Negative and Maximum in Terms of One Binary Operation," *American Journal of Mathematics*, *58* (1936), 193–94.

Wittgenstein, L., *Tractatus Logico-Philosophicus*, Eng. trans. D. Pears and B. McGuinness (London, Routledge, 1961).

Postscript
Henry Leonard at
Michigan State University

William J. Callaghan

I propose to give here an account of Henry Leonard's work as a teacher and administrator (specifically, as a department chairman) at Michigan State University. This is a little odd, since such employments, the second sort especially, are often viewed as very minor parts of a philosophic career. Reasons for viewing them dimly are not hard to find. Nevertheless Henry Leonard took this work seriously, so seriously that he sacrificed to it a good part of his purely philosophic potential. Why he did this, in the particular place he chose, and whether it was a good thing to do—these are questions that might come to mind, and so provide excuse for the following brief memoir. A good deal of that will necessarily consist of personal recollections.

Long before Leonard came to Michigan State University I was able to form some notion of his remarkable talents both as a teacher and as a philosopher. This came about through the good luck of drawing him as my tutor when I was a sophomore at Harvard. The year was 1934, and Leonard was then three years past the award of his Ph.D. About that time, there was an astonishing concentration of most able young philosophers at Harvard, all at roughly the same state in their professional

development. There was Leonard himself, William Frankena,
Paul Henle, Charles Stevenson, Willard Van Orman Quine,
John Goheen, Nelson Goodman, Arnold Isenberg—and the
list could be extended. We youngsters were more in awe of
them than of the illustrious senior members of the faculty. I
was, therefore, surprised and relieved to find Leonard so
pleasant and affable, so concerned to have me discover my
proper direction, not at all anxious to point me along his own
course. My interests were then heavily historical. Exploring
them under Leonard's supervision, I found myself studying
and using analytical and logical techniques of the then most
contemporary philosophy, techniques which—in my green
confidence—I had dismissed as irrelevant to any truly philosophical investigations. Leonard never argued for the general
validity and effectiveness of analytic methods—those values
simply became apparent in working along the natural grain of
the subject-matter.

I mentioned this because it was my only close view of
Leonard's remarkable skill and fairness as a teacher (one's
knowledge of a colleague's teaching procedures is always
indirect and limited). Later I could have observed that his
students preserved—even developed—their individual styles
while working with him. I might not have recognized, however, that this was his aim. And I might have supposed that this
was all Leonard aimed at, which would have been a mistake.
In fact he was seriously committed to an ethics of inquiry, one
compatible with very diverse techniques and objectives. Its
central precepts, however, had to be deduced from his practice,
since he did not fancy himself in the role of Moses, with his
students cast as chosen people.

In any event, he was remarkable as a teacher not through his
advocating such and such broad norms for inquiry but through
his ability to do something more difficult and more effective:
to hit upon the determinate mode of applying such a norm to

an actual piece of work in progress. That is the difficult trick, and Leonard was uniquely expert at it; and expert without evasion or cheating, without constricting the range of inquiry to match the capacities of familiar techniques, or distorting materials and results in accordance with methodological preconceptions.[1] What one directly learned from Leonard was how to work effectively at philosophic problems. One arrived indirectly at his view of the overall norms for philosophy as an activity. Some of these norms or maxims might be roughly phrased as follows. It is wrong to work with vaguely formulated concepts (heaven knows what stupidities may lurk in their murky intensions). The structures of key propositions must be carefully blueprinted (no conscientious builder of any complex structure would frame it at random). It cannot be assumed that one set of tools, with their special operating directions, is adequate for every task (thus *Principia Mathematica* could not be taken as the universal manual for practising philosophers). Again, no part of philosophy is completely insulated from any other (or from the total body of theory and practice). Today and tomorrow one may need to concentrate wholly on logic, but on some future day ontology (or X-ology) may decisively intrude.

These remarks have a strongly "practical" tone. The implicit code of an expert and responsible engineer or architect or shipwright would involve very similar maxims. And in fact Leonard—and also C. I. Lewis, his teacher and close friend—

1. A lecture course, given several times at Michigan State from about 1960 on, gave display to these gifts. Centering on *Process and Reality*, Leonard produced a clarification and systematization of Whitehead's concepts, working presuppositions and objectives which was a marvel of lucidity, meticulous analysis, sympathetic insight into another man's intentions, and philosophic resourcefulness. He imparted to Whitehead's system an altogether surprising degree of compatibility to ordinary reasonableness, as well as a pretty thoroughgoing cohesiveness. Neither of these qualities immediately strikes the eye on inspection of the source works.

always represented to me the best type of New Englander, a type of which Thoreau is a mutilated specimen. I am thinking of the cool, independent, resourceful, nonhistrionic individuals (and the smallest towns produced them), who built all those cleanly beautiful meetinghouses, all those magnificent sailing ships. Their complete, clearsighted and imaginative control of the materials and methods available to them is the impressive thing. It was this high standard of workmanship that Leonard passed on to his pupils.[2]

Now, where this sort of teaching is concerned, the situations are pretty similar whether one is talking about philosophy or— say—architecture. It is quite likely that the bad or indifferent worker in architecture will, in all felt sincerity, profess adherence to the same values and objectives which the expert realizes in his work. What is lacking in the former is the knowledge or energy or imagination to find the determinate modes of applying higher-level directives to the actual enterprise in hand. For example, few philosophers employ hazy or badly defined terms as a matter of principle. But probably still fewer have attended to the modes and functions of definitory devices with Leonard's carefulness, energy and system. And, Lord knows, there are strong temptations to stray unwittingly from the path of this virtue, and to produce slapdash clumsy work. Leonard's students became acutely aware of the manifold occasions for this kind of sinning and of the conscious intellectual practices which were the only guards against them. The best of his students were led to aim at one thing: fully conscious and carefully maintained control over whatever

2. Amusingly, but rightly, Leonard had an actual (one might say "personal") fondness for Socrates, based on this shared respect for intelligent competence in serious trades. He once scandalized a culture-struck class by referring to Socrates as a "cracker-barrel philosopher." When a solemn delegation visited him to protest this insult to an ancient sage, Leonard was scandalized in turn at their low estimate of the importance of cracker-barrel philosophizing.

instruments and themes were involved in the area of philosophic work they elected as their own.

The above is the best (a very poor best) that I can do in the way of suggesting the special quality and excellence of Leonard's teaching. It is probably intrinsically difficult to speak precisely, or even very usefully, on such matters. Otherwise pedagogics would not be the dark art which it is, with so very many painful failures to its account. Not that even the finest teacher does not have his failures, or at least encounter areas and situations in which his results fall below his highest achievements elsewhere. Thus Leonard was the best teacher I have ever known for groups of a size and quality to permit him to use his special gifts to effect his special aims. Thanks to extraordinary ingenuity and resourcefulness, his actual range was very broad. The giant, randomly collected lecture class, however, is by nature inimical to his kind of talent. His work under such conditions was solid and effective but always a little abrasive to his nerves. And he not only did not want but thought it intellectually immoral to employ the rhetorical and dramatic devices probably essential to the kind of teaching often described as "inspirational". No answer, in short, to the prayers of the assembly-line educationists for a lecturer whose potency can be enlarged simply by increasing the wattage of the public address system or the spread of the closed-circuit television network. Leonard's results were precisely those which cannot be achieved by increased efficiency in the reproduction of sign-tokens—whether by Gutenberg's or some later invention.

So much for the overall character of Leonard's teaching, in prelude to writing of particular occurrences at Michigan State University.[3] Leonard was asked and agreed to go there in

3. To be accurate, he joined not Michigan State University but Michigan State College. The single land-grant institution denoted by both titles did not adopt its present one until 1956. Until 1927, it had presented itself—with simple honesty—as Michigan Agricultural College.

1949. Until a short time before, psychology and philosophy had existed in East Lansing as a single, joint department. Such academic Siamese twins were at that time too common to be exhibited as curiosities. This invitation was to chair[4] an essentially new department with hardly any staff, with a program that was largely impromptu, caught up inside a mushrooming state institution, one heavily practical (or serviceable) in its overall aims. Almost certainly its administration would take an old-fashioned view of philosophy, would probably expect quantities of bad Royce—nondenominational lay preaching that was solemn, dialectical, declamatory, and irrelevant to either scientific or executive activities.

Both at the time and later, many of Leonard's friends were surprised and a little puzzled at his undertaking so chancey a venture. Certainly its chancey aspects were recognized by him, and he laid them out plainly to me in the process of inviting me to join his new department. But it was also clear, for all his low-key manner, that he found the possibilities of the situation attractive. "Wouldn't it be exciting to see what could be done?" To see, that is, what philosophy in its actual contemporary forms could and should accomplish in an aggressively modern state university with a large and growing variety of programs and interests. In the ten or twelve years since I had last seen Leonard, years almost entirely spent in nonscholarly activities, I had become rather naïvely concerned about the contribution philosophy could make to society at large. That society seemed less rational, less willing critically to assess beliefs and proposals for action, than was necessary or safe. In fact

4. Accuracy demands another aside: Leonard came not as "Chairman" but as "Head" of the department. Some dozen years later, as a by-product of a most mannerly faculty struggle for increased influence upon academic policies, heads lost their old, temporally unlimited authority, and took new titles—suggestive of a novel responsibility to the consensus of departmental aims and opinions.

Leonard himself had contributed to the development of this concern, as I realized later. At the time, however, I was surprised at his having such serious social aims; and, of course, reassured, delighted, and most ready to accompany him. It had hitherto seemed steadily the case that socially conscious philosophers were, nearly all of them, dogmatic doctrinaires, conspicuously unlikely to increase the public supply of reasonableness. But Leonard took this to be both possible and necessary, viewed it as a duty entirely compatible with those others involved in sound professional practice. Michigan State attracted him as being an environment where valuable results could be produced by the diffusion within it of principles of right reason. This is a simplistic and quixotic way of expressing his attitude, and he would have added all sorts of qualifications, but it does describe the simple core of it.

Violent postwar changes were well under way when Leonard arrived at Michigan State. There the general scheme of things had long been markedly paternalistic and authoritarian. The great G.I. invasion was just about at its peak in 1949. Already it had relaxed the strict old patterns, as far as student life and work were concerned. These soldiers-become-students had been, most of them, members of the swarming subculture of enlisted men. They were perfectly trained in the techniques of defending themselves against authority and of extracting creature comforts from whatever environment they found themselves in. Restrictive, *in loco parentis* regulations were circumvented with ease. Inadequate subsidies were eked out by skillful foraging raids upon the rich agricultural stations so providentially near to hand. Young lambs and calves, sucking pigs, poultry (all of distinguished blood-lines), the wild ducks on the campus-threading Red Cedar—these provided welcome, unofficial supplements to a diet which might else have proved monotonous. Their grouped hutments formed a sizeable village, the Temporary Housing Area, and they set up a City

Council which managed its affairs with firm and competent ingenuity.

A liberalized society for faculty members was much slower in coming. Differences in academic rank were consequential, but the distinction between a full professor and the least of the administrators had generic import. Department heads, for example, enjoyed the status, nearly, of hereditary chieftains of primitive clans. Their appointments owed scarcely anything to approval by the department's staff, and, once installed, they held their posts until death, retirement, or promotions transported them to different spheres. While they reigned, their capacities for rendering subordinates' lives miserable approximately equalled those of a first mate on a late-nineteenth-century square-rigger. And, stacked above them, were layers and layers of more tremendous authorities: directors of divisions, assistant deans, associate deans, deans, and still more august, figures, too august, really, for casual naming. To make matters more unsettling, no one not included in the upper hierarchy had the slightest understanding of the pecking-order which prevailed there.[5]

There is no need to point out how queer a setting this was for Henry Leonard. Still he was much better prepared to cope with it than casual acquaintances would have supposed. In spite of the almost quaint formality of his manners, he was an immense success with the turbulent G.I. element in the student body. They quickly perceived that he matched their own standards for independence and resourcefulness. His spontaneous, though invariable, courtesy also made a pleasant contrast to the glum, mechanical etiquette of the military establishment.

5. This caused genuine practical problems. Leonard once had to arrange a consultation involving three deans, etc. who ruled provinces with vast but vague boundaries. The meeting could not be laid on until he had acquired a room equipped with a perfectly square (or it may have been perfectly circular) table, around which all three could sit in obvious positional equality.

From the beginning, departmental decisions were arrived at in New England town-meeting style, with Leonard displaying no more pomp and stateliness than the moderator of such a session. Yankee equalitarianism, self- and other-respecting, was in his blood. Principles of this democratic sort were not only much to his credit but practically advantageous as well: this if only because the two already-on-the-scene members of the department were themselves nonauthoritarian types.[6] They were prepared to, and did, make the most strenuous contributions to a common enterprise in which each man had the full personal and professional respect of every other. By the same token, neither would have collaborated in the building of an academic satrapy. Since our group, including Leonard, numbered only four, procedural pomp and circumstance would have been absurd as well as annoying. (Not, however, unprecedented; subminiature reproductions of the court of the Sun King did then exist on our campus.)

We did not, however, adjust our aims and ambitions to our size. Leonard's belief that the business of philosophers was to be *generally* reasonable, to be concerned with the rationality of the methods and results of inquiry in the fields of chief human importance, attracted us all. With such (as I should say now) ingenuously confident aims, the risk of biting off more than one could chew simply had to be accepted. So Leonard began by designing a course program that stretched our resources to the limit. From the start (for practical considerations to be mentioned later) this program ran through the two graduate degrees. It involved a sheer quantity of teaching that was intimidating; even more daunting was the spread of subjects over which it ranged. Not every new thing that was needed was needed at once. Still, much more needed to be got under

6. The elder of this truly invaluable pair was the late John DeHaan, killed together with his wife in a highway accident in 1957. His much younger colleague, Lewis K. Zerby, is still a member of the department.

way than, on the face of it, we were qualified and trained to do. And we certainly did not think that, just because (say) a course in aesthetics would assist our overall and long-range aim to rationalize the university, we should be justified in laying on a bad course in aesthetics.

Down-Easters used to be, on good grounds, famous for their tact and ingenuity in managing things and materials. They could improvise, "make do," extract the utmost from the available resources. Leonard showed just such a Yankee knack in deploying the human resources available to him. One colleague (according to all his working papers, a Plato and Aristotle specialist) nursed a suppressed desire to teach a class in traditional logic. Another had a surprising, and surprisingly useful, side interest (in, say, Kant, where his special field was philosophy of science). A third could be lured into extended discussions of the "right way" to teach something or other totally unrepresented in his past pedagogical history. Leonard made adroit use of such clues and lures. The results should have ranged from poor to disastrous. In fact they were surprisingly good,[7] and a great deal of lively and valuable work was done. Leonard himself took part in these ventures into more or less alien fields. He taught a Plato course one year and a course in Leibniz a couple of years later. Both were real successes. But the really impressive thing was his alertness to the real (rather than the certified) competencies of his associates.

The departmental program which Leonard instituted, in scrupulously constant consultations with staff, was sound and comprehensive but not particularly novel. The immediate

7. The effects on individual careers were a different, less cheerful story. Even Leonard, very creative and most hard working, produced scarcely anything for publication until 1959, when—at Gödel's invitation—he began a two-year stay at the Princeton Institute for Advanced Studies. At the end of that period, his appointment to one of the four University Professorships maintained at Michigan State finally left him free to concentrate on philosophical researches. That release, as it turned out, came sadly late.

introduction of a two-term sequence in what was then identified as "mathematical" (or "symbolic", or "contemporary")
logic did strike some of our colleagues in the humanities as a
radical move. Identifying *Principia Mathematica* as the *Das
Kapital* of the Logical Positivist movement, they tagged us all
as party members. This, though far from a slander, was a
mistake, and one that complicated our working relations with
the English, History and Literature departments for many
years. A second and major constituent of our first program
was a three-term sequence in the history of philosophy. A
third was a freshman introduction, not to logic, but to the
requirements of sound and effective reasoning in general.
Cooperatively taught but planned by Leonard, this course
generated his book, *Principles of Right Reason.*

The book and the course both broke sharply from established patterns for dealing with beginners in philosophy. The
nature of the break was neatly and accurately defined by
James Wilkinson Miller in a review of the *Principles.*

> This excellent book is an extreme instance of the ten-
> dency, evident in many introductions, of taking logic as
> the nucleus, and surrounding it with a mass of material
> drawn from other subjects. But whereas in many older
> texts this eking out of logic has all the appearance of
> padding, Leonard knows exactly what he is doing, and
> fits contributions of semiotic, methodology, epistemology
> and logic into a coherent and purposeful whole.[8]

It was that coherent whole which Leonard viewed as important; pure logic—in spite of the gifts for the subject evidenced
by his contributions to it—struck him as having its greatest
value only in a wider philosophic context.

Still, the boundaries of that larger complex within which
logic acquired philosophic significance had an alarming

8. *Journal of Symbolic Logic, 23* (1958), 435–36.

tendency to swell and swell. "Darn it!," he once remarked, "everything creeps out and latches on to everything else!" And the *Principles of Right Reason*, though trimmed as far as his conscience allowed, considerably exceeded the average diameter of a freshman student's gullet. Neither the book nor the course was a complete success for the majority of these students. Both, however, had great value for a superior minority, and brought us many really brilliant young departmental majors.

Of course, no amounts of effort and ingenuity could produce a truly adequate program with only four men working in it. And it was a long time before staff additions produced any lessening of the average load. Instead the arrival of a new colleague was the signal for putting in new courses. Grave overburdening remained the rule until about 1956, the year in which we awarded our first Ph.D. degree. From then on the tide began, very slowly, to turn.[9]

I shall speak only briefly of those administrative performances of Leonard's which involved mainly extradepartmental relations. Some of these, though remote, were important. It was, for example, a genuine contribution to the development of Michigan State merely to maintain a department whose members were treated and worked together as professional

---

9. Some mention (brief as it has to be in the context) must be made of these men whose work so greatly aided Leonard's aims. And even the mere listing of their names, arrival dates, and specialities roughly indicates the pattern (and the painfully slow rate) of the department's growth. So I give these data:

Donald K. Marshall	1950	Plato and Aristotle
John F. A. Taylor	1952	Aesthetics and Ethics
Harold T. Walsh	1955	Logic, Contemporary Philosophy
Richard S. Rudner	1956	Philosophy of Science
Paul M. Hurrell	1957	Philosophy of Religion, History of Philosophy

equals.[10] Again, thanks to his post, Leonard could and did give valuable reinforcement to a liberal and energetic minority within a disturbingly passive academic senate. This really counted. The upper administration was much less opposed to change than the faculty pessimistically supposed. The chief opposition, often in Leonard's and other cases bitterly personal, came from old-guard members of the middle corps of officers—the academic equivalents of majors and lieutenant-colonels. Had this group not been infiltrated by liberals of Leonard's type and firmness, increase in the range and degree of faculty control over academic affairs would have proceeded at an intolerably slow rate. In fact, by the end of Leonard's administrative career, very considerable advances had been made.

State universities (especially in a state where there are several large ones, all rapidly expanding) present some administrative problems of a distracting sort. The universities as units compete to extract from the legislature the largest possible share of the total budget allocated for their collective support. Within each university, there is equally strenuous competition between the separate colleges, divisions, departments, etc. Where the character of a university is undergoing rapid change, such competition becomes almost desperate. And Michigan State, during Leonard's years, existed in a state of flux that would have unnerved Heraclitus. The College of Agriculture, long rich and powerful, was declining in importance, due to massive and rapid changes in the state's economy and population patterns. Explosive increases in the population

10. It would be wrong to suggest that Leonard's department was the only one of this character. There were others. The departments of English (under Russel Nye) and History (headed by Walter Fee) were eminently civilized communities among our near neighbors in the College of Arts and Science. But there also survived a good number of the antique fiefdoms; also, traditions and regulations were such that a change in the headship could always bring about a relapse into despotism.

of our schools set our College of Education to growing at the rate of Jack's beanstalk. The pure sciences, steadily outpacing by steadily greater margins the manuals for their application, forced radical changes in both the methods and the fields of scientific work. Other broad cultural changes made it imperative to undertake serious programs in humanistic studies; and so on and so on, while all the time more and more students crowded in. The result was a situation in which old patterns of priorities for support disintegrated. The future was so uncertain that no new guidelines of any clarity could be laid down. Administrators at every level were caught in a *sauve-qui-peut* struggle for money and for official endorsement of their projects for the future.

Any head of department had reason to dread these melées. Deans, by comparison, fought deadly but dignified combats with their peers. Each had a quite limited number of serious opponents to assail or guard against. For directors of divisions matters were more difficult, but for a department head they were nearly intolerable, and not merely because he was at the bottom of the heap. On the higher levels, what was at issue was the total budget for a corporate entity—a college, a division, a department. It was much harder to take the outcome cooly when it directly determined ranks and salaries for known individuals, with whom one worked side by side in a shared professional endeavor. To a man of Leonard's sensitivity and scruples, the failure to achieve an adequate budget for his department could be most painful and discouraging.

Some departments (and divisions and colleges) sallied out upon these foraging expeditions from well-protected bases, with small likelihood of really damaging defeat. That they had important and continuing roles to play in the university's growth was an acknowledged fact. Their roles were fairly well defined or rapidly became so. Agriculture, education, the natural sciences (especially in their applied aspects), business administration—these and some others enjoyed such favorable situations. Novel enterprises which clearly linked on to such established concerns (e.g. the School of Packaging, a natural accessory to both Business and Agriculture) could count on sharing their prosperity from the very start. The social sciences prospered less well and less uniformly. Economics (agricultural and plain) was in good state; so also—thanks to generous federal subventions—was political science. Some others, e.g. psychology, had nearly as many downs as ups.

That vaguely defined collection of studies often called the humanities was distinctly disadvantaged. The decision to cultivate these fields of scholarship had been recent and un-enthusiastic. The university had a long tradition[11] of hard-headed practicality which generated scepticism with regard to the value of purely liberal inquiries and exercises. For-tunately, many of the liberal arts had something besides their intrinsic merits to justify the expenditure they involved. After all, English, foreign languages, history, even art and music, were taught in the primary and secondary schools. And the training of teachers was a major postwar obligation at Michigan State as at most other large tax-supported educa-tional establishments. But philosophy could urge no such claim to a share in the tax dollars of frugal and industrious Michiganders. To all appearances it was totally and brazenly impractical.

11. Curiously, the founding fathers of Michigan Agricultural College held wider and more generous views of education. One of its earliest presidents, Theophilus C. Abbot (in office from 1862 to 1885), taught English, history, and philosophy (with a special—and acute—interest in inductive logic and the methodology of science). He opened his house to students, and delighted in reading Shakespeare and Milton with them. Cf. Madison Kuhn, *Michigan State The First Hundred Years* (East Lansing, Michigan, M.S.U. Press, 1956), pp. 89–90.

It must also be remembered that our principal administrators took a rather old-fashioned view of philosophy.[12] By and large, "philosophy" signified to them what is sometimes spoken of as "life philosophy"—religious-toned, dialectically argued, artificially impassioned discourse in support of conventional theses in theology, politics, and morals. Such discourse has a close affinity to the orations traditionally laid on for the Fourth of July or Mother's Day. In all decency, a certain part of the community budget should be made available to these orators, but in all prudence that part should be small.

It was within such an institutional and attitudinal context that Leonard undertook to build a philosophy department at Michigan State. Everything was in short supply—students, staff, catalogued course offerings, working quarters, and operating budget. And each shortage made all the others more trying. We all agreed with Leonard that it was precisely such large and multifarious universities as our own that required wide-ranging programs in philosophy, at both graduate and undergraduate levels. But the programs needed to be planned and manned and shown to be valuable to large enrollments, so as to convince the administration to provide us the funds that would permit us to carry out just those actions. A systematic, long-range plan for meeting such difficulties was out of the question. We had to proceed like someone working on a terribly tangled and snarled fishline. A little slack here would be used to undo a twist there, and so on.

12. Very old-fashioned indeed: years after Leonard's first struggles to establish the department, an administrator at one of the many levels overlaying ours inquired, in honest startlement, "But since when has philosophy had anything to do with science?" The answer, "Since Thales," was tactless and no help. One freakish episode in the history of philosophy, nineteenth-century idealism, had produced a deep and lasting blindness with respect to philosophy's long-run aims.

Fortunately, the history of such an operation can only be outlined, not detailed, since in detail it would be as maddening as the original work. In general, Leonard's first and major effort was to install good courses that would bring us good students, both majors for our own department and minors in departments to which our work had real relevance. This he managed, as I have already said, by a finesse and ingenuity that compensated for extremely limited staff resources. He was also extremely shrewd in establishing, at the very start, a program of graduate studies. That struck some of us as very rash, but it was a thoroughly sensible move. The best of our graduate students, installed[13] as teaching assistants and assistant instructors, permitted a substantial increase in enrollments. And out of this came the increases in our budget which, as they slowly accumulated, made it possible to bring in new permanent staff. Smaller, but still necessary, gains also required elaborate planning and maneuvering. The acquisition of an ancient but functional mimeograph machine, for example, was a not-too-minor triumph. And that surely carries me as far into detail as is tolerable. The point is this: working with fantastically limited resources, Leonard had by 1959 built up a really solid department of philosophy, with a full and carefully designed program of courses, and a large student

13. "Installed" has a matter-of-course connotation which fails to do justice to the facts. For many years, our budget made provision for only one teaching assistant. The University, however, had "extension" and "adult education" classes underway throughout the whole state of Michigan. We acquired some of this work, on the thin fiction that the teacher was being compensated by "released time plus travel costs." In such cases, the department, not the man, received the proportion of his salary equivalent to his off-campus teaching load. We used this money to add to the roster of teaching assistants. The men doing this work were, of course (or is the right term "incredibly"?), volunteers. Like many volunteers, they sometimes regretted their impetuosity. Especially in the wintertime, hundred-mile drives over secondary highways in dark of night could be unpleasant.

enrollment of excellent quality. What is perhaps still more important, he had established philosophy as a subject of genuine significance in the university's total work. With the old, though natural enough, misconception of philosophy removed, the old and equally natural reluctance to support its study was greatly reduced.

One last thing: this memoir has lately been ascribing an excessively solemn quality to the department and to Leonard's direction of it. One might take him for a Schweitzer, and us for a collection of zealot disciples. Really Leonard was anything but a missionary with a gospel, and we were a thoroughly non-solemn lot. Leonard believed that teaching philosophy was, or rightly managed could be, valuable and important work. One could take it seriously however, without succumbing to messianic delusions, and in fact such delusions are fatal to doing the work well. Of course, Leonard realized that philo-sophy has to be advanced as well as expounded (New Eng-landers generally distrust the policy of dipping into capital to meet current expenses). But he also thought that philosophy has both obligations and opportunities outside its own boundaries. Finally, he believed that the natural environment for philosophy's survival and growth was the academic one. Firmly to establish its practice within a large university was, therefore, serious professional work, even at the cost of reduced personal contributions to the profession's literature. Leonard's talents were so extraordinary that I often find myself regretting that he made this decision. I do not, however, believe that it was a mistaken one.

Selected Bibliography

BOOKS

Belnap, Nuel D. Jr., *An Analysis of Questions: Preliminary Report*, Santa Monica, System Development Corp., 1963.

Beth, E. W., *Mathematical Thought*, Dordrecht, Reidel, 1965.

Curry, H. B., and Feys, R., *Combinatory Logic, 1* (Amsterdam, North Holland, 1958).

Church, Alonzo, *Introduction to Mathematical Logic, 1* (Princeton, Princeton University Press, 1956).

Geach, P. and Black, M., *The Philosophical Writings of Gottlob Frege*, Oxford, Blackwell, 1952.

Harrah, D., *Communication: A Logical Model*, Cambridge, Mass., M.I.T. Press, 1963.

Hintikka, Jaakko, *Knowledge and Belief*, Ithaca, Cornell University Press, 1962.

Hume, David, *A Treatise of Human Nature*, Selby-Bigge Edition.

Kaplan, David, *Foundations of Intensional Logic*, Ann Arbor, University Microfilm, 1964.

Kleene, S., *Introduction to Mathematics*, Amsterdam, North Holland, 1952.

Leonard, Henry S., *Principles of Reasoning*, New York, Dover, 1967.

Lewis, C. I., and Langford, C. H., *Symbolic Logic*, 2nd ed. New York, Dover, 1959.

Prior, A., *Time and Modality*, Oxford, Oxford University Press, 1957.

Ramsey, F. P., "Truth and Probability," in *Foundations of Mathematics and other Essays*, London, Routledge, Kegan-Paul, 1931.

Reichenbach, Hans, *The Philosophy of Space and Time*, Eng. trans. M. Reichenbach and J. Freund, New York, Dover, 1958.

Sartre, J. P., *Transcendance of the Ego*, Eng. trans. F. Williams and R. Kirkpatrick, New York, Farrar, Straus, 1957.

Sellars, Wilfrid, *Science and Metaphysics*, London, Routledge, Kegan-Paul, 1968.

Strawson, P. F., *Introduction to Logical Theory*, London, Methuen, 1952.

Quine, W. V., *Methods of Logic*, rev. ed., New York, Holt, 1959.

Quine, W. V., *Word and Object*, Cambridge, Mass., M.I.T. Press, 1960.

Quine, W. V., *Set Theory and Its Logic*, Cambridge, The Belknap Press, 1963.

ARTICLES

Castañeda, Hector, "On the Logic of Self-Knowledge," *Nous*, *1* (1967), 9–21.

Feyerabend, P., "Reichenbach's Interpretation of Quantum-Mechanics," *Philosophical Studies*, *4* (1958), 49–59.

Fitch, F. B., "The System CΔ of Combinatory Logic," *Journal of Symbolic Logic*, *28* (1963), 87–97.

Hintikka, Jaakko, "On the Logic of Existence and Necessity. I Existence," *The Monist*, *50* (1966), 55–76.

———, "Individuals, Possible Worlds, and Epistemic Logic," *Nous*, *1* (1967), 33–62.

Hintikka, K. J. J., "Existential Presuppositions and Existential Commitments," *Journal of Philosophy*, *56* (1959), 125–37.

———, "Modality as Referential Opacity," *Ajatus*, *20* (1957), 49–63.

Kripke, Saul A., "Semantical Considerations on Modal Logic," *Acta Philosophica Fennica*, *16* (1963), 83–94.

Lambert, Karel, "Existential Import Revisited," *Notre Dame Journal of Formal Logic*, *4* (1963), 288–92.

Leonard, Henry S., "The Logic of Existence," *Philosophical Studies*, *7* (1956), 49–64.

————, "Essences, Attributes, and Predicates," Presidential Address, American Philosophical Association (Western Division) Milwaukee, May 1964.

————, "Authorship and Purpose," *Philosophy of Science*, 26 (1959), 277–94.

Massey, Gerald J., "The Theory of Truth Tabulary Connectives, Both Truth Functional and Modal," *Journal of Symbolic Logic*, 31 (1966), 593–608.

Meyer, Robert K., and Lambert, Karel, "Universally Free Logic and Standard Quantification Theory," *Journal of Symbolic Logic*, 33 (1968), 8–26.

Montague, R., "Logical Necessity, Physical Necessity, Ethics, and Quantifiers," *Inquiry*, 4 (1960), 259–69.

Putnam, H., "Three-Valued Logic," *Philosophical Studies*, 5 (1957), 73–80.

Scott, Dana, "Existence and Description in Formal Logic," in A. J. Ayer, et al., eds., *Bertrand Russell: Philosopher of the Century*, Boston, Little Brown, 1967.

Strawson, P. F., "On Referring," *Mind*, 59 (1950), 320–44.

Thomason, R., and Leblanc, H., "Completeness Theorems for Some Presupposition-Free Logics," *Fundamenta Mathematicae*, 1968, 62 (1968), 123–64.

van Fraassen, Bas C., "The Completeness of Free Logic," *Zeitschrift für mathematische Logik und Grundlagen der Mathematik*, 12 (1966), 219–34.

————, "Singular Terms, Truth-Value Gaps, and Free Logic," *Journal of Philosophy*, 63 (1966), 481–95.

———— and Lambert, Karel, "On Free Description Theory," *Zeitschrift für mathematische Logik under Grundlagen der Mathematik*, 13 (1967), 225–40.

Vickers, J., "Some Features of Theories of Belief," *Journal of Philosophy*, 63 (1966), 197–201.

————, "Remarks on Coherence and Subjective Probability," *Philosophy of Science*, 32 (1965), 32–38.

Index

Abbot, T. C., 309 n.

Aboutness, 7–8, 244–45; as "logical" connection between volition and action, 244–45

Abstraction, 256 n., 257–58, 265, 272–75; axioms of, 258; equations, 273–75

Action, 199, 202–04, 206–11, 214, 217, 239–43, 247; "act of will," 208; "basic actions," 202, 210–11, 217; human, 199, 202–04, 214, 240, 243; intentional, 207, 210; logic of, 206; minimal, 241–42; nonminimal, 241; purposive activity, 209

"*Actus voluntatis elicitus*," 215

Adams, Ernest, 51 n.

Aesthetics, 306 n.

Agency, 199–200, 202, 206–07, 208 n., 212, 214, 216, 243, 246

Analytic contingencies, 182

"Ancestral," Frege's definition, 213

Anselm, St., 194–95

Answers, 27–36; direct, 27–28, 33; nominal, 27; real, 27

Aquinas, St. Thomas, 195

Aristotle, 116, 220–22, 226, 238, 243, 247, 252, 261 n., 304, 306 n., 307 n.; Aristotelian framework, 221–22; notions of priority, 220

Assertibility, 228

Augustine, St., 210 n. f.

Axiomization, 117, 121–22, 125–26, 129–31, 135, 140–42

Ayer, A. J., 97

Barcan Principle, 125; Converse Barcan Principle, 125

"Bare particular," 231

Bayesians, 54, 62

Behavioristic parameters, 53

Belief, 4, 39–41, 43–63, 95, 245; cause of perceptual, 245; frequentist, 43–46, 54, 62; laws of probability, 45; mathematical, 63–64; partial, 43–46, 50–51, 53–54, 56, 59–61, 63; perceptual taking, 245; religious, 58; subjectivist, 43–46, 51–54, 56

Belnap, Nuel D., Jr., 23–37, 82

Bergmann, G., 222–23, 226

Beth, E. W., 69 n., 88

Binary stroke, 280–82

Bivalence, 69, 73, 88, 164–66, 171

Black, M., 156 n., 168 n., 256 n.

Bohr, N., 108, 110, 112

"Bundle theory," 231

Buridan, J., 138 n.

Butler, Bishop Joseph, 222